D1309264

Prentice Hall

GRAMMAR HANDBOOK

Grade 8

Upper Saddle River, New Jersey
Boston, Massachusetts
Chandler, Arizona
Glenview, Illinois

Prentice Hall Grammar Handbook Consulting Author
We wish to thank Jeff Anderson who guided the pedagogical approach to grammar instruction utilized in this handbook.

Grateful acknowledgment is made to the following for copyrighted material:

Gelston Hinds, Jr. o/b/o Amy Ling
"Grandma Ling" by Amy Ling from *Bridge: An Asian American Perspective, Vol. 7, No. 3.* Copyright © 1980 by Amy Ling.

Little, Brown and Company, Inc.
"Ode to Enchanted Light" from *Odes to Opposites* by Pablo Neruda. Copyright © 1995 by Pablo Neruda and Fundacion Pablo Neruda (Odes in Spanish). Copyright © 1995 by Ken Krabbenhoft (Odes in English); Copyright © 1995 by Ferris Cook (Illustrations and Compilation).

Longman Publishing Group, A Division of Pearson Education, Inc.
"Writing in a Second Language" *from Writing: A Guide for College and Beyond (2nd Edition)* by Lester Faigley. Copyright © 2010 by Pearson Education, Inc.

Note: Every effort has been made to locate the copyright owner of material reproduced in this component. Omissions brought to our attention will be corrected in subsequent editions.

Credits

Cover
Photos provided by istockphoto.com

Illustrations
Monika Melnychuk

Photographs
All interior photos provided by Shutterstock, Inc.

ISBN-13: 978-0-13-363841-7
ISBN-10:   0-13-363841-3
8 9 10 V056 15

GRAMMAR

CONTENTS

USAGE

CONTENTS

Numbered tags like this **ELL** are used on instruction pages of the Grammar Handbook to indicate where to find a related tip in the English Learner's Resource.

CHAPTER 1

NOUNS and PRONOUNS

Use a balance of nouns and pronouns in your writing to help you create sentences that flow smoothly.

WRITE GUY *Jeff Anderson, M.Ed.*

WHAT DO YOU NOTICE?

Focus on nouns and pronouns as you zoom in on sentences from "The Adventure of The Speckled Band" by Arthur Conan Doyle.

MENTOR TEXT

> Sherlock Holmes ran her over with one of his quick, all-comprehensive glances.
> "You must not fear," said he soothingly, bending forward and patting her forearm.

Now, ask yourself the following questions:

- How do you know that the personal pronouns *his* and *he* refer to Sherlock Holmes?
- How can you tell whether the personal pronoun *you* refers to Holmes or to the woman identified as *her*?

You can tell that *he* and *his* refer to Sherlock Holmes because those are the personal pronouns used for males, and Holmes is the only male the author mentions. The personal pronoun *you* must refer to the woman because Holmes is the narrator. If he was speaking of himself, he would say *I* instead.

Grammar for Writers Writers use personal pronouns to create sentences that readers can understand and follow. Check that you matched nouns and pronouns correctly in your writing.

Is the pizza for you or her?

That's an easy one! It's for me.

1

1.1 Nouns

Nouns are naming words. Words such as *friend*, *sky*, *dog*, *love*, *courage*, and *Seattle* are nouns.

RULE 1.1.1

A **noun** names something.

Most nouns fall into four main groups.

People, Places, Things, and Ideas

The nouns in the chart are grouped under four headings. You may know most of the nouns under the first three headings. You may not have realized that all the words in the fourth group are nouns.

PEOPLE	PLACES	THINGS	IDEAS
veterinarian	Lake Mead	bumblebee	strength
Dr. Robinson	classroom	collar	honesty
Americans	kennel	motorcycle	willingness
leader	Bunker Hill	notebook	obedience

See Practice 1.1A

Concrete and Abstract Nouns

Nouns may be classified as **concrete** or **abstract.** In the chart above, *People*, *Places*, and *Things* are concrete nouns. *Ideas* are abstract nouns.

RULE 1.1.2

A **concrete noun** names something that can be recognized through any of the five senses. An **abstract noun** names something that cannot be recognized through the senses.

CONCRETE NOUNS			
pencil	dog	tractor	river
ABSTRACT NOUNS			
courage	fun	honor	exploration

See Practice 1.1B

Collective Nouns

A few nouns name groups of people or things. A *pack*, for example, is "a group of dogs or other animals that travel together." These nouns are called **collective nouns.**

> A **collective noun** names a group of people or things.

1.1.3 RULE

COLLECTIVE NOUNS		
club	herd	army
troop	orchestra	committee
class	team	group

See Practice 1.1C

Count and Non-count Nouns

Nouns can be grouped as **count** or **non-count** nouns.

> **Count nouns** name things that can be counted. **Non-count nouns** name things that cannot be counted.

1.1.4 RULE

COUNT NOUNS	NON-COUNT NOUNS
orange	thunder
bench	rice
street	grass

Count nouns can take an article and can be plural.

EXAMPLE   a bench   the bench   three benches

Non-count nouns do not take an indefinite article (*a* or *an*) and cannot be plural:

EXAMPLES   We cut the grass on Saturday.
(*not* We cut *a* grass on Saturday.)

She needs clothing for the vacation.
(*not* She needs clothing**s** for the vacation.)

See Practice 1.1D

Read the sentences. Then, write the nouns in each sentence.

EXAMPLE   The powerful body of the lion gives it a proud appearance.

ANSWER   *body, lion, appearance*

1. The camels are a popular attraction at the zoo.

2. Many scientists find oceans fascinating to study.

3. Most pets offer love to their owners.

4. Some people like only certain types of flowers.

5. Jamal's friends are coming to his house to see a movie.

6. A dictionary is a kind of reference book.

7. We invited Hector to play golf.

8. Kevin and Louisa walked near the ocean.

9. Lyle bought milk at the store.

10. Martin needs new shoes for playing basketball.

Read the sentences. Then, write the nouns in each sentence, and label each one *concrete* or *abstract*.

EXAMPLE   Josie sometimes behaves foolishly despite her cleverness.

ANSWER   *Josie* — concrete
cleverness — abstract

11. We saw some crabs scuttling across the sand.

12. Dad always reminds us of the importance of self-respect.

13. Sometimes a herd of buffalo grazes near that road.

14. The senator vowed to work toward equality.

15. The teacher showed no enthusiasm for my idea.

16. The detective only wanted to discover the truth.

17. Justice is an important principle in a democracy.

18. My friend showed her sympathy by sending a card.

19. Jason has always had a terrible fear of insects.

20. Leslie often uses humor to hide her discomfort.

SPEAKING APPLICATION

Tell a partner about a sporting event you've watched. Your partner should listen for and name three nouns that you use.

WRITING APPLICATION

Use sentence 18 as a model, and write three more sentences that each contain two concrete nouns and one abstract noun.

PRACTICE 1.1C ▷ Finding Collective Nouns

Read the pairs of nouns. Each pair includes one collective noun. Write the collective noun.

EXAMPLE   squad, men

ANSWER   *squad*

1. panel, judges
2. crew, pilot
3. family, parent
4. professor, faculty
5. person, audience
6. band, guitarist
7. jury, peer
8. face, crowd
9. bunch, flower
10. singer, choir

PRACTICE 1.1D ▷ Identifying Count and Non-count Nouns

Read the sentences. Then, list the count and non-count nouns. One sentence has only count nouns.

EXAMPLE   A player must have endurance to play soccer well.

ANSWER   *Count noun — player*
           Non-count nouns — endurance, soccer

11. Water quickly filled the boat.
12. My little brother has great fun with his toy airplane.
13. We watched the lightning from the safety of the porch.
14. The group of friends went to the game together.
15. He always says there is no excuse for boredom.
16. That dog is not getting enough nutrition.
17. His intelligence was obvious to the teacher.
18. Right now the refrigerator is in storage.
19. Mom's wisdom is a gift that I value.
20. Travel is one leisure activity the whole family enjoys.

SPEAKING APPLICATION

With a partner, take turns describing a vacation or day trip you enjoyed. Your partner should listen for and name at least one collective noun, one count noun, and one non-count noun.

WRITING APPLICATION

Use sentence 20 as a model, and write two more sentences that each contain one non-count noun and two count nouns.

Recognizing Compound Nouns

Some nouns are made up of two or more words. *Classroom* is a **compound noun** made up of *class* and *room*.

> **A compound noun** is one noun made by joining two or more words.

Compound nouns are written in three different ways: as single words, as hyphenated words, and as two or more separate words.

COMPOUND NOUNS		
SINGLE WORDS	HYPHENATED WORDS	SEPARATE WORDS
crossbar	by-product	dinner jacket
firefighter	right-hander	pole vault
thunderstorm	middle-distance	pen pal
classroom	mother-in-law	chief justice

See Practice 1.1E

Using Common and Proper Nouns

All nouns can be divided into two large groups: **common nouns** and **proper nouns.**

EL2

> **A common noun** names any one of a class of people, places, things, or ideas. **A proper noun** names a specific person, place, thing, or idea.

Common nouns are not capitalized. Proper nouns are always capitalized.

COMMON NOUNS	PROPER NOUNS
inventor	Alexander Graham Bell
village	Tarrytown
story	"The Tell-Tale Heart"
organization	American Red Cross
idea	Gem Theory of Disease

See Practice 1.1F

PRACTICE 1.1E ▷ Identifying Compound Nouns

Read the sentences. Then, write the compound nouns, and draw a line between the words that make up each compound noun. One sentence has two compound nouns.

EXAMPLE   We won the game because of good teamwork.

ANSWER   *team | work*

1. Gigi wants to be a famous songwriter.

2. There was a car accident near the high school.

3. The baseball got lost in the tall grass.

4. Please stop by the post office on your way to the store.

5. Ellie's aunt drives a tractor-trailer for a living.

6. Pedro's self-confidence grew after he made his first two baskets.

7. All the cheerleaders arrived at the game early.

8. The jet stream has an influence on weather and climate.

9. An earthquake is a sudden movement of the earth's crust.

10. The greenhouse is full of thriving houseplants.

PRACTICE 1.1F ▷ Using Common and Proper Nouns

Read the sentences. Then, rewrite them, replacing the underlined words with proper nouns.

EXAMPLE   The trailer for <u>that movie</u> was funny.

ANSWER   *The trailer for <u>Marley and Me</u> was funny.*

11. I have read almost every book by <u>this author</u>.

12. The science program at <u>the school</u> is very good.

13. Juanita is moving to <u>that street</u> next month.

14. The athlete I admire most is <u>that player</u>.

15. We will meet at <u>a theater</u> to see the dance performance.

16. During the vacation, Carly got to see the <u>famous bridge</u>.

17. My grandmother has been receiving <u>that newspaper</u> for many years.

18. Jenna read <u>a short story</u> for her literature class.

19. The exhibit has several paintings by <u>a famous artist</u>.

20. Have you ever seen <u>that national monument</u>?

SPEAKING APPLICATION

With a partner, take turns describing your town or city. Your partner should listen for two compound nouns and two proper nouns.

WRITING APPLICATION

Write three sentences. In your sentences, include at least one compound noun, one common noun, and one proper noun.

1.2 Pronouns

Pronouns are words that take the place of nouns. They are used rather than repeating a noun again and again. Pronouns make sentences clearer and more interesting.

A **pronoun** is a word that takes the place of a noun or a group of words acting as a noun.

Imagine, for example, that you are writing about Uncle Mike. If you were using only nouns, you might write the following sentence:

WITH NOUNS   Uncle Mike was late because **Uncle Mike** had to make **Uncle Mike's** mashed potatoes.

WITH PRONOUNS   Uncle Mike was late because **he** had to make **his** mashed potatoes.

Sometimes a pronoun takes the place of a noun in the same sentence.

EXAMPLES   My sister opened **her** presents first.
pronoun

Many people say finding a hobby has helped **them**.
pronoun

A pronoun can also take the place of a noun used in an earlier sentence.

EXAMPLES   My sister ate her soup first. **She** was hungry.
pronoun

Visitors must take off their shoes. **They** can then put on slippers.
pronoun

A pronoun may take the place of an entire group of words.

EXAMPLE   Trying to make our family's recipe was hard work. **It** took a lot of time.
pronoun

Antecedents of Pronouns

The word or group of words that a pronoun replaces or refers to is called an **antecedent.**

> An **antecedent** is the noun (or group of words acting as a noun) to which a pronoun refers.

1.2.2 RULE

EXAMPLES   The **doctors** described how **they** performed **their**
            antecedent   pronoun   pronoun
            jobs.

            Finally, the **doctor** spoke. **She** seemed to think
                        antecedent   pronoun
            the patient was fine.

            How Michael was saved is amazing. **It** is a story
                    antecedent   pronoun
            that he'll tell often.

            Although **she** was a pediatrician, **Tara** also
                     pronoun   antecedent
            diagnosed adults.

See Practice 1.2A

Some kinds of pronouns do not have any antecedent.

EXAMPLES   **Everyone** at the party knew the truth.
            indefinite pronoun

            Who cooked the food?
            indefinite pronoun

See Practice 1.2B

The indefinite pronouns *everyone* and *who* do not have a specific antecedent because their meaning is clear without one.

PRACTICE 1.2A Recognizing Pronouns and Antecedents

Read the sentences. Then, write each pronoun and its antecedent.

EXAMPLE   The park has closed its gates for the day.

ANSWER   *its, park*

1. Many people say they have seen strange objects in the sky.
2. When Tamesa read *Oliver Twist* for the first time, she cried.
3. Jamal called his mother as soon as the karate class was over.
4. That tree is colorful, but it only blooms for a few weeks each year.
5. Serena, would you give your speech now?
6. The four boys walked to the gate with their tickets in hand.
7. Because of his injury, the dancer could not perform.
8. If she had wanted to, Cheryl could have won the spelling bee.
9. Jerome said, "I would like to read a book about space travel."
10. Arthur C. Clarke entertains readers, but he suggests ideas to them, too.

PRACTICE 1.2B Supplying Pronouns for Antecedents

Read the sentences. Then, write each sentence, filling in the blank with the appropriate pronoun. Correctly identify and underline the antecedent of the pronoun you supply.

EXAMPLE   Mom, could _____ please give the boys a ride?

ANSWER   *Mom, could you please give the boys a ride?*

11. "_____ fixed the DVD player," said Ann.
12. Since Phoebe moved, _____ has been getting better grades.
13. "Girls, _____ will have to clean up this mess right now," commanded Ms. Chavez.
14. Bryant tried to call his mother, but _____ was not in the office.
15. The brothers joined the team as soon as _____ could.
16. The book is not as difficult as _____ first chapter suggests.
17. The Garcias said _____ would volunteer at the food bank.
18. Uncle Gene donated _____ used clothing to charity.
19. Somehow Amy managed to lose _____ clarinet.
20. According to Dad, all dogs can behave well if _____ are trained properly.

SPEAKING APPLICATION

Tell a partner about a movie you saw recently. Have your partner listen for and name at least two pronouns and their antecedents.

WRITING APPLICATION

Write three sentences about animals. Use at least one pronoun and antecedent in each sentence. Circle each pronoun and draw an arrow to the antecedent.

Recognizing Personal Pronouns

The pronouns used most often are **personal pronouns**.

> **Personal pronouns** refer to (1) the person speaking or writing, (2) the person listening or reading, or (3) the topic (person, place, thing, or idea) being discussed or written about.

1.2.3 RULE

The first-person pronouns *I, me, my, mine, we, us, our,* and *ours* refer to the person or persons speaking or writing.

EXAMPLES   **I** like the latest edition of the book.

Please hand **us** the china plates.

The second-person pronouns *you, your,* and *yours* refer to the person or persons spoken or written to.

EXAMPLES   **You** should see that movie.

Your DVD player isn't working.

The third-person pronouns *he, him, his, she, her, hers, it, its, they, them, their,* and *theirs* refer to the person, place, thing, or idea being spoken or written about.

EXAMPLES   **He** wants to watch the inaugural speech.

They wrote letters to the new president.

Some personal pronouns show possession. Although they can function as adjectives, they are still identified as personal pronouns because they take the place of possessive nouns.

EXAMPLES   **Joe's** nutrition book will be published soon.
            possessive noun

            His recipes in the book are delicious.
            possessive pronoun

The chart on the next page presents the personal pronouns.

PERSONAL PRONOUNS		
	SINGULAR	PLURAL
First person	I, me, my, mine	we, us, our, ours
Second person	you, your, yours	you, your, yours
Third person	he, him, his, she, her, hers, it, its	they, them, their, theirs

See Practice 1.2C

Reflexive and Intensive Pronouns

The ending -*self* or -*selves* can be added to some pronouns to form **reflexive** or **intensive pronouns.** These two types of pronouns look the same, but they function differently within a sentence.

REFLEXIVE AND INTENSIVE PRONOUNS		
	SINGULAR	PLURAL
First person	myself	ourselves
Second person	yourself	yourselves
Third person	himself, herself, itself	themselves

RULE 1.2.4

A reflexive pronoun directs the action of the verb toward its subject. Reflexive pronouns point back to a noun or pronoun earlier in the sentence.

A reflexive pronoun is essential to the meaning of a sentence.

REFLEXIVE **Tara** helped **herself** to some cookies.
noun reflexive pronoun

They made **themselves** homemade cookies.
pronoun reflexive pronoun

See Practice 1.2D

RULE 1.2.5

An intensive pronoun simply adds emphasis to a noun or pronoun in the same sentence.

An intensive pronoun is not essential to the meaning of the sentence.

INTENSIVE The mayor **herself** attended the carnival.

PRACTICE 1.2C ▷ Recognizing Personal Pronouns

Read the sentences. Then, write the personal pronouns in each sentence.

EXAMPLE   Carlos thought he would enjoy his vacation.

ANSWER   *he, his*

1. Mason brushed his cat's fur carefully.

2. At the game, we supported our team by cheering loudly.

3. Will you please close the door?

4. José decided he would practice his soccer skills.

5. Rosa could see her dog standing at the bowl eating its food.

6. The students wanted to perform a skit, so first they wrote a script.

7. My brother would sell his car, but it is not worth much.

8. The Johnsons bought their house in 1998, and they are still happy with it.

9. Mr. Montoya made us tacos and rice.

10. I believe you left your jacket in the car, Josh.

PRACTICE 1.2D ▷ Supplying Reflexive and Intensive Pronouns

Read the sentences. Write the reflexive or intensive pronoun that completes each sentence.

EXAMPLE   The audience members prepared _____ for an exciting performance.

ANSWER   *themselves*

11. Luis _____ can do several card tricks.

12. The cellist gave _____ a stage name.

13. Viewers found for _____ a new kind of hero in Captain Kirk.

14. Wonder Woman could not fly by _____.

15. I _____ can't understand why more people don't recycle.

16. The researchers _____ are unsure about the results.

17. Dan is sick, so I may have to finish the project _____.

18. The actors treated _____ to snacks at the opening night party.

19. Marianne gave _____ a chance to catch her breath.

20. Fix _____ a sandwich and let's go!

SPEAKING APPLICATION

Tell a partner a funny story about your family. Your partner should listen for and name at least two personal pronouns.

WRITING APPLICATION

Write three sentences, using a reflexive or an intensive pronoun in each.

Demonstrative Pronouns

Demonstrative pronouns point to people, places, and things, much as you point to them with your finger.

RULE

1.2.6

> A **demonstrative pronoun** points to a specific person, place, or thing.

There are two singular and two plural demonstrative pronouns.

DEMONSTRATIVE PRONOUNS			
SINGULAR		PLURAL	
this	that	these	those

This and *these* point to what is near the speaker or writer. *That* and *those* point to what is more distant.

NEAR   **This** rack is where I keep my videos.

         These are my favorite bands to listen to.

FAR   Is **that** the road to take?

         Those smoothies look good.

See Practice 1.2E

Using Relative Pronouns

Relative pronouns are connecting words.

RULE

1.2.7

> A **relative pronoun** begins a subordinate clause and connects it to another idea in the same sentence.

There are five relative pronouns.

RELATIVE PRONOUNS				
that	which	who	whom	whose

The chart on the next page gives examples of relative pronouns connecting subordinate clauses to independent clauses. (See Chapter 7 to find out more about relative pronouns and clauses.)

INDEPENDENT CLAUSES	SUBORDINATE CLAUSES
Here is the recipe	that Bonnie lost.
Ricky bought our old computer,	which needs repairs.
She is a teacher	who has an unusual gift.
Is this the child	whom you saw earlier?
He is the one	whose car has a new stereo.
Here is the restaurant	that was described in the article.
Charlie found his ball	that was under the table.

See Practice 1.2F

Interrogative Pronouns

To interrogate means "to ask questions."

> An **interrogative pronoun** is used to begin a question.

1.2.8 RULE

All five interrogative pronouns begin with *w.*

INTERROGATIVE PRONOUNS				
what	which	who	whom	whose

Most interrogative pronouns do not have antecedents.

EXAMPLES **What** did the principal say?

Which is the best place to invest money?

Who wants to see a movie?

From **whom** will you receive the best directions?

See Practice 1.2G

Whose cake was chosen for the taste testing?

Indefinite Pronouns

> An **indefinite pronoun** refers to a person, place, thing, or idea that is not specifically named.

EXAMPLES   **Everything** is ready for our trip to Europe.

Everyone really wants to see Rome first.

Anyone can afford to travel by bus.

Something fell off the table when I bumped it.

An indefinite pronoun can function either as an adjective or as the subject of a sentence.

ADJECTIVE   **Both** girls want to be veterinarians.

SUBJECT   **Both** want to be veterinarians.

A few indefinite pronouns can be either singular or plural, depending on their use in the sentence.

INDEFINITE PRONOUNS		PLURAL	SINGULAR OR PLURAL
SINGULAR			
another	much	both	all
anybody	neither	few	any
anyone	nobody	many	more
anything	no one	others	most
each	nothing	several	none
either	one		some
everybody	other		
everyone	somebody		
everything	someone		
little	something		

See Practice 1.2H

PRACTICE 1.2E Identifying Demonstrative Pronouns

Read the sentences. Then, write the demonstrative pronoun and the noun to which it refers.

EXAMPLE   Isn't that an interesting painting?

ANSWER   *that, painting*

1. That was an important decision you made.
2. This is the largest stadium in the state.
3. Are these the shoes you were asking me about?
4. Skis are expensive, so be careful with those!
5. That is not the movie I would have chosen.
6. "I'd like to try some of that," said Brandon, pointing to the salad.
7. My advice to you is this: Be patient.
8. "May I please see those?" Janelle asked, looking at the earrings.
9. Are these the treats you want to buy for the dog?
10. Those are the instructions for the printer.

PRACTICE 1.2F Supplying Relative Pronouns

Read the sentences. Then, write the correct relative pronoun (e.g., *whose, that, which*) for each sentence.

EXAMPLE   She bought some shoes _____ matched her purse.

ANSWER   *that*

11. One leader _____ our country will never forget is George Washington.
12. I could not find a dress _____ fit properly.
13. The woman _____ writes that column is not a journalist.
14. These sandals, _____ I wear often, are very comfortable.
15. Ernesto, _____ is bringing the dip, has not arrived yet.
16. Can you find a frame _____ will fit this photo?
17. Consuela is the girl _____ pen I borrowed.
18. The singer _____ we liked best sang two solos.
19. Solar panels, _____ harness the sun's energy, are good for the environment.
20. The birds _____ we saw at the lake were herons.

SPEAKING APPLICATION

With a partner, take turns describing a favorite hobby. Use at least one demonstrative pronoun and one relative pronoun (e.g., *whose, that, which*), and ask your partner to identify them.

WRITING APPLICATION

Write three sentences using relative pronouns (e.g., *whose, that, which*).

PRACTICE 1.2G > Identifying Interrogative Pronouns

Read the sentences. Then, write the interrogative pronoun in each sentence.

EXAMPLE   What is the largest species of bird?

ANSWER   *What*

1. Who took you to the museum?

2. Whose is the cellphone with the red holder?

3. To whom should we send the package?

4. Which is the jacket you got for your birthday?

5. What is the yogurt flavor you like best?

6. Who left his backpack lying on the floor?

7. What does that symbol on your cap represent?

8. Whom did you sit with at the game?

9. Which is the best dish to order here?

10. Whom will you get to help with the forms?

PRACTICE 1.2H > Supplying Indefinite Pronouns

Read the sentences. Then, write an appropriate indefinite pronoun for each sentence.

EXAMPLE   _____ of my friends are going to see a professional basketball game tomorrow.

ANSWER   *Some*

11. _____ of the actors did not know their lines.

12. Has _____ eaten the rest of the soup?

13. _____ of the host's hints proved helpful.

14. A _____ of us are going surfing next week.

15. Carmen finally asked _____ for directions.

16. _____ of these books are slightly damaged.

17. _____ has to pay an entry fee this time.

18. _____ in the audience laughed at the comedian.

19. I will see the movie with _____ from my family.

20. The teacher encouraged _____ of the students to study.

SPEAKING APPLICATION

With a partner, take turns describing a school event. Your partner should listen for and name two interrogative pronouns and two indefinite pronouns.

WRITING APPLICATION

Write two sentences with interrogative pronouns and two sentences with indefinite pronouns.

VERBS

Use strong verbs to convey actions in clear and powerful ways in your writing.

CHAPTER 2

WRITE GUY *Jeff Anderson, M.Ed.*

WHAT DO YOU NOTICE?

Seek out the verbs as you zoom in on this sentence from the story "Who Can Replace a Man?" by Brian Aldiss.

MENTOR TEXT

> When he swung suddenly to face them as they loomed over him, they saw that his countenance was ravaged by starvation.

Now, ask yourself the following questions:

- Which words are action verbs in this sentence?
- Which words make up a verb phrase in this sentence?

Swung, face, loomed, and *saw* are action verbs; they describe the specific actions of *he* or *they* in the sentence. The words *was* and *ravaged* form the verb phrase *was ravaged.* The word *was* is a helping verb, and the word *ravaged* is the main verb.

Grammar for Writers Writers can use action verbs to add dimension to their writing. Choose action verbs that bring your sentences to life and that help readers picture scenes as they unfold.

I was relaxed during the test.

It looks as if your helping verb helped!

2.1 Action Verbs

Verbs such as *walk, sailed, played, migrate, raced, crossed, learn,* and *arrive* all show some kind of action.

EL5

RULE 2.1.1

An **action verb** tells what action someone or something is performing.

EXAMPLES   Tara **carries** all her science books.

The old truck **chugged** into the garage.

I **believe** it's hurricane season.

Joshua **remembered** to bring the script.

The verb *carries* explains what Tara did with the books. The verb *chugged* tells what the truck did. The verb *believe* explains my action about the hurricane season. The verb *remembered* explains Joshua's action with the script.

Some actions, such as *carries* or *chugged,* can be seen. Some actions, such as *believe* or *remembered,* cannot be seen.

See Practice 2.1A

Using Transitive Verbs

RULE 2.1.2

An action verb is **transitive** if the receiver of the action is named in the sentence. The receiver of the action is called the **object** of the verb.

EXAMPLES   Bonnie **opened** the **drawer** with difficulty.
                          verb   object

The bicyclist suddenly **hit** a **pothole**.
                                verb   object

In the first example, *opened* is transitive because the object of the verb—*drawer*—names what Bonnie opened. In the second example, *hit* is transitive because the object of the verb—*pothole*—tells what the bicyclist hit.

EL5   ## Using Intransitive Verbs

> An action verb is **intransitive** if there is no receiver of the action named in the sentence. An intransitive verb does not have an object.

2.1.3 RULE

EXAMPLES

The conference call **began** .

The motorcyclist **raced** through the traffic jam.

The teaching staff **gathered** in the teachers' lounge.

My doorbell **rang** at midnight!

Some action verbs can be transitive or intransitive. You need to determine if the verb has an object or not.

TRANSITIVE VERB   Chuck **painted** the **garage door** .

INTRANSITIVE VERB   The student **painted** in art class.

TRANSITIVE VERB   Jody **sang** a funny **song** .

INTRANSITIVE VERB   The chorus **sang** on stage.

TRANSITIVE VERB   Will **flew** his small **plane** .

See Practice 2.1B   INTRANSITIVE VERB   The small plane **flew** over the bridge.

PRACTICE 2.1A > Finding Action Verbs

Read the sentences. Then, write each action verb.

EXAMPLE   Ants live in colonies and dig underground.

ANSWER   *live, dig*

1. Athletes from many countries compete in the Olympics.
2. The band marched onto the field and played the national anthem.
3. Jason wonders about getting into college.
4. The subway pulled away from the platform.
5. Rosa bought a handmade basket and filled it with dried flowers.
6. Sometimes Aunt Lucy thinks of her lost cat and cries.
7. Chop the onions into small pieces.
8. I dream of a bright future for all children.
9. Brianna opened the door for her little brother.
10. Plants use carbon dioxide and produce oxygen.

PRACTICE 2.1B > Identifying Transitive and Intransitive Verbs

Read the sentences. Write each verb and label it *transitive* or *intransitive*.

EXAMPLE   New York City offers many attractions for tourists.

ANSWER   *offers* — transitive

11. During World War II, Japan cooperated with Germany.
12. Brenda took a trip to Arizona with her family.
13. Vendors usually sell pretzels at baseball games.
14. Each boy named his favorite sport.
15. My brother ran in the 100-yard dash.
16. The game lasted for almost two hours.
17. Please explain your actions to the principal.
18. The dog slept peacefully on the floor all morning.
19. After a long train ride, we reached the village.
20. Receiving loud applause, the dancer grinned broadly.

SPEAKING APPLICATION

Tell a partner about a form of exercise you enjoy. Your partner should listen for and name at least two transitive verbs and two intransitive verbs.

WRITING APPLICATION

Write two sentences with transitive verbs and two sentences with intransitive verbs.

2.2 Linking Verbs

Some widely used verbs do not show action. They are called **linking verbs**.

2.2.1 RULE

A **linking verb** is a verb that connects a subject with a word that describes or identifies it.

EXAMPLES

Joshua **was** an army **soldier**.
subject / linking verb / predicate nominative
(IDENTIFIES)

The **winners** of first place **were** **Heather and I**.
subject / linking verb / predicate nominative
(IDENTIFIES)

We **were** extremely **tired** after our workout.
subject / linking verb / predicate adjective
(DESCRIBES)

Recognizing Forms of *Be*

In English, the most common linking verb is *be.* This verb has many forms.

FORMS OF *BE*		
am	can be	has been
are	could be	have been
is	may be	had been
was	might be	could have been
were	must be	may have been
am being	shall be	might have been
are being	should be	must have been
is being	will be	shall have been
was being	would be	should have been
were being		will have been
		would have been

Using Other Linking Verbs

Several other verbs also function as linking verbs. They connect the parts of a sentence in the same way as the forms of *be*. In the sentence below, *calm* describes *father*.

EXAMPLE

Her **father** **remained** **calm** after the news.
subject   linking verb   predicate adjective

OTHER LINKING VERBS		
appear	look	sound
become	remain	stay
feel	seem	taste
grow	smell	turn

Action Verb or Linking Verb?

Some verbs can be used either as linking verbs or action verbs.

LINKING

The sky **looked** black.
(*Looked* links *sky* and *black.*)

ACTION

The reporter **looked** at the sky.
(The reporter performed an action.)

LINKING

The puppy **grew** impatient.
(*Grew* links *puppy* and *impatient.*)

ACTION

The gardener **grew** flowers.
(The gardener performed an action.)

To test whether a verb is a linking verb or an action verb, replace the verb with *is, am,* or *are.* If the sentence still makes sense, then the verb is a linking verb.

EXAMPLE

The puppy **is** impatient.
linking verb

See Practice 2.2A
See Practice 2.2B

PRACTICE 2.2A ▷	Identifying Action Verbs and Linking Verbs

Read the sentences. Write the verb in each sentence, and label it either *action* or *linking*.

EXAMPLE   Marcus turned pale at the accident site.

ANSWER   *turned* — linking

1. My uncle in Indiana grows vegetables in his garden.
2. The teams stayed in a hotel near the stadium.
3. Those burritos look delicious and healthful.
4. For some reason Lupita remains cheerful all the time.
5. Sometimes a rash appears on his face.
6. Heather looked through the binoculars.
7. The lawyer appears very calm and confident.
8. That orange smells delightful.
9. Dad tasted the peach for me.
10. Suddenly, the sky became darker.

PRACTICE 2.2B ▷	Using *Be* and Other Linking Verbs

Read the pairs of words below. For each pair of words, write a sentence that uses a linking verb to connect them.

EXAMPLE   plane   late

ANSWER   *Because of snow, the plane was late.*

11. server   happy
12. they   early
13. Dickens   writer
14. plan   excellent
15. sauce   salty
16. actress   daughter
17. sister   athlete
18. children   afraid
19. painting   work
20. runner   exhausted

SPEAKING APPLICATION

With a partner, take turns describing a special meal you have had. Your partner should listen for and name at least one action verb and one linking verb.

WRITING APPLICATION

Write one sentence using *taste* as a linking verb and another sentence using it as an action verb. Then do the same with one of these verbs: *smell*, *stay*, *look*, or *grow*.

2.3 Helping Verbs

Sometimes, a verb in a sentence is just one word. Often, however, a verb will be made up of several words. This type of verb is called a **verb phrase**.

Helping verbs are added before another verb to make a **verb phrase**.

EL5

Notice how these helping verbs change the meaning of the verb *jump*.

EXAMPLES   jump   **might have** jumped

          had jumped   **should have** jumped

          will have jumped   **will be** jumping

Recognizing Helping Verbs

EL6

Forms of *Be* Forms of *be* are often used as helping verbs.

SOME FORMS OF *BE* USED AS HELPING VERBS	
HELPING VERBS	MAIN VERBS
am	growing
has been	warned
was being	told
will be	reminded
will have been	waiting
is	opening
was being	trained
should be	written
had been	sent
might have been	played

See Practice 2.3A

26   Verbs

Other Helping Verbs Many different verb phrases can be formed using one or more of these helping verbs. The chart below shows just a few.

HELPING VERBS	MAIN VERBS	VERB PHRASES
do	remember	do remember
has	written	has written
would	hope	would hope
shall	see	shall see
can	believe	can believe
could	finish	could finish
may	attempt	may attempt
must have	thought	must have thought
should have	grown	should have grown
might	win	might win
will	jump	will jump
have	planned	have planned
does	want	does want

Sometimes the words in a verb phrase are separated by other words, such as *not* or *certainly*. The parts of the verb phrase in certain types of questions may also be separated.

WORDS SEPARATED

He **could** certainly **have come** today.

This **has** not **occurred** to me before.

Aunt Grace **has** certainly not **learned** how to cook!

She **had** certainly **written** a long term paper.

Did you ever **expect** to see a full eclipse?

When **will** we **arrive** at the hotel?

Did you ever **expect** the cake to be so good?

Carolyn **must** not **have taken** the test.

Would you ever **want** to go to Europe?

See Practice 2.3B

| PRACTICE 2.3A | Identifying Helping and Main Verbs |

Read the sentences. Write *main verb* if the underlined verb is a main verb. Write *helping verb* if it is a helping verb.

EXAMPLE   Our cat, Sophie, <u>has been</u> living with us for eight years.

ANSWER   *helping verb*

1. They <u>have</u> often hiked to the top of the mountain.

2. Alisa <u>went</u> to the hockey game on Tuesday night.

3. What time are you <u>going</u> to the Earth Day festival?

4. Yes, he did <u>explain</u> his project to the teacher.

5. Rosita <u>could have</u> won first place.

6. The clerk carefully <u>wrapped</u> the vase for shipping.

7. The singers are <u>preparing</u> for the concert.

8. The speaker <u>has been</u> delayed because of traffic.

9. A walk in the park <u>is</u> a pleasant experience.

10. Zach <u>is</u> bringing his tennis racquet.

| PRACTICE 2.3B | Using Verb Phrases |

Read the verb phrases. Use each verb phrase in an original sentence.

EXAMPLE   have been decorating

ANSWER   *The girls have been decorating their room.*

11. has arrived

12. will help

13. has asked

14. have been saving

15. may wish

16. should have gone

17. must have disagreed

18. have been studying

19. could hear

20. was reaching

SPEAKING APPLICATION

With a partner, take turns telling a brief story about a pet or other animal. Your partner should listen for and name at least two verb phrases.

WRITING APPLICATION

Write three sentences about your favorite school subject. Use a verb phrase in each sentence.

CHAPTER 3

ADJECTIVES and ADVERBS

Use adjectives and adverbs in your descriptions to help your readers create mental pictures as they read.

WRITE GUY *Jeff Anderson, M.Ed.*

WHAT DO YOU NOTICE?

Watch for adjectives and adverbs as you zoom in on these sentences from Maya Angelou's autobiography, *I Know Why the Caged Bird Sings.*

MENTOR TEXT

> Her sounds began cascading gently. I knew from listening to a thousand preachers that she was nearing the end of her reading, and I hadn't really heard, heard to understand, a single word.

Now, ask yourself the following questions:

- Which verbs do the adverbs *gently* and *really* modify?
- Which word is an adjective that describes an amount, and which noun does it modify?

The adverb *gently* modifies *cascading,* telling readers in what way the words were spoken. The adverb *really* modifies *heard* and describes to what extent Angelou heard the words. The adjective *thousand* modifies *preachers.* A thousand is probably an exaggeration, but it creates a vivid picture for the reader.

Grammar for Writers To craft memorable descriptions, writers carefully select adjectives and adverbs. Before choosing an adjective or adverb, ask yourself if and how it will help your reader see what you are describing.

Is *truly* an adverb?

Yes, *truly* is truly an adverb.

3.1 Adjectives

Adjectives are words that make language come alive by adding description or information.

Adjectives help make nouns more specific. For example, *car* is a general word, but a *red two-door car* is more specific. Adjectives such as *red* and *two-door* make nouns and pronouns clearer and more vivid.

An **adjective** is a word that describes a noun or pronoun.

Adjectives are often called *modifiers*, because they modify, or change, the meaning of a noun or pronoun. You can use more than one adjective to modify a noun or pronoun. Notice how *dress* is modified by each set of adjectives below.

EXAMPLES   **old-fashioned** dress

new **black** dress

women's **evening** dress

sparkly **blue** dress

Adjectives answer several questions about nouns and pronouns. They tell *What kind? Which one? How many?* or *How much?* Numeral adjectives, such as *eleven,* tell exactly how many. In the chart below, notice how adjectives answer these questions.

WHAT KIND?	WHICH ONE?	HOW MANY?	HOW MUCH?
brick house	that judge	one daffodil	no time
white flowers	each answer	both trees	enough raisins
serious argument	those books	several jars	many hobbies
colorful shirts	this student	four books	some cars

Adjective Position An adjective usually comes before the noun it modifies, as do all the adjectives in the chart on the previous page. Sometimes, however, adjectives come after the nouns they modify.

EXAMPLES

The publishing world, **complex** and **serious**, is sometimes very fast-paced.

noun   adjective   adjective

The subway platform, **crowded** and **dark**, frightened us.

noun   adjective   adjective

Colors, **vivid** and **bold**, filled the walls of the room.

noun   adjective   adjective

Adjectives that modify pronouns usually come after linking verbs. Sometimes, however, adjectives may come before the pronoun.

AFTER

She was **shy** and **quiet**.

pronoun   adjective   adjective

He is **anxious** and **hopeful**.

pronoun   adjective   adjective

She is **talkative**.

pronoun   adjective

BEFORE

Timid yet **confident**, **she** walked into the class.

adjective   adjective   pronoun

Peaceful and **happy**, **she** sat on a park bench.

adjective   adjective   pronoun

Intelligent and **hardworking**, **she** always did well on exams.

adjective   adjective   pronoun

See Practice 3.1A
See Practice 3.1B

PRACTICE 3.1A Identifying Adjectives

Read the sentences. Then, write each adjective and list the question it answers. (*What kind? Which one? How many? How much?*)

EXAMPLE Put some dip in that bowl, please.

ANSWER *some* — How much?
that — Which one?

1. A large man stepped from the red truck.

2. Few people could climb to the top of those mountains.

3. Leanne, tired from cleaning, took a long nap on the couch.

4. Bernice wore a wide-brimmed hat with a green cotton ribbon.

5. Several citizens have complained about that dangerous intersection.

6. Each artist sold two portraits at the outdoor festival.

7. Jan made four calls to the company but received no help.

8. They packed the antique posters in a large box.

9. We saw many birds in the three days we spent at that cabin by the lake.

10. This sculpture has a smooth surface and little detail.

PRACTICE 3.1B Identifying Adjectives and Words They Modify

Read the sentences. Then, write the adjectives and the words they modify.

EXAMPLE The many colors of fall were featured in the beautiful photograph.

ANSWER *many, colors*
beautiful, photograph

11. A cheerful girl skipped across the field.

12. That rude, thoughtless comment was inappropriate.

13. The tall receiver reached for the pass and made a great catch.

14. The third attempt to break the record was successful.

15. The horse, muscular and graceful, trotted around the ring.

16. Sometimes I enjoy the cold, brisk days of winter.

17. Serena received a bouquet of fresh flowers.

18. This state boasts many natural wonders.

19. The lake, sparkling and clear, looked refreshing.

20. That young woman is a talented violinist with the local symphony.

SPEAKING APPLICATION

Tell a partner about a piece of artwork you like. Have your partner listen for and name at least four adjectives and the words they modify.

WRITING APPLICATION

Write three sentences about your favorite season. Use at least one adjective in each sentence.

EL4

Articles

Three frequently used adjectives are the words *a, an,* and *the.* They are called **articles**. Articles can be **definite** or **indefinite**. Both types indicate that a noun will soon follow.

> *The* is a **definite article.** It points to a specific person, place, thing, or idea. *A* and *an* are **indefinite articles.** They point to any member of a group of similar people, places, things, or ideas.

3.1.2 RULE

DEFINITE   Mr. Halpern is **the** one to see. (a specific person)

Go into **the** house, and I'll meet you. (a specific place)

I want to drive **the** new car. (a specific thing)

INDEFINITE   I want to see **a** concert. (any concert)

Please take **an** envelope. (any envelope)

You should ask **a** friend to go with you. (any friend)

A is used before consonant sounds. *An* is used before vowel sounds. You choose between *a* and *an* based on sound. Some letters are tricky. The letter *h,* a consonant, may sound like either a consonant or a vowel. The letters *o* and *u* are vowels, but they may sometimes sound like consonants.

USING *A* AND *AN*	
A WITH CONSONANT SOUNDS	*AN* WITH VOWEL SOUNDS
a black wallet	an endangered species
a happy occasion (*h* sound)	an honest friend (no *h* sound)
a one-lane road (*w* sound)	an old car (*o* sound)
a Union general (*y* sound)	an umbrella (*u* sound)
a jeep	an egg
a pear	an individual
a universal remote (*y* sound)	an angry horn

See Practice 3.1C

PRACTICE 3.1C > **Identifying Definite and Indefinite Articles**

Read the sentences. Then, write the articles and label them
definite or *indefinite*.

EXAMPLE   Uncle Ian used a metal detector to find the watch.

ANSWER   *a* — indefinite
            the — definite

1. Most of the research can be done at the downtown library.

2. A treasure is said to be hidden in the cave.

3. A family of ducks was trying to cross the street.

4. Have you seen the senator yet?

5. Randall bought a new hockey stick and a helmet.

6. Our science teacher explained the theory well.

7. The alley leading to the parking lot is blocked off.

8. Read the book on the Vietnam War, and then write a report.

9. We spent an entire week working on the social studies project.

10. Tracy is hoping for an island vacation or a luxury cruise.

SPEAKING APPLICATION

Tell a partner what chores
you are responsible for at
home. Your partner should
listen for and name two
definite articles and two
indefinite articles.

WRITING APPLICATION

Use sentence 3 as a model,
and write two more
sentences that each contain
one indefinite article and
one definite article.

Using Proper Adjectives

A **proper adjective** begins with a capital letter. There are two types of proper adjectives.

> **A proper adjective** is (1) a proper noun used as an adjective or (2) an adjective formed from a proper noun.

3.1.3 RULE

A proper noun used as an adjective does *not* change its form. It is merely placed in front of another noun.

PROPER NOUNS	USED AS PROPER ADJECTIVES
Truman	the Truman Library (*Which* library?)
Florida	Florida wetlands (*Which* wetlands?)
December	December weather (*What kind* of weather?)

When an adjective is formed from a proper noun, the proper noun will change its form. Notice that endings such as *-n, -ian,* or *-ese* have been added to the proper nouns in the chart below or the spelling has been changed.

PROPER NOUNS	PROPER ADJECTIVES FORMED FROM PROPER NOUNS
America	American history (*Which kind* of history?)
Japan	Japanese cities (*Which* cities?)
Norway	Norwegian legends (*Which* legends?)
Inca	Incan empire (*Which* empire?)
Florida	Floridian sunset (*Which* sunset?)

See Practice 3.1D

Using Nouns as Adjectives

Nouns can sometimes be used as adjectives. A noun used as an adjective usually comes directly before another noun and answers the question *What kind?* or *Which one?*

NOUNS	USED AS ADJECTIVES
shoe	a shoe salesperson (*What kind* of salesperson?)
waterfowl	the waterfowl refuge (*Which* refuge?)
court	a court date (*What kind* of date?)
morning	a morning appointment (*What kind* of appointment?)

Using Compound Adjectives

Adjectives, like nouns, can be compound.

3.1.4

A **compound adjective** is made up of more than one word.

Most **compound adjectives** are written as hyphenated words. Some are written as combined words, as in "a *runaway* horse." If you are unsure about how to write a compound adjective, look up the word in a dictionary.

HYPHENATED	COMBINED
a well-known actress	a featherweight boxer
a full-time job	a freshwater lake
snow-covered mountains	a sideways glance
one-sided opinions	heartbreaking news
so-called experts	a nearsighted witness

See Practice 3.1E

PRACTICE 3.1D > Using Proper Adjectives

Read the sentences. Then, rewrite each sentence to include a proper adjective before the underlined noun.

EXAMPLE   Carmen enjoyed the <u>play</u>.

ANSWER   *Carmen enjoyed the Shakespearean play.*

1. That store carries some expensive <u>antiques</u>.
2. My neighbor adopted a <u>cat</u>.
3. My mother collects <u>jewelry</u>.
4. Last week we learned about <u>explorers</u>.
5. The dancers performed traditional <u>dances</u>.
6. Aunt Carol invited us to her house for a <u>feast</u>.
7. We saw many <u>tourists</u> in Italy.
8. I'd like a book about the fashions of the <u>era</u>.
9. Meet me in the library after <u>class</u>.
10. Jason enjoys studying ancient <u>coins</u>.

PRACTICE 3.1E > Recognizing Nouns Used as Adjectives

Read the sentences. Write the noun, proper noun, or compound noun used as an adjective. Then, write the noun that the adjective modifies.

EXAMPLE   Dad used a whole bag of Idaho potatoes in the soup.

ANSWER   *Idaho, potatoes*

11. The evening sky was laced with orange and pink.
12. We spent the second day of our trip driving across the California desert.
13. Piano music could be heard from the street.
14. You will find the subway station just three blocks from here.
15. Isn't Texas toast much thicker than regular toast?
16. The students constructed a life-sized statue of Abraham Lincoln.
17. The art festival will be held at the park near the river.
18. Jenna sighed when she first saw the lovely lakeside cabin.
19. The January temperatures were unusually mild that year.
20. All of the seventh-grade teachers calmly led their students out of the building.

SPEAKING APPLICATION

Tell a partner about a country you would like to visit. Have your partner listen for and name two nouns used as adjectives, as well as one proper adjective.

WRITING APPLICATION

Write sentences using each of the following as adjectives: a noun, a compound noun, and a proper noun. Then, write one sentence using a proper adjective.

Using Pronouns as Adjectives

Pronouns, like nouns, can sometimes be used as adjectives.

A pronoun becomes an adjective if it modifies a noun.

EXAMPLES We saw the dress on **this** side of the mall.

Which store has the nicest dress?

In the first example, the demonstrative pronoun *this* modifies *side,* and in the second example, the interrogative pronoun *which* modifies *store.*

Using Possessive Nouns and Pronouns as Adjectives

The following personal pronouns are often **possessive adjectives:** *my, your, her, his, its, our,* and *their.* They are adjectives because they come before nouns and answer the question *Which one?* They are pronouns because they have antecedents.

EXAMPLES The **children** clapped **their** hands.
antecedent · pronoun

The **library** wants to upgrade **its** computers.
antecedent · pronoun

In the first example, *their* is an adjective because it modifies *hands.* At the same time, it is a pronoun because it refers to the antecedent *children.*

In the second example, *its* is an adjective because it modifies *computers.* The word *its* is also a pronoun because it refers to the antecedent *library.*

Note About Possessive Nouns Possessive nouns function as adjectives when they modify a noun.

EXAMPLES The slide is in the **Browns'** backyard.

The **cat's** tail is orange and white.

See Practice 3.1F

Using Demonstrative Adjectives

This, that, these, and *those*—the four demonstrative pronouns—can also be **demonstrative adjectives.**

PRONOUN   We bought **that** .

ADJECTIVE   **That** man is the new principal.

PRONOUN   Why did you buy **these** ?

ADJECTIVE   **These** children are waiting for frozen yogurt.

Using Interrogative Adjectives

Which, what, and *whose*—three of the interrogative pronouns—can be **interrogative adjectives.**

PRONOUN   **Which** is your favorite dish?

ADJECTIVE   **Which** sauce do you like the best?

PRONOUN   **Whose** is that?

ADJECTIVE   **Whose** poodle can that be?

Using Indefinite Adjectives

A number of indefinite pronouns—*both, few, many, each, most,* and *all,* among others—can also be used as **indefinite adjectives.**

PRONOUN   I ordered one of **each** .

ADJECTIVE   **Each** student gets to choose.

PRONOUN   I don't need **any** .

See Practice 3.1G   ADJECTIVE   I don't need **any** advice.

> **PRACTICE 3.1F** **Recognizing Possessive Nouns and Pronouns Used as Adjectives**

Read the sentences. Then, write the possessive noun or pronoun used as an adjective in each sentence.

EXAMPLE   The club treasurer understands her responsibilities.

ANSWER   *her*

1. Everyone found the dancers' performance inspiring.

2. Did you call your cousin last night?

3. I will share my sandwich with you if you like.

4. The Jacksons' house is the one on the corner.

5. Lily's mother goes to yoga class twice a week.

6. Jada and Lewis will give their presentation on ancient Rome.

7. I think that book is about Lincoln's presidency.

8. The boy finally found his backpack near the bus stop.

9. Our dance last weekend was a big success.

10. The puppy knocked over its water bowl and made a mess.

> **PRACTICE 3.1G** **Identifying Demonstrative, Interrogative, and Indefinite Adjectives**

Read the sentences. Then, write the adjective in each sentence and label it *demonstrative*, *interrogative*, or *indefinite*.

EXAMPLE   This marvel of geology attracts tourists from across the country.

ANSWER   *This* — demonstrative

11. Could you hand me one of those pears, please?

12. Which poem are you going to recite in class?

13. This watch was a gift from a friend.

14. Both students gave excellent presentations.

15. There are many acts auditioning for the show.

16. What kind of music do you like most?

17. I need to organize these books and then dust the shelves.

18. Have you made some necklaces to give as gifts?

19. Whose sculptures will be on display at the gallery?

20. Each child made a mobile to take home.

SPEAKING APPLICATION

With a partner, take turns describing a concert or play you have seen. Have your partner listen for and name at least one possessive noun and one possessive pronoun used as an adjective.

WRITING APPLICATION

Write four sentences about the ocean. In your sentences, use at least one demonstrative adjective, one interrogative adjective, and one indefinite adjective.

3.2 Adverbs

Adverbs can modify three different parts of speech. They make the meaning of verbs, adjectives, or other adverbs more precise.

3.2.1 RULE

> An **adverb** modifies a verb, an adjective, or another adverb.

Although adverbs may modify adjectives and other adverbs, they generally modify verbs.

Using Adverbs That Modify Verbs

Adverbs that modify verbs will answer one of these four questions: *Where? When? In what way? To what extent?* These adverbs are also known as *adverbs of place, adverbs of time, adverbs of manner,* and *adverbs of degree.*

ADVERBS THAT MODIFY VERBS			
WHERE?	**WHEN?**	**IN WHAT WAY?**	**TO WHAT EXTENT?**
push upward	will leave soon	works carefully	hardly ate
fell there	comes daily	speaks well	really surprised
stay nearby	swims often	chews noisily	almost cried
go outside	exhibits yearly	acted willingly	partly finished
is here	report later	walk quietly	nearly won
jump away	come tomorrow	smiled happily	fully agree
drove down	went yesterday	moved gracefully	totally oppose

Negative adverbs, such as *not, never,* and *nowhere,* also modify verbs.

EXAMPLES   Heather **never arrived** at the dinner.
                          adverb   verb

He **could not answer** the judge.
       verb   adverb verb

Continuing to argue had **led nowhere**.
                                        verb   adverb

See Practice 3.2A

Using Adverbs That Modify Adjectives

An adverb modifying an adjective answers only one question: *To what extent?*

> **When adverbs modify adjectives or adverbs, they answer the question *To what extent?***

ADVERBS THAT MODIFY ADJECTIVES	
very upset	extremely tall
definitely wrong	not hungry

EXAMPLE   The snow can be **very beautiful**.

The adverb *very* modifies the adjective *beautiful*.

EXAMPLE   The mountain is **extremely snowy**.

The adverb *extremely* modifies the adjective *snowy*.

Adverbs Modifying Other Adverbs

When adverbs modify other adverbs, they again answer the question *To what extent?*

ADVERBS MODIFYING ADVERBS	
traveled less slowly	move very cautiously
lost too easily	lived almost happily

EXAMPLE   Owls are **hardly ever** seen in the daytime.

The adverb *hardly* modifies the adverb *ever*.

EXAMPLE   When writing, my hand cramps **too quickly**.

The adverb *too* modifies the adverb *quickly*.

See Practice 3.2B

PRACTICE 3.2A Identifying How Adverbs Modify Verbs

Read the sentences. Write the adverb in each sentence and list the question it answers. (*When? Where? In what way? To what extent?*)

EXAMPLE   To get to the stadium, turn right at the light.

ANSWER   *right* — In what way?

1. Harriet Tubman was known everywhere along the Underground Railroad.

2. Tanya opened the door to the barn cautiously.

3. The engine sputtered and then stopped.

4. Approval for the Brooklyn Bridge was finally given in 1869.

5. The cat napped quietly on the back of the couch.

6. She immediately called the police about the robbery.

7. Silently, the cougar leapt from the rock.

8. Jason has almost finished the jigsaw puzzle.

9. Gina and Alexis played soccer outside.

10. The new school is nearly completed.

PRACTICE 3.2B Recognizing Adverbs and Words They Modify

Read the sentences. Write the word that each underlined adverb modifies. Then, write whether that word is a *verb*, an *adjective*, or an *adverb*.

EXAMPLE   Jake <u>expertly</u> applied the glue to the fabric.

ANSWER   *applied* — verb

11. My little sister is learning to speak <u>more</u> clearly.

12. The running back's movements seemed <u>rather</u> sluggish.

13. We tried to catch the hamster, but it was moving <u>too</u> fast.

14. The beef stew simmered <u>slowly</u> on the stove.

15. Caleb gave the teacher his term paper <u>late</u>.

16. At the awards ceremony, Consuela seemed <u>slightly</u> upset.

17. The police officers approached the building <u>quite</u> cautiously.

18. My brother <u>quickly</u> swept the front porch.

19. The dance team purchased an <u>almost</u> new CD player.

20. My mother speaks Portuguese <u>extremely</u> well.

SPEAKING APPLICATION

With a partner, take turns describing the ideal pet. Your partner should listen for three adjectives and tell what words the adjectives modify.

WRITING APPLICATION

Write three sentences about birds. In the first sentence, use an adverb that modifies a verb. In the second sentence, use an adverb that modifies an adjective. In the third, use an adverb that modifies another adverb.

Finding Adverbs in Sentences

Adverbs can be found in different places in sentences. The chart below shows examples of possible locations for adverbs. Arrows point to the words that the adverbs modify.

LOCATION OF ADVERBS IN SENTENCES	
LOCATION	EXAMPLE
At the beginning of a sentence	Carefully, she approached the puppy.
At the end of a sentence	She approached the puppy carefully.
Before a verb	She carefully approached the puppy.
After a verb	She tiptoed silently toward the puppy.
Between parts of a verb phrase	She had carefully approached the puppy.
Before an adjective	The puppy was always quiet.
Before another adverb	The puppy whined rather quietly.

Conjunctive adverbs **Conjunctive adverbs** are adverbs that join independent clauses. (See Chapter 5 for more about conjunctive adverbs.)

EXAMPLES   Her computer broke; **therefore** , she couldn't finish
                                    conjunctive adverb
her essay.

Tara bought a new outfit at the mall; **however** ,
                                            conjunctive adverb
she forgot to take the tags off.

See Practice 3.2C

Adverb or Adjective?

Some words can function as adverbs or as adjectives, depending on their use in a sentence.

> If a noun or pronoun is modified by a word, that modifying word is an **adjective.** If a verb, adjective, or adverb is modified by a word, that modifying word is an **adverb.**

3.2.3 RULE

An adjective will modify a noun or pronoun and will answer one of the questions *What kind? Which one? How many?* or *How much?*

An adverb will modify a verb, an adjective, or another adverb and will answer one of the questions *Where? When? In what way?* or *To what extent?*

ADVERB MODIFYING VERB

Teachers **work** **hard**.
            verb   adverb

When the puppies reached the door, they **stepped** **inside**.
      verb   adverb

ADJECTIVE MODIFYING NOUN

Teachers accomplish **hard** **tasks**.
          adjective   noun

This is the **right** **spot** to see the sun rise
         adjective noun
over the mountains.

While most words ending in *-ly* are adverbs, some are not. Several adjectives also end in *-ly*. These adjectives are formed by adding *-ly* to nouns.

ADJECTIVES WITH *-LY* ENDINGS

a **lovely** dress

a **costly** meal

EXAMPLES

At the mall we found a **lovely** dress.

Eating out is fun, but that was a **costly** meal.

See Practice 3.2D

PRACTICE 3.2C > Locating Adverbs

Read the sentences. Then, write each adverb and the word or words it modifies.

EXAMPLE   I have often wondered about that run-down building.

ANSWER   *often, have wondered*

1. Usually I finish my homework before dinner.
2. Many fans arrived at the game early.
3. My friend Harriet is a very kind person.
4. These candied yams are especially delicious.
5. The home team was defeated rather easily by the visitors.
6. The little child spoke too softly to be heard.
7. Jeanette has made this gravy awfully thick.
8. Serena awoke early on the day of the spelling bee.
9. She squinted because the sun was shining so brightly.
10. Please order the tickets soon.

PRACTICE 3.2D > Recognizing Adverbs and Adjectives

Read the sentences. Then, write whether each underlined word is an *adjective* or an *adverb*.

EXAMPLE   I worked <u>hard</u> to pass the test.

ANSWER   *adverb*

11. When it rains, we eat lunch <u>inside</u>.
12. The batter swung at an <u>inside</u> pitch.
13. Sam eats breakfast before his <u>early</u> class.
14. Please try to arrive <u>early</u> on Saturday.
15. The restaurant is too <u>far</u> from our house.
16. That's Kai in the <u>far</u> corner.
17. My dog sensed that a storm was <u>near</u>.
18. Is your school <u>near</u> here?
19. The students studied for their <u>weekly</u> quiz.
20. I receive the magazine <u>weekly</u>.

SPEAKING APPLICATION

With a partner, take turns telling about a typical evening at your home. Your partner should listen for and name at least three adverbs.

WRITING APPLICATION

Use sentences 19 and 20 as models, and write one sentence in which *weekly* is used as an adjective and one sentence in which *weekly* is used as an adverb.

CHAPTER 4

PREPOSITIONS

Build meaning into your sentences by using prepositions to create relationships between words.

WRITE GUY *Jeff Anderson, M.Ed.*

WHAT DO YOU NOTICE?

Spot the prepositions as you zoom in on these sentences from the essay "Science and the Sense of Wonder" by Isaac Asimov.

MENTOR TEXT

> Should I stare lovingly at a single leaf and willingly remain ignorant of the forest? Should I be satisfied to watch the sun glinting off a single pebble and scorn any knowledge of a beach?

Now, ask yourself the following questions:

- In the two prepositional phrases that begin with the preposition *of*, what are the objects of the prepositions?
- In the two prepositional phrases that contain the word *single*, what are the prepositions and their objects?

In the phrase *of the forest*, *forest* is the object of the preposition. The noun *beach* is the object of the preposition in the phrase *of a beach*. In the phrase *at a single leaf*, the preposition is *at* and the object is *leaf*. In the phrase *off a single pebble*, the preposition is *off* and the object is *pebble*.

Grammar for Writers Choosing one preposition over another can change the meaning of a sentence. Use prepositions in your writing that convey the meaning you intend.

I need to study before tomorrow's test.

Well, definitely not after it!

4.1 Prepositions

Prepositions function as connectors, relating one word to another within a sentence.

They allow a speaker or writer to express the link between separate items. **Prepositions** can convey information about location, time, or direction or provide details.

RULE 4.1.1

A **preposition** relates the noun or pronoun following it to another word in the sentence.

EXAMPLES

RELATES   RELATES

The flower fell **onto** the surface **of** the counter.
preposition   noun   preposition   noun

RELATES

The puppy ran **across** the patio and
preposition   noun

RELATES

hid **inside** his doghouse.
preposition   noun

In the first example, the flower fell where? (onto the surface)
It was the surface of what? (the counter) In the second example,
the puppy ran where? (across the patio) The puppy hid where?
(inside his doghouse)

FIFTY COMMON PREPOSITIONS				
about	behind	during	off	to
above	below	except	on	toward
across	beneath	for	onto	under
after	beside	from	opposite	underneath
against	besides	in	out	until
along	between	inside	outside	up
among	beyond	into	over	upon
around	but	like	past	with
at	by	near	since	within
before	down	of	through	without

See Practice 4.1A

Compound Prepositions Prepositions consisting of more than one word are called **compound prepositions.** Some of them are listed in the chart below:

COMPOUND PREPOSITIONS		
according to	by means of	instead of
ahead of	in addition to	in view of
apart from	in back of	next to
aside from	in front of	on account of
as of	in place of	on top of
because of	in spite of	out of

Because prepositions have different meanings, using a particular preposition will affect the way other words in a sentence relate to one another. In the first sentence, for example, notice how each preposition changes the relationship between *parade* and *City Hall.*

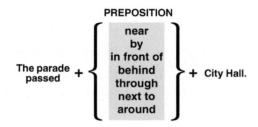

In this sentence, the preposition changes the relationship between *girls* and *gym.*

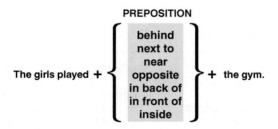

See Practice 4.1B

PRACTICE 4.1A > Identifying Prepositions

Read the sentences. Then, write the preposition in each sentence.

EXAMPLE   Our dog runs from the house when he hears the bathwater running.

ANSWER   *from*

1. The plants are on the porch.
2. Where are the photos from our vacation?
3. The boat chugged along the wide river.
4. We can ask Mrs. Lopez about the math test.
5. During the winter we often go skiing.
6. We found the teddy bear underneath the child's blankets.
7. The boys strolled into the pizza parlor.
8. The traffic snaked slowly through the town.
9. Before dinner Sara always walks the dogs.
10. After all the excitement, I could not find my suitcase.

PRACTICE 4.1B > Identifying Compound Prepositions

Read the sentences. Then, write the compound preposition in each sentence.

EXAMPLE   The flight was canceled because of the storm.

ANSWER   *because of*

11. The flower seeds can be found next to the gardening tools.
12. I'd like a salad instead of fries, please.
13. In spite of the trouble, we arrived at the train station in time.
14. According to the book jacket, this is the story of an adventure at sea.
15. Keeley gave her sister a nice gift in addition to the birthday card.
16. A crowd had gathered in front of the building.
17. As of last night, the concert was canceled.
18. Put the dog treats on top of the refrigerator.
19. The shuttle arrived ahead of time, but we were ready.
20. Darren started the game in place of the usual point guard.

SPEAKING APPLICATION

With a partner, take turns describing the street on which you live. Your partner should listen for and name at least three different prepositions.

WRITING APPLICATION

Use sentence 1 as a model, and write three more sentences that contain prepositions. Include at least one compound preposition in your sentences.

Prepositions Used in Sentences

A preposition is never used by itself in a sentence. Instead, it appears as part of a phrase containing one or more other words.

> A **preposition** in a sentence always introduces a **prepositional phrase.**

Prepositional Phrases

A **prepositional phrase** is a group of words that begins with a preposition and ends with a noun or pronoun. The noun or pronoun following the preposition is the **object of the preposition.**

Some prepositional phrases contain just two words—the preposition and its object. Others are longer because they contain modifiers.

EXAMPLES

during **school**
  preposition   object

from the **White House**
preposition   object

in place of the old, used **sneakers**
   preposition   object

inside the warm, new **house**
preposition   object

with **time**
preposition object

according to the new **manager**
    preposition   object

See Practice 4.1C
See Practice 4.1D

Prepositional phrases convey information about location, time, or direction or provide details. (See Chapter 11 to learn about prepositional phrases and their influence on subject–verb agreement.)

Preposition or Adverb?

Some words can be used either as prepositions or as adverbs. The following chart lists some examples. When the word is used as a preposition, it begins a prepositional phrase and is followed by the object of the preposition. If the word has no object, it is probably being used as an adverb.

PREPOSITION OR ADVERB		
above	inside	outside
after	nearby	past
around	opposite	underneath
before	out	within

PREPOSITION	The broken glass was **outside** the cabinet.
ADVERB	The woman saw the broken glass **outside**.
PREPOSITION	She appeared **before** the committee.
ADVERB	She had not seen that **before**.
PREPOSITION	The girl ran **past** the classroom door.
ADVERB	The teacher walked **past** quickly.
PREPOSITION	She sat **inside** the salon.
ADVERB	Please go **inside** tomorrow.
PREPOSITION	The teacher sat **behind** the students.
ADVERB	The student lingered **behind**.
PREPOSITION	The book was on the shelf **above** the table.
ADVERB	Confetti fell on them from **above**.

See Practice 4.1E
See Practice 4.1F

PRACTICE 4.1C ▷ Recognizing Prepositional Phrases

Read the sentences. Write the prepositional phrase in each sentence, and underline the object of the preposition.

EXAMPLE   Beyond that small mountain range is a Hopi reservation.

ANSWER   *Beyond that small mountain <u>range</u>*

1. The postal carrier left a box outside the house.
2. The puppy wriggled under the heavy blankets.
3. The package warned consumers of many dangers.
4. You will see a stained-glass window near the front door.
5. What are those weeds growing between the fence slats?
6. Three deer could be seen grazing by the road.
7. She looked beautiful in her new outfit.
8. In spite of his concerns, Mr. Grant mailed the letter.
9. In front of my aunt's house stands a large, old maple tree.
10. June tried to see ahead of the traffic but could not spot anything.

PRACTICE 4.1D ▷ Distinguishing Prepositions and Prepositional Phrases

Read the sentences. Write the prepositional phrases. Then, underline the preposition in each phrase.

EXAMPLE   Because of the heavy traffic, the Garcias arrived late.

ANSWER   *<u>Because of</u> the heavy traffic*

11. Use the large baking dish for that casserole.
12. The dog was so excited that he ran into the wall.
13. According to the label, this dish soap is highly concentrated.
14. The trampoline in the backyard has had much use.
15. The dirty towels are on top of the washing machine.
16. Scott threw the ball toward first base.
17. Without your help, we never could have succeeded.
18. Jumping off the high dive can be frightening.
19. Let's have pancakes instead of scrambled eggs.
20. The girls took a long hike through the woods.

SPEAKING APPLICATION

Tell a partner how you usually celebrate your birthday. Your partner should listen for and name at least three prepositional phrases.

WRITING APPLICATION

Use sentence 16 as a model, and write three more sentences that each contain a prepositional phrase.

PRACTICE 4.1E ▷ Distinguishing Prepositions and Adverbs

Read the sentences. Label each underlined word *preposition* or *adverb*.

EXAMPLE   Greg picked up the rock and looked <u>underneath</u>.

ANSWER   *adverb*

1. Nina jogged <u>through</u> the park on her way home from school.

2. If you can't get through the gate, just go <u>around</u>.

3. The tourists had to travel <u>along</u> the main road for three more miles.

4. Janelle gets nervous whenever a storm comes <u>near</u>.

5. We watched the parade go <u>by</u>.

6. Wiggling its tiny body, the puppy tried to slip <u>through</u> the door.

7. I called to her, but she ran <u>outside</u>.

8. A festive crowd had gathered <u>near</u> the parade route.

9. Sam found a lot of dust <u>behind</u> the couch.

10. Please walk <u>along</u> quietly until you reach the ticket counter.

PRACTICE 4.1F ▷ Supplying Prepositions and Prepositional Phrases

Read the sentences. Then, expand each sentence by adding a prepositional phrase that begins with a preposition of your choice, or use one of these prepositions: *in, for, on, of, by, from, with, into, between, through, about.*

EXAMPLE   The hamster is running.

ANSWER   *The hamster is running on its exercise wheel.*

11. The dog is trying to climb.

12. We make breakfast and then get dressed.

13. Kevin likes pizza.

14. We found the perfect camping site.

15. Karli works every day.

16. Dad promised to help us.

17. Several rows of pansies were planted.

18. One of the ushers smiled.

19. The softball game has been postponed.

20. The parking lot is full.

SPEAKING APPLICATION

Tell a partner a story about your best friend. Your partner should listen for and name at least one preposition and one adverb that could also be used as a preposition.

WRITING APPLICATION

Write a sentence that contains a preposition. Then write a second sentence that uses the same word as an adverb.

CHAPTER 5

CONJUNCTIONS *and* INTERJECTIONS

Use conjunctions to show relationships between ideas in your writing; add interjections to affect the mood.

WRITE GUY *Jeff Anderson, M.Ed.*

WHAT DO YOU NOTICE?

Search for conjunctions as you zoom in on this sentence from the essay "The Trouble With Television" by Robert MacNeil.

MENTOR TEXT

> Literacy may not be an inalienable human right, but it is one that the highly literate Founding Fathers might not have found unreasonable or even unattainable.

Now, ask yourself the following questions:

- Why does the author use the coordinating conjunction *but*?
- How does the use of *or* differ from the use of *but* in the sentence?

The author uses a comma followed by *but* to connect two sentences. The first sentence is *literacy may not be an inalienable right,* and the second is *it is one that the highly literate Founding Fathers might not have found unreasonable or even unattainable.* The use of *or* differs from the use of *but* because *or* connects two adjectives, *unreasonable* and *unattainable*.

Grammar for Writers Conjunctions help writers show relationships between ideas. Use conjunctions in your writing to infuse variety and interest.

Should I put the conjunction here or there?

I think you need one here *and* there.

5.1 Conjunctions

Conjunctions are like links in a chain: They help you join words and ideas.

RULE 5.1.1

A **conjunction** connects words or groups of words.

Conjunctions fall into three groups: **Coordinating conjunctions, correlative conjunctions,** and **subordinating conjunctions**.

Coordinating Conjunctions

RULE 5.1.2

Coordinating conjunctions connect words of the same kind, such as two or more nouns or verbs. They can also connect larger groups of words, such as prepositional phrases or even complete sentences.

COORDINATING CONJUNCTIONS						
and	but	for	nor	or	so	yet

In the following examples, notice the coordinating conjunctions that connect the highlighted words.

Connecting Nouns	My dad and his boss met for lunch to close the deal.
Connecting Verbs	They brought my soup but forgot to bring the salad.
Connecting Prepositional Phrases	Put the vegetables onto the table or into the basket.
Connecting Two Sentences	The roast was still in the oven, yet it was time to eat.

See Practice 5.1A

Correlative Conjunctions

Correlative conjunctions are *pairs* of words that connect similar kinds of words or groups of words.

CORRELATIVE CONJUNCTIONS		
both . . . and	neither . . . nor	whether . . . or
either . . . or	not only . . . but also	

Notice the correlative conjunctions in the following examples.

Connecting Nouns	Either the blanket or the quilt will work.
Connecting Pronouns	Neither my sister nor I know the story.
Connecting Verbs	Every afternoon, he both calls and e-mails.
Connecting Prepositional Phrases	He's arriving today—whether by car or by bus, I can't say.
Connecting Two Clauses	Not only do they skate, but also they ski.

See Practice 5.1B

Subordinating Conjunctions

> **Subordinating conjunctions** connect two ideas by making one idea dependent on the other.

5.1.3 RULE

FREQUENTLY USED SUBORDINATING CONJUNCTIONS				
after	as soon as	if	though	whenever
although	as though	in order that	till	where
as	because	since	unless	wherever
as if	before	so that	until	while
as long as	even though	than	when	

The Dependent Idea The subordinating conjunction always introduces the dependent idea. The subordinating conjunction connects the dependent idea to the main idea.

EXAMPLES   I made the plans **after** **I heard the weather report** .

When **she called yesterday** , I was worried something was wrong.

The examples show that the main idea can come at the beginning or at the end of the sentence. Look at the difference in punctuation. When the dependent idea comes first, it must be separated from the main idea with a comma. If the dependent idea comes second, no comma is necessary.

See Practice 5.1C

Conjunctive Adverbs

Conjunctive adverbs are used as conjunctions to connect complete ideas. They are often used as transitions, connecting different ideas by showing comparisons, contrasts, or results.

CONJUNCTIVE ADVERBS	
accordingly	indeed
again	instead
also	moreover
besides	nevertheless
consequently	otherwise
finally	then
furthermore	therefore
however	thus

Notice the punctuation that is used before and after the conjunctive adverbs in the following examples. (See Chapter 13 for more about punctuation with conjunctive adverbs.)

EXAMPLES   This restaurant has great food; **otherwise** , I wouldn't eat here.

Our dinner reservations are at 7:00 P.M. sharp; **therefore** , we should hurry.

See Practice 5.1D

Supplying Coordinating Conjunctions

Read the sentences. Then, write each sentence, replacing the blank with a coordinating conjunction that makes sense in the sentence.

EXAMPLE   I knew it was getting late, _____ I could not put the book down.

ANSWER   *I knew it was getting late, yet I could not put the book down.*

1. A good athlete must have strength _____ endurance.

2. Get in the car now, _____ you'll have to find another ride.

3. The quarterback delivered the pass quickly _____ accurately.

4. With time _____ patience, you can train your dog.

5. I must study tonight, _____ I have a science test in the morning.

6. The Jacksons drive a small _____ comfortable car.

7. Gina has not called, _____ she has sent me an e-mail.

8. Today is Josh's birthday, _____ we are cooking dinner for him.

9. You can put that plant in the kitchen _____ in the living room.

10. Mom remembered the gift _____ then left it in the car.

Writing Sentences With Correlative Conjunctions

Write ten sentences, using each of the correlative conjunctions below.

EXAMPLE   whether . . . or

ANSWER   *I don't know whether I will go to the museum or stay home.*

Please decide whether you would like cereal or eggs for breakfast.

11. both . . . and
12. either . . . or
13. neither . . . nor
14. not only . . . but also
15. whether . . . or
16. both . . . and
17. either . . . or
18. neither . . . nor
19. not only . . . but also
20. whether . . . or

SPEAKING APPLICATION

Tell a partner about a band you like. Your partner should listen for and name at least one coordinating conjunction and one correlative conjunction.

WRITING APPLICATION

Write two sentences about the weather. In the first sentence, use a coordinating conjunction. In the second, use a correlative conjunction.

PRACTICE 5.1C > **Identifying Subordinating Conjunctions**

Read the sentences. Then, write the subordinating conjunction (e.g., *because*, *since*) in each sentence.

EXAMPLE   Unless you notify the book club, you will receive a new book every month.

ANSWER   *Unless*

1. Sheryl might win the spelling bee if she spends some time studying.

2. Jamal went into the diner while everyone else waited outside.

3. Although I like my little brother, he does annoy me sometimes.

4. As soon as I have all the supplies, I will build my own kite.

5. Aunt Jo always takes us out for lunch when she is in town.

6. I can't go to the movies because I have to watch my little sister tonight.

7. I haven't seen Leona since she visited last year.

8. Jerome wants a bicycle so that he can ride to school.

9. When our lost cat was returned to us, we all cried for joy.

10. Even though I have other friends, I really miss Amanda.

PRACTICE 5.1D > **Identifying Conjunctive Adverbs**

Read the sentences. Then, write the conjunctive adverb in each sentence.

EXAMPLE   Rosa is very smart; indeed, she is the smartest person I know.

ANSWER   *indeed*

11. Consuela wanted to take photography; however, she could not fit it in.

12. Mom is out shopping today; therefore, we'll have to fix our own lunch.

13. Rescue workers helped the frightened passengers; finally, the ordeal was over.

14. I want to get a snack; besides, the concert won't start for at least fifteen minutes.

15. Rama had not used the software before; nevertheless, she was willing to try.

16. Jamal might like that group; moreover, he might buy their CDs.

17. The auditorium was filled to capacity; consequently, some people were turned away.

18. Please make sure the thermostat is turned down; otherwise, we will be wasting fuel.

19. They decided not to go to Phoenix; instead, they spent the weekend at the beach.

20. Her test scores were low; furthermore, she had missed several classes.

SPEAKING APPLICATION

Tell a partner about a career you have considered. Have your partner listen for and name at least one subordinating conjunction (e.g., *because*, *since*).

WRITING APPLICATION

Write one sentence with a subordinating conjunction at the beginning and one with a subordinating conjunction in the middle. Finally, write a sentence using a conjunctive adverb.

5.2 Interjections

The **interjection** is the part of speech that is used the least. Its only use is to express feelings or emotions.

> An **interjection** expresses feeling or emotion and functions independently from the rest of a sentence.

5.2.1 RULE

An interjection has no grammatical relationship to any other word in a sentence. It is, therefore, set off from the rest of the sentence with a comma or an exclamation mark.

Interjections can express different feelings or emotions.

JOY	**Wow!** This place is fun.
SURPRISE	**Oh**, I must have called you by accident.
PAIN	**Ouch!** That was sharp.
IMPATIENCE	**Hey!** How long is the line?
HESITATION	I, **uh**, thought you had already left.

Interjections are used more in speech than in writing. They are informal, rather than formal, expressions. When you do see them in writing, they are often included in dialogue. The following chart lists words often used as interjections.

INTERJECTIONS			
ah	gosh	nonsense	ugh
aha	great	oh	uh
alas	heavens	oops	um
boy	hey	ouch	well
darn	huh	psst	what
eureka	hurray	shh	whew
fine	my	terrible	wonderful
golly	never	terrific	wow

See Practice 5.2A
See Practice 5.2B

Read the sentences. Write the interjection in each sentence. Then, write what emotion the interjection conveys.

EXAMPLE   Wow! Look at that gymnast on the parallel bars!

ANSWER   *Wow* — *surprise*

1. Hey! Don't touch that cellphone.
2. Gosh, can't you be a little nicer?
3. Darn, my bicycle chain broke.
4. Ouch! That pan is still hot.
5. Whew, that was a close one.
6. Hurray! I won a prize in the sweepstakes!
7. I, uh, think I forgot to bring my lunch.
8. Gee, I never thought I'd see you here.
9. Aha! I have the answer.
10. Fine, take all the crackers you want.

Read the sentences. Rewrite each sentence, using an appropriate interjection in place of the feeling shown in parentheses. Use a comma or an exclamation mark after each interjection.

EXAMPLE   (anger) The stain did not come out of this shirt.

ANSWER   *Darn! The stain did not come out of this shirt.*

11. (surprise) I can't believe the president shook my hand.
12. (impatience) We're going to miss the kickoff.
13. (dislike) That coat is the ugliest thing I've ever seen.
14. (pain) I stubbed my toe on the coffee table.
15. (joy) We are all so happy you got the award.
16. (annoyance) Would you kindly stop talking for just one minute?
17. (anger) You know you're not allowed to do that.
18. (relief) I thought the plane would never land.
19. (joy) I'm leaving for vacation tomorrow.
20. (surprise) I thought you'd forgotten our anniversary.

SPEAKING APPLICATION

With a partner, take turns telling about a memorable experience. Your partner should listen for and name at least two interjections.

WRITING APPLICATION

Write four sentences with interjections. Use commas to punctuate any interjections showing mild emotion, and use exclamation marks with those that show strong emotion.

PRACTICE 1 ▷ **Writing Sentences With Nouns**

Write five sentences, each using one of the following kinds of nouns. Circle those nouns, and underline any other nouns you use.

1. a common noun and a proper noun that name a person

2. a common noun and a proper noun that name a place

3. an abstract noun and a collective noun

4. a single-word compound noun and a hyphenated compound noun

5. a count noun and a non-count noun

PRACTICE 2 ▷ **Identifying Pronouns**

Read the sentences. Then, write the pronoun or pronouns that each sentence contains. Label each pronoun *personal, reflexive, intensive, demonstrative, relative, interrogative, or indefinite.*

1. We heard reports that a hurricane was coming.

2. Whose is that coat, and why is it here?

3. The chef himself made this sandwich for me.

4. Something was making everyone sleepy.

5. She took care of the problem herself.

6. Who wants something from the deli?

7. This is her best movie in years.

8. The house, which needs paint, was once ours.

9. Roger convinced himself that he was right.

10. I myself understand everything that you said.

PRACTICE 3 ▷ **Using Action and Linking Verbs**

Write two sentences for each word below. In the first sentence, use the word as an action verb; in the second sentence, use it as a linking verb.

1. look

2. feel

3. grow

4. sound

5. appear

PRACTICE 4 ▷ **Identifying Helping Verbs and Main Verbs in Verb Phrases**

Read the sentences. Then, write the complete verb phrase in each sentence. Label the parts of each verb phrase *helping* or *main.*

1. Mina has been my friend since kindergarten.

2. The waiter is carrying a large tray of food.

3. I did not see you on the bus this morning.

4. Dad's trip has been postponed until Monday.

5. Peter will never arrive on time.

6. Everyone can sing along.

7. She would not tell me the answer.

8. The hotel was completely renovated last year.

9. The ballgame should be over soon.

10. Have you ever visited Mexico?

Continued on next page ▶

Cumulative Review Chapters 1–5

 PRACTICE 5 Revising Sentences With Adjectives and Adverbs

Read the sentences. Then, rewrite each sentence by adding at least one adjective to modify a noun or a pronoun or one adverb to modify a verb, an adjective, or another adverb.

1. Clara knitted a scarf.
2. The day was warm.
3. The child ran up the steps.
4. The nurse spoke to Dad.
5. A vase of flowers sat on the table.
6. The ambulance driver tore through the streets.
7. An alligator crawled onto the road.
8. The man yelled from the other side of the room.
9. The trees stood like soldiers along the stream.
10. Have you eaten in that restaurant?

 PRACTICE 6 Writing Sentences With Prepositions and Adverbs

Write ten sentences describing outdoor activities. In your first five sentences, use the prepositional phrases in items 1–5. In your next five sentences, use the words in items 6–10 as adverbs.

1. beyond the gate
2. after an hour
3. outside the building
4. across the street
5. along the edge
6. beyond
7. after
8. outside
9. across
10. along

PRACTICE 7 Identifying Conjunctions

Read the sentences. Then, identify each underlined word or pair of words as a *coordinating conjunction*, a *subordinating conjunction*, *correlative conjunctions*, or a *conjunctive adverb*.

1. I saw Karen, <u>but</u> she did not see me.
2. Everyone hurried to class <u>after</u> the bell rang.
3. <u>Both</u> Neil <u>and</u> Fran are away for the summer.
4. I know the answer; <u>therefore</u>, I'll raise my hand.
5. Myra <u>or</u> her brother will walk the dog.

PRACTICE 8 Revising to Include Interjections

Rewrite the following dialogue, adding interjections to show the speakers' emotions. Use either a comma or an exclamation mark after each interjection.

RAUL: Did you see that tornado yesterday?

AMANDA: Mom and I saw it when we were driving home from the supermarket.

RAUL: I'm glad you are both all right.

AMANDA: It was pretty scary for a few minutes.

RAUL: At least we know what to do in emergencies.

AMANDA: Yes. Mom and I were talking about that.

RAUL: As Mom always says, it's important to have a plan.

BASIC SENTENCE PARTS

While it is important to pair interesting subjects and verbs in your writing, your sentences should also have strong finishes with well-chosen direct objects.

WRITE GUY *Jeff Anderson, M.Ed.*

WHAT DO YOU NOTICE?

Track down the sentence parts as you zoom in on this verse from the poem "Ode to Enchanted Light" by Pablo Neruda.

MENTOR TEXT

> A cicada sends
> its sawing song
> high into the empty air.

Now, ask yourself the following questions:

- What are the subject and verb in this verse?
- What is the direct object of the verb?

The subject is *cicada,* and the verb is *sends*. The noun *song* is the direct object because it receives the action of the verb *sends*. You can figure this out by asking *what* the cicada sends.

Grammar for Writers Strong writing shows how people, things, and events affect one another. To craft dynamic sentences, consider the relationships among your subjects, verbs, and direct objects.

My brother hid my favorite game.

Looks like your game is the direct object of his game.

6.1 The Basic Sentence

There are many kinds of sentences. Some are short; others are long. Some are simple, and others are more complex. In order to be considered complete, a sentence must have two things: a subject and a verb.

The Two Basic Parts of a Sentence

Every sentence, regardless of its length, must have a subject and a verb.

RULE 6.1.1 A complete **sentence** contains a subject and a verb and expresses a complete thought.

The Subject

A sentence must have a **subject.** Most subjects are nouns or pronouns. The subject is usually, but not always, found near the beginning of the sentence.

RULE 6.1.2 The **subject** of a sentence is the word or group of words that names the person, place, thing, or idea that performs the action or is described. It answers the question *Who?* or *What?* before the verb.

EXAMPLES

The **pantry** is full.

Mr. Halpern broke his new mug.

He knows how to fix it.

Glue will fix the mug.

The noun *pantry* is the subject in the first sentence. It tells *what* is *full*. In the next sentence, the proper noun *Mr. Halpern* tells *who* broke his mug. The pronoun *he* in the third sentence tells *who can fix it.*

EL5

The Verb

As one of the basic parts of a sentence, the **verb** tells something about the subject.

> The **verb** in a sentence tells what the subject does, what is done to the subject, or what the condition of the subject is.

6.1.3 RULE

EXAMPLES   My sister **won** first place.

Her speech **was presented** at the ceremony.

She **seemed** nervous.

Won tells what *my sister* did. *Was presented* explains what was done with *the speech. Seemed*, a linking verb, tells something about the condition of *she* by linking the subject to *nervous*.

See Practice 6.1A

Using Subjects and Verbs to Express Complete Thoughts

Every basic sentence must express a complete thought.

> A sentence is a group of words with a subject and a verb that expresses a complete thought and can stand by itself and still make sense.

6.1.4 RULE

INCOMPLETE
THOUGHT   in the pantry in the kitchen

(This group of words cannot stand by itself as a sentence.)

This incomplete thought contains two prepositional phrases. The phrases can become a sentence only after *both* a subject and a verb are added to them.

COMPLETE
THOUGHT   The **pasta** **is** in the pantry in the kitchen.
                subject   verb

(This group of words can stand by itself as a sentence.)

See Practice 6.1B   In grammar, incomplete thoughts are often called **fragments.**

PRACTICE 6.1A **Finding Subjects and Verbs**

Read the sentences. Write the subject and verb of each sentence.

EXAMPLE   My injured wrist is bothering me again.

ANSWER   *wrist, is bothering*

1. The creation of a television show is a complex process.

2. A very pleased teacher addressed her first-period class.

3. Tomorrow they will begin their long journey.

4. The book describes the causes of World War II.

5. On special occasions Keiko wears a Japanese kimono.

6. Different dogs need different kinds of training.

7. We have enjoyed our time at the Native American pueblo.

8. Over the summer Juan visited several national parks.

9. The reasons for my decision are good ones.

10. Your hospitality has been delightful.

PRACTICE 6.1B **Recognizing Complete Thoughts**

Read the following groups of words. If a group of words expresses a complete thought, write *complete*. If a group of words expresses an incomplete thought, write *incomplete*.

EXAMPLE   To survive the drought.

ANSWER   *incomplete*

11. Rodents living underground.

12. If the police do not get here soon.

13. Jamal borrowed two novels from his cousin.

14. The bridge was washed out by the flooding.

15. This afternoon we will go swimming.

16. In the building next to the barbershop.

17. Julio and Felicia decided to mow the lawn.

18. A long report about the American Revolution.

19. Because she was very interested in politics.

20. Mr. Cruz can no longer depend on that old computer.

SPEAKING APPLICATION

With a partner, take turns describing a recent assembly at school. Your partner should listen for and name the subject and verb in each of your sentences.

WRITING APPLICATION

Write three sentences about the beach. Make sure each sentence expresses a complete thought. Underline each subject and circle each verb.

6.2 Complete Subjects and Predicates

Have you ever seen tiles laid on a floor? First, a line is drawn in the center of the room. One tile is placed to the left of the line, and another is placed to the right. Then, more tiles are added in the same way: one to the left and one to the right.

Imagine that the first tile on the left is a subject and the first tile on the right is a verb. You would then have a subject and a verb separated by a vertical line, as shown in the example.

EXAMPLE   **Hair** | **fell**.

Now, in the same way that you would add a few more tiles if you were tiling a floor, add a few more words.

EXAMPLE   Blonde **hair** | **fell** on the floor.

At this point, you could add still more words.

EXAMPLE   Margaret's long blonde **hair** | **fell** on the floor in piles.

{EL8}

The centerline is important in laying tiles. It is just as important in dividing these sentences into two parts. All the words to the left of the line in the preceding examples are part of the **complete subject.** The main noun in the complete subject, *hair*, is often called the **simple subject.**

> The **complete subject** of a sentence consists of the subject and any words related to it.

6.2.1 RULE

As in the examples above, the complete subject may be just one word—*hair*—or several words—*Margaret's long blonde hair*.

Look at the example sentences again, plus one with new words added.

EXAMPLES   Blonde **hair** | **fell** on the floor.

Margaret's long blonde **hair** | **fell** on the floor in piles.

Margaret's long blonde **hair** | **had fallen** on the floor when it was cut.

All the words to the right of the line in the preceding examples are part of the **complete predicate.** The verb *fell*, or a verb phrase such as *had fallen*, on the other hand, is often called the **simple predicate.**

See Practice 6.2A

> The **complete predicate** of a sentence consists of the verb and any words related to it.

EL8

As the examples show, a complete predicate may be just the verb itself or the verb and several other words.

Many sentences do not divide so neatly into subject and predicate. Look at the subjects and predicates in the following sentences.

EXAMPLES   **After the movie** , my **friends** **went home** .

With the waves crashing , the **surfers** **jumped into the water** .

In these sentences, part of the predicate comes *before* the subject, and the rest of the predicate follows the subject.

As you have seen, a complete simple sentence contains a simple subject and a simple predicate. In addition, a complete simple sentence expresses a complete thought.

See Practice 6.2B

PRACTICE 6.2A Identifying Complete Subjects and Predicates

Read the sentences. Rewrite each sentence, and draw a vertical line between the complete subject and the complete predicate. Then, underline the subject once and the verb twice.

EXAMPLE   A terrible tornado was sweeping across the county.

ANSWER   *A terrible tornado | was sweeping across the county.*

1. The woman in blue danced in front of the stage.

2. The two bicycles sat in the garage for months.

3. Heather described her anxieties about the social studies exam.

4. The cherry tree in their backyard has burst into flower.

5. Bernice makes her own jewelry with beads.

6. Small red spots appeared on the little boy's face.

7. Alicia grinned at the children in the park.

8. A large statue of a cowboy stands in the courtyard.

9. Her sister was enjoying the drive.

10. The lawyer's argument did not persuade the judge.

PRACTICE 6.2B Writing Complete Sentences

Read the items. Each item contains either a complete subject or a complete predicate. Rewrite each item along with the missing part to create complete sentences.

EXAMPLE   _____ drove onto the sidewalk.

ANSWER   *The taxi driver drove onto the sidewalk.*

11. The set for the school play _____.

12. _____ played three songs at halftime.

13. The young basketball coach _____.

14. _____ was hard to fix.

15. My favorite social studies project _____.

16. _____ is much lower now.

17. The local library _____.

18. _____ is a movie I would like to see.

19. The girl and her family _____.

20. _____ might win the chess tournament.

SPEAKING APPLICATION

Tell a partner about a Web site that you have found useful for research. Your partner should listen for the complete subject and complete predicate in each of your sentences.

WRITING APPLICATION

Use sentence 1 as a model, and write three complete sentences of your own. Make sure each of your sentences has a subject and a verb.

6.3 Compound Subjects and Compound Verbs

Some sentences have more than one subject. Some have more than one verb.

Recognizing Compound Subjects

A sentence containing more than one subject is said to have a **compound subject.**

RULE 6.3.1

A **compound subject** is two or more subjects that have the same verb and are joined by a conjunction such as *and* or *or*.

EXAMPLES

Parrots and hamsters **are** small house pets.
compound subject   verb

Singers, dancers, and other artists **can learn**
compound subject   verb
to perform together.

Recognizing Compound Verbs

A sentence with two or more verbs is said to have a **compound verb.**

RULE 6.3.2

A **compound verb** is two or more verbs that have the same subject and are joined by a conjunction such as *and* or *or*.

EXAMPLES

The **committee** **may or may not succeed**.
       subject   compound verb

She **plans, organizes, and hosts** all the
subject   compound verb
charity events.

Sometimes a sentence will have both a compound subject and a compound verb.

EXAMPLE

Jim and Tara **danced and sang** at the party.
compound subject   compound verb

See Practice 6.3A
See Practice 6.3B

PRACTICE 6.3A ▷ **Recognizing Compound Subjects and Compound Verbs**

Read the sentences. Write the compound subject and/or the compound verb in each sentence.

EXAMPLE   The dolphins and the trainer work well together and give an entertaining show.

ANSWER   *dolphins, trainer* — *compound subject*
work, give — *compound verb*

1. Toys for dogs and birdseed can be found in Aisle 3.

2. At the skate park Tamesa and Randall got some minor scrapes.

3. My sister jogs or rides her bike almost every day.

4. The host and the contestants smiled and waved at the audience.

5. The squirrel chattered loudly and then scampered across a low branch.

6. Bananas, granola, or fresh peaches taste great with plain yogurt.

7. The trail winds up the mountain and gradually narrows near the top.

8. Phoenix and Tucson are both large cities in Arizona.

9. The bear stomped into the river, caught a salmon, and brought it to her cubs.

10. Balloons or flowers can make a room more festive and lift everyone's spirits.

SPEAKING APPLICATION

Take turns telling a partner about an exciting amusement park ride you have heard about or experienced. Your partner should listen for and name at least one compound subject and one compound verb.

WRITING APPLICATION

Use sentence 2 as a model, and write two more sentences that contain compound subjects. Then, use sentence 5 as a model to write two sentences that contain compound verbs.

PRACTICE 6.3B ▷ **Combining Sentences With Compound Subjects and Compound Verbs**

Read the sentences. Combine each pair of sentences by using compound subjects or compound verbs.

EXAMPLE The kite dipped suddenly. Then it wrapped itself around a tree.

ANSWER *The kite dipped suddenly and then wrapped itself around a tree.*

1. Russia traded with the Vikings. France traded with the Vikings.

2. Silent film actors delighted audiences. Silent film actors entertained audiences.

3. Langston Hughes was born in Missouri. He grew up in Kansas and Ohio.

4. Joggers crowd the park every afternoon. Cyclists crowd the park every afternoon.

5. Carlos has a broken leg. He is not able to go hiking with us.

6. The rattlesnake gave a warning. Then it struck Joe's leg.

7. Near the wall, daisies grew in abundance. Bluebonnets grew in abundance.

8. The dentist will clean your teeth. His assistant might clean them instead.

9. Deanna searched the Internet. Deanna found a Web site with some pictures of monarch butterflies.

10. Greeting cards can be found near the front of the store. Wrapping paper can be found near the front, too.

SPEAKING APPLICATION

Take turns telling a partner about a museum you have heard about or visited. Your partner should listen for and name at least one compound subject and one compound verb.

WRITING APPLICATION

Write two sentences with compound subjects and two sentences with compound verbs.

6.4 Hard-to-Find Subjects

It can be difficult to identify simple subjects in certain sentences. These sentences do not follow **normal word order** in which the subject comes before the verb. Sometimes the subject will follow the verb or part of a verb phrase. This is called **inverted word order**. Questions are often presented in inverted word order.

NORMAL WORD ORDER

The **ceremony** **will begin** at 6:00 P.M.
    subject   verb

INVERTED WORD ORDER

When **will** the **ceremony** **begin**?
     verb   subject   verb

Sometimes the subject will not actually be stated in the sentence. It will be understood to be the pronoun *you*. This is often true in sentences that express commands or requests.

The Subject of a Command or Request

When a sentence commands or requests someone to do something, the subject is often unstated.

> **The subject of a command or request is understood to be the pronoun *you*.**

6.4.1

RULE

COMMANDS OR REQUESTS	HOW THE SENTENCES ARE UNDERSTOOD
Wait!	You wait!
Stop at once!	You stop at once!
Please sit down.	You please sit down.
Tara, take a message.	Tara, you take a message.
Mike, get the groceries.	Mike, you get the groceries.

See Practice 6.4A

Even though a command or request may begin with the name of the person spoken to, the subject is still understood to be *you*.

Finding Subjects in Questions

Questions are often presented in inverted word order. You will usually find the subject in the middle of the sentence.

> **In questions, the subject often follows the verb.**

Some questions in inverted word order begin with the words *what, which, whom, whose, when, where, why,* and *how.* Others begin with the verb itself or with a helping verb.

EXAMPLES How **are** the **puppies** this morning?

Did you hold them yet?

Have you found owners for them yet?

If you ever have trouble finding the subject in a question, use this trick: Change the question into a statement. The subject will then appear in normal word order before the verb.

QUESTIONS	REWORDED AS STATEMENTS
How is your sister?	Your sister is how today.
What did the manager say?	The manager did say what.
Were the grades posted?	The grades were posted today.
Did she bring the tickets with her?	She did bring the tickets with her.

Not every question is in inverted word order. Some are in normal word order, with the subject before the verb. Questions beginning with *who, whose,* or *which* often follow normal word order.

EXAMPLES **Who has** the keys?

Whose **car can go** the fastest?

Which **car would handle** the best?

See Practice 6.4B

PRACTICE 6.4A >	Identifying Subjects in Commands or Requests

Read the sentences. Write the subject of each sentence.

EXAMPLE   Just imagine the size of the solar system.

ANSWER   *you*

1. Listen to the lyrics carefully.
2. Jasmine, try to start the car now.
3. After finishing lunch, please clean the dishes.
4. Terri, practice the piano now.
5. Tell me about the marathon, Ernesto.
6. Carmen, choose only the freshest fruits.
7. Just throw those pillows onto the couch for now.
8. Angela, give your sister this book.
9. Please chop the onions while I peel the potatoes.
10. Measure the amount of snow that fell last night.

PRACTICE 6.4B >	Finding Subjects in Questions

Read the questions. Write the subject of each question. If you have trouble finding the subject in a question, change the question into a statement.

EXAMPLE   Has the speaker arrived at the convention center?

ANSWER   *speaker*

11. What did the governor say?
12. Will the fruit stay fresh for three days?
13. Has Mr. Hernandez seen the art exhibit?
14. Why have they blocked off this road?
15. When did the news reach the school?
16. Did the veterinarian cure the cat?
17. Are the actors ready to take the stage?
18. Which train did you take this morning?
19. Whom did the technician call?
20. How is the patient today?

SPEAKING APPLICATION

With a partner, take turns describing an outdoor adventure. Use at least one sentence that is a direction or an order and one that is a question, and have your partner name the subjects.

WRITING APPLICATION

Write one sentence that is a direction or an order and one that is a question. Underline the subject in each sentence.

Finding the Subject in Sentences Beginning With *There* or *Here*

Sentences beginning with *there* or *here* are usually in inverted word order.

> **There** or **here** is never the subject of a sentence.

There or *here* can be used in two ways at the beginning of sentences. First, it can be used to start the sentence.

SENTENCE
STARTER

There are two choices for new head chef.

Here is where their first concert was performed.

There or *here* can also be used as an adverb at the beginning of sentences. As adverbs, these two words point out *where* and modify the verbs.

ADVERB

There is the famous painter.

Here is the first painting he ever sold.

Be alert to sentences beginning with *there* and *here*. They are probably in inverted word order, with the verb appearing before the subject. If you cannot find the subject, reword the sentence in normal word order. If *there* is just a sentence starter, you can drop it from your reworded sentence.

SENTENCES BEGINNING WITH *THERE* OR *HERE*	REWORDED WITH SUBJECT BEFORE VERB
There is a mistake on the exam.	A mistake is there on the exam.
Here comes the instructor of the exam.	The instructor of the exam comes here.

See Practice 6.4C

Finding the Subject in Sentences Inverted for Emphasis

Sometimes a subject is intentionally put after its verb to draw attention to the subject.

> **In some sentences, the subject follows the verb in order to emphasize the subject, or make it stand out.**

6.4.4 RULE

In the following examples, notice how the order of the words builds suspense by leading up to the subject.

EXAMPLES

Wandering in the midst of the large crowd **was**
   verb   verb
a lost **puppy**.
       subject

Running through the yard **was** a **group** of
  verb   verb   subject
giggling children.

Hiding under the big leafy bush **was** the
  verb   verb
white **rabbit**.
     subject

You can reword sentences such as these in normal word order to make it easier to find the subject.

INVERTED WORD ORDER	REWORDED WITH SUBJECT BEFORE VERB
Wandering in the midst of the large crowd was a lost puppy.	The puppy was wandering in the midst of the large crowd.
Running through the yard was a group of giggling children.	A group of giggling children was running through the yard.
Hiding under the big leafy bush was the white rabbit.	The white rabbit was hiding under the big leafy bush.

See Practice 6.4D

PRACTICE 6.4C **Identifying Subjects in Sentences Beginning With *Here* or *There***

Read the sentences. Write the subject of each sentence.

EXAMPLE   There might be another solution to that problem.

ANSWER   *solution*

1. There is a fly in the kitchen.
2. Here is the button from your coat.
3. Here comes your biggest fan.
4. There are the missing pieces from the puzzle.
5. Here are your shoes.
6. There are twenty passengers on that bus.
7. There should be a better way.
8. Here is the most difficult question of all.
9. There goes the superhero now!
10. Here comes another group of students.

PRACTICE 6.4D **Identifying Subjects in Sentences Inverted for Emphasis**

Read the sentences. Write the subject of each sentence.

EXAMPLE   From deep in the trench came the squeals of a puppy.

ANSWER   *squeals*

11. Next to the old firehouse is a French bakery.
12. On the top of the building sits an elegant dome.
13. Alongside the elderly lady were two young girls with backpacks.
14. Off the bench sprang an eager backup quarterback.
15. In the middle of the courtyard stood a huge, decorative water fountain.
16. All over the floor lay old photographs from the albums.
17. On that hill once stood a small chapel.
18. Not far from the lake was an old abandoned house.
19. Out of the shadows stepped a dark figure.
20. In a tiny cottage deep in the woods lived a mysterious old man.

SPEAKING APPLICATION

Tell a partner about a scary moment you experienced or imagined. Your partner should listen for one sentence beginning with *here* or *there* and one sentence with inverted word order for emphasis.

WRITING APPLICATION

Use sentence 19 as a model, and write two more sentences with inverted word order. Underline the subject in each sentence.

6.5 Complements

Often, a subject and verb alone can express a complete thought. For example, *Birds fly* can stand by itself as a sentence, even though it contains only two words, a subject and a verb.

Other times, however, the thought begun by a subject and its verb must be completed with other words. For example, *Heather collected, The coach told, Our teacher was, Michael feels,* and *Kelly won* all contain a subject and verb, but none expresses a complete thought. All these ideas need **complements**.

A **complement** is a word or group of words that completes the meaning of a sentence.

6.5.1 RULE

Complements are usually nouns, pronouns, or adjectives. They are located right after or very close to the verb. The complements are shown below in blue. The complements answer questions about the subject or verb in order to complete the sentence.

DIFFERENT KINDS OF COMPLEMENTS

Heather **collected** **books**.
subject · verb · complement

The **coach** **told** **us** the **rules**.
subject · verb · complements

Our **teacher** **was** **tired**.
subject · verb complement

Michael **feels** **sick**.
subject · verb complement

Kelly **won** the **high jump**.
subject · verb · complement

This section will describe three types of complements: **direct objects, indirect objects,** and **subject complements.** All complements add information about the subjects or verbs in the sentence. They paint a clearer picture that helps the reader understand the writer's thoughts.

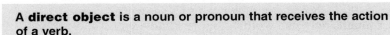

Recognizing Direct Objects

Direct objects follow action verbs.

> A **direct object** is a noun or pronoun that receives the action of a verb.

You can find a direct object by asking *What?* or *Whom?* after an action verb.

EXAMPLES   My older **sister** **found** the hidden **passageway**.
subject   verb   direct object

I **called** **Matt** later that night.
subject verb   direct object

My friend **Kris** **likes** a relaxing **swim**
subject   verb   direct object
before bedtime.

Passageway, Matt, and *swim* are the direct objects of the verbs in the examples. In the first sentence, *passageway* answers the question *Found what?* In the second sentence, *Matt* answers the question *Called whom?* In the third sentence, *swim* answers the question *Likes what?*

Compound Direct Objects
Like subjects and verbs, direct objects can be compound. That is, one verb can have two or more direct objects.

EXAMPLES   The **cat** **eats** **tuna** and other **food**.
subject verb   direct   direct object
object

The **board** **chose** **Mrs. Fried**,
subject   verb   direct object

Mrs. Kennedy, and **Mrs. Greene** to organize
direct object   direct object
the event.

See Practice 6.5A
See Practice 6.5B

PRACTICE 6.5A Recognizing Direct Objects

Read the sentences. Write the direct object or the compound direct object in each sentence.

EXAMPLE   Jan told Vince and him about the movie.

ANSWER   *Vince, him*

1. Sari brought a gift to the party.

2. The enthusiastic tourists took many pictures.

3. Jermaine attended a festive parade.

4. He bought pants, shoes, and a baseball cap.

5. In the morning Mom will take me to the soccer match.

6. The new bicycle has ten speeds and special wheels.

7. Please ask Ted and them about the plans for tonight.

8. For his birthday my father got a sweater and a tie.

9. Tyrell twisted his ankle yesterday.

10. The pandas were eating bamboo.

PRACTICE 6.5B Adding Complements

Read the sentences. Rewrite the sentences, and fill in the blanks with appropriate direct objects. Use both nouns and pronouns.

EXAMPLE   The ship reached ____ very late.

ANSWER   *The ship reached port very late.*

11. Tell ____ about the concert.

12. I want ____ and ____ to join the team.

13. Alicia asked ____ about the science teacher.

14. At the store, get some ____, ____, and ____.

15. I saw ____ in the park this morning.

16. Then she took ____ on a long drive.

17. Last night Terri wrote ____ for class.

18. The boys do not have ____ for the play.

19. The children greeted ____ and ____ warmly.

20. Sara built a ____ and a ____ in woodworking class.

SPEAKING APPLICATION

With a partner, take turns describing how to fix a favorite snack. Your partner should listen for and name at least two direct objects.

WRITING APPLICATION

Use sentence 20 as a model, and write two sentences with compound direct objects.

Distinguishing Between Direct Objects, Adverbs, and Objects of Prepositions

Not all action verbs have direct objects. Be careful not to confuse a direct object with an adverb or with the object of a preposition. If you are unsure if a word or phrase is a direct object, ask yourself who or what is receiving the action of the verb.

RULE 6.5.3

> **A direct object is never an adverb or the noun or pronoun at the end of a prepositional phrase.**

Compare the following examples. Notice that the action verb *drove* has a direct object in only the first sentence.

EXAMPLES

Rich **drove** his **motorcycle** .
subject   verb   direct object

Rich **drove** **slowly** .
subject   verb   adverb

Rich **drove** **through the park** .
subject   verb   prepositional phrase

Each example shows a very common sentence type. The first consists of a subject, a verb, and a direct object. The noun *motorcycle* is the direct object of the verb *drove*.

The second example consists of a subject, a verb, and an adverb. Nothing after the verb in the sentence answers the question *What?* so there is no direct object. *Slowly* modifies the verb and tells *how* Rich drove.

The third example consists of a subject, a verb, and a prepositional phrase. Again, no noun or pronoun answers the question *What?* after the verb. The prepositional phrase tells *where* Rich drove.

Notice also that a single sentence can contain more than one of these three parts.

EXAMPLE

Rich **drove** his **motorcycle** **slowly**
subject   verb   direct object   adverb

through the park .
prepositional phrase

See Practice 6.5C

Finding Direct Objects in Questions

In normal word order, a direct object follows a verb. In questions that are in inverted word order, however, the direct object often appears before the verb and subject.

> **A direct object in a question will sometimes be found before the verb.**

In the following chart, questions are paired with sentences reworded in normal word order. Compare the positions of the direct objects in each. Direct objects are highlighted in pink, subjects are highlighted in yellow, and verbs are highlighted in orange.

QUESTIONS	REWORDED IN NORMAL WORD ORDER
When did the teacher begin the test?	The teacher did begin the text when.
Whom will you ask to the dance?	You will ask whom to the dance.
What does the puppy eat?	The puppy does eat what.
Which car do you like, the red sports car or the black convertible?	You do like which car, the red sports car or the black convertible.
Whom did you meet at the store?	You did meet whom at the store.

In each of the five questions, the direct object appears before, rather than after, the verb. To locate the direct object in a question, put the sentence into normal word order with the subject appearing before the verb. Then, the direct object will be found in its usual position after the verb.

See Practice 6.5D

PRACTICE 6.5C > Distinguishing Direct Object, Adverb, and Object of a Preposition

Read the sentences. Label each underlined word *DO* for direct object, *ADV* for adverb, or *OP* for object of a preposition.

EXAMPLE   Stepping off the ferry, the passengers smiled <u>broadly</u>.

ANSWER   *ADV*

1. In the spring Colin plants <u>peppers</u> in his garden.

2. Near noon we stopped at a roadside <u>diner</u>.

3. Marcus really wants a new <u>pair</u> of in-line skates.

4. In high school my sister played <u>basketball</u>.

5. He leapt <u>suddenly</u> onto the stage.

6. Mr. McNabb changes his <u>mind</u> frequently.

7. I made these <u>candles</u> from a kit.

8. Much to our disappointment, the team played <u>poorly</u>.

9. Rosita has taken her sister to the <u>park</u>.

10. He opened the package <u>eagerly</u>.

PRACTICE 6.5D > Finding Direct Objects in Questions

Read the questions. Write the direct object in each question.

EXAMPLE   Whom did you visit in Spokane?

ANSWER   *Whom*

11. Which shoes did she lose?

12. When will the electrician fix the wiring?

13. What reasons did he give?

14. Which role in the skit do you want?

15. Whom does the host expect?

16. Where did Raphael leave the scissors?

17. When will the workers finish the bridge?

18. What did you order for Gabriel?

19. How many movies did you see this year?

20. What did you write in the e-mail?

SPEAKING APPLICATION

Tell a partner about your favorite television show. Your partner should listen for and name at least two direct objects, one adverb, and one object of a preposition.

WRITING APPLICATION

Write three sentences with direct objects. Make at least one of your sentences a question.

Recognizing Indirect Objects

Sentences with a direct object may also contain another kind of complement, called an **indirect object.** A sentence cannot have an indirect object unless it has a direct object.

> An **indirect object** is a noun or pronoun that comes after an action verb and before a direct object. It names the person or thing to which something is given or for which something is done.

6.5.5 RULE

An indirect object answers the questions *To* or *for whom?* or *To* or *for what?* after an action verb. To find an indirect object, find the direct object first. Then, ask the appropriate question.

EXAMPLE   **Grandpa read us a book** before bedtime.
                            indirect   direct
                            object   object

(Read *what?* [*book*])
(Read the book *to whom?* [*us*])

Keep in mind the following pattern: *Subject + Verb + Indirect Object + Direct Object.* An indirect object will almost always come between the verb and the direct object in a sentence.

Compound Indirect Objects

Like a subject, verb, or direct object, an indirect object can be compound.

EXAMPLES   **Tara gave** each **dog and cat** a
             subject verb   compound indirect object

             treat .
             direct object

(Gave *what?* [*treat*])
(Gave a treat *to what?* [*each dog and cat*])

             Aunt Sarah offered Kate and me
             subject   verb   compound indirect object

             sunglasses and lemonade .
                     compound direct object

(Offered *what?* [*sunglasses and lemonade*])
(Offered sunglasses and lemonade to *whom?* [*Kate and me*])

See Practice 6.5E

Distinguishing Between Indirect Objects and Objects of Prepositions

Do not confuse an indirect object with the object of a preposition.

RULE 6.5.6

> **An indirect object never follows the preposition *to* or *for* in a sentence.**

Compare the following examples.

EXAMPLES   Betsy bought **her** a **stereo** .
                          indirect   direct object
                          object

Betsy bought a **stereo** for **her** .
                  direct object   object of
                                    preposition

In the first example above, *her* is an indirect object. It comes after the verb *bought* and before the direct object *stereo*. In the second example, *her* is the object of the preposition *for* and follows the direct object *stereo*.

EXAMPLES   Brian gave **Nicole** a **letter** .
                          indirect   direct
                          object   object

Brian gave a **letter** to **Nicole** .
                direct   object of
                object   preposition

To find the indirect object in the first example above, you must first find the direct object. Ask yourself what Brian gave. He gave a letter, so *letter* is the direct object. Then, ask yourself to whom Brian gave the letter. He gave it to *Nicole*, so *Nicole* is the indirect object.

Use the same questions in the second example. Again, *letter* is the direct object of *gave*; however, *Nicole* is no longer the indirect object. Instead, it is the object of the preposition *to*.

See Practice 6.5F

PRACTICE 6.5E **Recognizing Indirect Objects**

Read the sentences. Write the indirect object in each sentence.

EXAMPLE   The museum gives visitors an educational experience.

ANSWER   *visitors*

1. The zoo veterinarian gave the tiger excellent care.

2. Aunt Polly bought me a ticket to the show.

3. Mrs. Jefferson will give Mark and Terrence their assignment.

4. Would you show us the dance steps?

5. The clerk sold the girls some rings from the display case.

6. For his birthday, order Dad a pair of slippers.

7. The principal handed Rama and me our certificates.

8. I will give the teacher the answers she wants.

9. Did Ira buy his mother a necklace?

10. Pass your cousin the plate of chicken.

PRACTICE 6.5F **Distinguishing Indirect Object and Object of a Preposition**

Read the sentences. Write whether the underlined word is an *indirect object* or an *object of a preposition*.

EXAMPLE   The tour guide gave the brochures to the <u>visitors</u>.

ANSWER   *object of a preposition*

11. Tamika gave the CD to her <u>friend</u>.

12. Mom ordered <u>me</u> a new pair of contact lenses.

13. The director read <u>us</u> the stage directions.

14. Have you made a burrito for your <u>brother</u>?

15. Show your <u>mother</u> that funny cartoon.

16. In the lobby, a lady gave a phone number to <u>him</u>.

17. Have you read <u>Jody</u> your poem yet?

18. Jorge told the story to the <u>children</u>.

19. At the concert we handed the <u>usher</u> our tickets.

20. I have saved some mashed potatoes for <u>Jake</u>.

SPEAKING APPLICATION

With a partner, take turns describing a game. Your partner should listen for and name at least two indirect objects.

WRITING APPLICATION

Use sentence 5 as a model, and write three sentences with indirect objects.

Subject Complements

Both direct objects and indirect objects are complements used with action verbs. Linking verbs, however, have a different kind of complement called a **subject complement.** Like direct and indirect objects, subject complements add information to a sentence. However, subject complements give readers more information about the subject of the sentence, not the verb.

RULE 6.5.7

> A **subject complement** is a noun, pronoun, or adjective that follows a linking verb and provides important details about the subject.

Predicate Nouns and Pronouns

Both nouns and pronouns are sometimes used as subject complements after linking verbs.

RULE 6.5.8

> A **predicate noun** or **predicate pronoun** follows a linking verb and renames or identifies the subject of the sentence.

It is easy to recognize predicate nouns and predicate pronouns. The linking verb acts much like an equal sign between the subject and the noun or pronoun that follows the verb. Both the subject and the predicate noun or pronoun refer to the same person or thing.

EXAMPLES

Rosa **will** be **chair** of the department.
subject verb   predicate noun

(The predicate noun *chair* renames the subject *Rosa.*)

My first **dog** **was** a **poodle** .
subject verb   predicate noun

(The predicate noun *poodle* identifies the subject *dog.*)

The **winners** **were** **they** .
subject   verb   predicate
pronoun

(The predicate pronoun *they* identifies the subject *winners.*)   See Practice 6.5G

Predicate Adjectives

A linking verb can also be followed by a
predicate adjective.

> A **predicate adjective** follows a linking verb and describes
> the subject of the sentence.

A predicate adjective is considered part of the complete predicate
of a sentence because it comes after a linking verb. In spite of
this, a predicate adjective does not modify the words in the
predicate. Instead, it describes the noun or pronoun that serves as
the subject of the linking verb.

EXAMPLES   The **trip** to Washington, D.C., **was long**.
            subject   verb   predicate
                                                         adjective
(The predicate adjective *long* describes the subject *trip*.)

The **senator seemed** very **anxious**
    subject   verb   predicate adjective
to speak to the audience.

(The predicate adjective *anxious* describes the subject
senator.)

Compound Subject Complements

Like other sentence parts, subject complements can be
compound.

> A **compound subject complement** consists of two or
> more predicate nouns, pronouns, or adjectives joined by a
> conjunction such as *and* or *or*.

EXAMPLES   My two favorite **fruits are pears and apples**.
                             subject verb compound predicate noun

The **sand felt hot and grainy**.
    subject verb compound predicate
                          adjective

The **basket was** full of **carrots and tomatoes**.
    subject verb   compound predicate adjective

See Practice 6.5H

PRACTICE 6.5G > **Identifying Predicate Nouns and Predicate Pronouns**

Read the sentences. Write the predicate noun or predicate pronoun in each sentence.

EXAMPLE   At the scene, police were the ones who found evidence of a break-in.

ANSWER   *ones*

1. Ecuador is a small country in South America.
2. Barack Obama became president in 2009.
3. Baseball is my favorite sport in the summer.
4. The Alps are an important part of the beauty of Switzerland.
5. The best singer has never been he.
6. Callie should be the new treasurer of the student council.
7. The border collie is a dog with a great deal of energy.
8. My uncle is a funny guy and also a wonderful chef.
9. In this short story, the main character is a sailor.
10. At the school play, the ushers were Sasha and Riley.

PRACTICE 6.5H > **Identifying Predicate Adjectives**

Read the sentences. Write the predicate adjective in each sentence.

EXAMPLE   Those mountains stay snowy for most of the year.

ANSWER   *snowy*

11. A visit to an art gallery can be enjoyable.
12. The beauty of Costa Rica is breathtaking.
13. Maya's sprint times have been remarkable.
14. The governor's words were inspiring to the people of the state.
15. During the ride my baby sister seemed cranky.
16. Most of her school clothing was new.
17. The straw in that basket is very colorful.
18. This water seems quite muddy.
19. Tanya has always been honest about her feelings.
20. The desert looks beautiful in the twilight.

SPEAKING APPLICATION

With a partner, take turns describing a music video you like. Your partner should listen for and name at least one predicate noun, one predicate pronoun, and one predicate adjective.

WRITING APPLICATION

Write three sentences about sports. In the first sentence, use a predicate noun. In the second sentence, use a predicate pronoun. In the third, use a predicate adjective.

CHAPTER 7

PHRASES *and* CLAUSES

Use phrases and clauses in a variety of ways to add interest to your writing.

WRITE GUY *Jeff Anderson, M.Ed.*

WHAT DO YOU NOTICE?

Uncover the phrases as you zoom in on lines from the poem "Grandma Ling" by Amy Ling.

> **MENTOR TEXT**
>
> She smiled, stretched her arms
> to take to heart the eldest daughter
> of her youngest son a quarter century away.

Now, ask yourself the following questions:

- In the second line, how are the words *to take* different from the words *to heart*?
- What is the purpose of the prepositional phrase *of her youngest son* in the third line?

The words *to take* form the infinitive of the verb *take;* infinitives usually use the word *to* before the verb. In the phrase *to heart,* the word *to* is used as a preposition. *To heart* is a prepositional phrase, and the noun *heart* is the object of the preposition. The prepositional phrase *of her youngest son* acts as an adjective modifying the noun *daughter.*

Grammar for Writers Phrases allow writers to provide more information about the nouns and verbs in their sentences. Use phrases to construct lively sentences that flow smoothly.

Your infinitive phrase is very long.

I wrote it to stretch to infinity.

7.1 Phrases

Sentences are usually built with more than just a subject and a predicate. **Phrases** play an important role in sentences by adding more information.

> A **phrase** is a group of words that functions in a sentence as a single part of speech. Phrases do not contain a subject and a verb.

Prepositional Phrases

A **prepositional phrase** has at least two parts, a preposition and a noun or pronoun that is the object of the preposition.

EXAMPLES

behind **trees**
prep   object

near **meadows**
prep   object

The object of the preposition may be modified by one or more adjectives.

EXAMPLES

behind serene tall **trees**
prep   adj   adj   object

near beautiful green **meadows**
prep   adj   adj   object

The object may also be a compound, consisting of two or more objects connected by a conjunction such as *and* or *nor*.

EXAMPLES

behind quiet serene **trees** and **meadows**
prep   adj   adj   object   object

near beautiful green **meadows** and **gardens**
prep   adj   adj   object   object

See Practice 7.1A

In a sentence, some prepositional phrases can act as adjectives that modify a noun or pronoun. Other prepositional phrases can act as adverbs that modify a verb, adjective, or adverb.

Using Prepositional Phrases That Act as Adjectives

A prepositional phrase that acts as an adjective in a sentence is called an **adjective phrase** or **adjectival phrase.**

> An **adjective phrase** or **adjectival phrase** is a prepositional phrase that modifies a noun or pronoun by telling *what kind* or *which one.*

7.1.2 RULE

Unlike one-word adjectives, which usually come before the nouns or pronouns they modify, adjectival phrases usually come after the nouns or pronouns they modify.

ONE-WORD ADJECTIVES	ADJECTIVAL PHRASES
The green meadow started here.	The meadow with two oak trees began there.
The worried forest ranger stopped us.	The forest ranger with the worried face stopped us.

Adjectival phrases answer the same questions as one-word adjectives do. *What kind* of meadow began there? *Which* ranger stopped us?

USES OF ADJECTIVAL PHRASES	
Modifying a Subject	The sound of the hail worried us.
Modifying a Direct Object	It beat against the gutters on the house.

When two adjectival phrases appear in a row, the second phrase may modify the object of the preposition in the first phrase or both phrases may modify the same noun or pronoun.

ADJECTIVAL PHRASES IN A ROW	
Modifying the Object of a Preposition	The skylight on the roof of the house broke.
Modifying the Same Noun	There was the scent of baking in the house.

See Practice 7.1B

Using Prepositional Phrases That Act as Adverbs

A prepositional phrase that acts as an adverb modifies the same parts of speech as a one-word adverb does.

> An **adverbial phrase** or **adverb phrase** is a prepositional phrase that modifies a verb, an adjective, or an adverb. Adverbial phrases point out *where, when, in what way,* or *to what extent.*

Adverbial phrases are used in the same way as one-word adverbs, but they sometimes provide more precise details.

ONE-WORD ADVERBS	ADVERBIAL PHRASES
Bring your books here.	Bring your books into the library.
The class began early.	The class began at exactly 9:00 A.M.

Adverbial phrases can modify verbs, adjectives, and adverbs.

USES OF ADVERBIAL PHRASES	
Modifying a Verb	Rain poured down in heavy sheets. (Poured *in what way?*)
Modifying an Adjective	The sun was cold for early June. (Cold *in what way?*)
Modifying an Adverb	The fire suddenly spread without warning. (Suddenly *to what extent?*)

Adverbial phrases, unlike adjectival phrases, are not always located near the words they modify in a sentence.

═══ MODIFIES ═══

EXAMPLE   **During the high tide** , the boats were docked.

Two or more adverbial phrases can also be located in different parts of the sentence and still modify the same word.

═══ MODIFIES ═══   ═══ MODIFIES ═══

EXAMPLE   **In an instant** , the mice ran **through the kitchen** .

See Practice 7.1C
See Practice 7.1D

PRACTICE 7.1A ▷ **Identifying Prepositional Phrases**

Read the sentences. Then, write the prepositional phrase in each sentence, and underline the object of the preposition.

EXAMPLE   I left the box on the table.

ANSWER   *on the table*

1. In the morning we ate a light breakfast.
2. The shy child was hiding behind the couch.
3. The ice skater performed her routine without any mistakes.
4. The article about the new computer was very interesting.
5. During summer vacation we often play softball.
6. The clerk at the checkout counter operated her cash register very rapidly.
7. I usually do some stretches before my swim.
8. Have you traveled to Austin before, or is this your first trip here?
9. Some audience members near the stage stood up and blocked my view.
10. The young couple from next door came to visit.

PRACTICE 7.1B ▷ **Identifying Adjectival Phrases**

Read the sentences. Then, write the adjectival phrase in each sentence. One sentence has two adjectival phrases.

EXAMPLE   A flock of sheep grazed in the field.

ANSWER   *of sheep*

11. I bought a jacket with a high collar.
12. The shoes in the closet have never been worn.
13. This is not the highway to the beach.
14. I am reading a good book about pirates.
15. The house beside the river was flooded last spring.
16. The speaker at the podium knew everyone in the room.
17. After five minutes, the sound of the thunder grew louder.
18. When does the train on Track 20 leave for Chicago?
19. High in the tree perched a cat with white stripes.
20. Jane sat with Tom at a table with wobbly legs.

SPEAKING APPLICATION

With a partner, take turns describing a store or a restaurant that you have visited. Your partner should listen for and name a prepositional phrase and an adjectival phrase that you use.

WRITING APPLICATION

Write three sentences about something you are wearing. Use at least one adjectival phrase in each sentence.

PRACTICE 7.1C
Identifying Adverbial Phrases

Read the sentences. Then, write the adverbial phrase in each sentence. One sentence has two adverbial phrases.

EXAMPLE   On the shelf you will find a phone directory for this area.

ANSWER   *On the shelf*

1. The bus stops at the corner every hour.
2. The runner slid safely into third base.
3. Everyone is hoping for an early spring.
4. Without a compass, you may lose your way.
5. The manager was pleased with Jane's work.
6. After three years, the new park was finally finished.
7. On weekday mornings, the restaurant opens before six o'clock.
8. The students in Miss Jackson's class studied hard for the midterm.
9. The star of the show fell on the ice.
10. None of the answers seemed right to me.

PRACTICE 7.1D
Writing Adjectival and Adverbial Phrases

Read the sentences. Then, rewrite each sentence, adding the adjectival or adverbial phrases as directed in parentheses.

EXAMPLE   The house needs many repairs. (adjectival phrase)

ANSWER   *The house with the broken windows needs many repairs.*

11. That woman is a nurse. (adjectival phrase)
12. Mom uses a thermos. (adverbial phrase)
13. Attendance was surprisingly low. (adjectival phrase)
14. Carl enjoys gardening. (adverbial phrase)
15. We celebrated our victory. (adverbial phrase)
16. A strong smell filled the room. (adjectival phrase)
17. The shopkeeper installed a burglar alarm. (adverbial phrase)
18. The dancers learned the new steps. (two adjectival phrases)
19. I met the new mayor. (two adverbial phrases)
20. This can has a big dent. (adjectival phrase, adverbial phrase)

SPEAKING APPLICATION

With a partner, take turns describing a highway, a house, or something else being built or repaired. Your partner should listen for and name three adverbial phrases that you use.

WRITING APPLICATION

Write four sentences about a sport you play or watch on television. Use a prepositional phrase in each sentence, and write whether it is an adjectival phrase or an adverbial phrase. Use at least one of each type.

Using Appositives and Appositive Phrases

Appositives, like adjectival phrases, give information about nouns or pronouns.

> An **appositive** is a noun or pronoun placed after another noun or pronoun to identify, rename, or explain the preceding word.

7.1.4 RULE

Appositives are very useful in writing because they give additional information without using many words.

┌─ MODIFIES ─┐

EXAMPLES The florist **Kathy Perkins** prepared a beautiful floral arrangement.

┌─ MODIFIES ─┐

I admire the author **William Shakespeare**.

An appositive with its own modifiers creates an **appositive phrase.**

> An **appositive phrase** is a noun or pronoun with modifiers. It is placed next to a noun or pronoun and adds information or details.

7.1.5 RULE

The modifiers in an appositive phrase can be adjectives or adjectival phrases.

EXAMPLES Uncle Joe, my **favorite** **uncle**, cooks
        adjective noun
     Thanksgiving dinner.

     On the kitchen wall is a platter, an heirloom
     in my family for years.
       adj phrase

Appositives and appositive phrases can also be a compound.

See Practice 7.1E

See Practice 7.1F EXAMPLE Actors, **old** and **young**, performed together.
          compound noun

PRACTICE 7.1E > Identifying Appositives and Appositive Phrases

Read the sentences. Then, write the appositive or appositive phrase in each sentence.

EXAMPLE   I met with John English, publisher of the local newspaper.

ANSWER   *publisher of the local newspaper*

1. Jan painted her room in her favorite color, blue.

2. The magazine article, a brief history of tea, was quite interesting.

3. My brother's car, a very old station wagon, often breaks down.

4. Only the first-prize winner, Cynthia, gets to make a speech.

5. Jim is studying meteorology, the science of atmospheric activity such as the weather.

6. My sister Jane joined her friends in the diner.

7. I admire my friend Carlos, a talented actor.

8. The vegetables carrots and spinach are good sources of vitamins.

9. A popular bunch of musicians, they always draw a large crowd.

10. Author Mark Twain was born in Missouri.

PRACTICE 7.1F > Combining Sentences With Appositive Phrases

Read the sentences. Combine each pair of sentences by using an appositive phrase.

EXAMPLE   Pedro Salazar is a great athlete. He is the quarterback on our team.

ANSWER   *Pedro Salazar, the quarterback on our team, is a great athlete.*

11. People often use the rose as a symbol of love. It is a beautiful flower.

12. Emily Dickinson was a famous poet. She rarely left her home in her later years.

13. Skiing is a winter sport. Skiing requires special warm clothing.

14. Vermeer is now a famous artist. He had trouble earning a living.

15. Bobcats are large cats found in the wild. They sometimes attack deer.

16. San Antonio is a city with a strong Mexican heritage. The Alamo is in San Antonio.

17. I hope to reach my goal before I am twenty. My goal is to win an Olympic medal.

18. Julie performs in the school musical each year. She is a talented singer.

19. Our hotel is in the French Quarter. That is a famous neighborhood in New Orleans.

20. Victoria ruled at a time of prosperity for her nation. She was Britain's queen for many years.

SPEAKING APPLICATION

With a partner, take turns describing the planets. Include at least three appositive phrases. Your partner should listen for and name three appositive phrases that you use.

WRITING APPLICATION

Write three sentences about different presidents of the United States. Use an appositive phrase in each sentence. Underline each appositive phrase.

Using Verbals and Verbal Phrases

A **verbal** is any verb form that is used in a sentence not as a verb but as another part of speech.

Like verbs, verbals can be modified by an adverb or adverbial phrase. They can also be followed by a complement. A verbal used with a modifier or a complement is called a **verbal phrase.**

Participles

Participles are verb forms with two basic uses. When they are used with helping verbs, they are verbs. When they are used alone to modify nouns or pronouns, they become adjectives.

EL6

> A **participle** is a form of a verb that is often used as an adjective.

7.1.6

RULE

There are two kinds of participles, **present participles** and **past participles.** Each kind can be recognized by its ending.

All present participles end in *-ing*.

EXAMPLES talking   doing   eating   wanting

Most past participles end either in *-ed* or in *-d*.

EXAMPLES opened   jumped   played   moved

Other past participles end in *-n*, *-t*, *-en*, or another irregular ending.

EXAMPLES grown   felt   bought   eaten   held

Both present and past participles can be used in sentences as adjectives. They tell *what kind* or *which one*.

PRESENT PARTICIPLES	PAST PARTICIPLES
They scheduled a walking tour.	Chilled water is refreshing.
Talking quickly, he explained what happened.	At the time, she felt concerned.

See Practice 7.1G

Participle or Verb?

Sometimes, verb phrases (verbs with helping verbs) are confused with participles. A verb phrase always begins with a helping verb. A participle used as an adjective stands by itself and modifies a noun or pronoun.

VERB PHRASES	PARTICIPLES
The boy was racing around the yard.	The racing jockey rode around the track.
Her assistant may have scheduled the meeting earlier.	I spoke at the scheduled meeting.

Participial Phrases

A participle can be expanded into a participial phrase by adding a complement or modifier.

RULE

7.1.7

> A **participial phrase** is a present or past participle and its modifiers. The entire phrase acts as an adjective in a sentence.

Participial phrases can be formed by adding an adverb, an adverbial phrase, or a complement to a participle.

EXAMPLES   The coach, **demonstrating quickly**, explained the play.

The well-known coach, **honored by the victory**, led the team.

The first participial phrase contains the adverb *quickly* added to the participle *demonstrating*. The second includes the adverbial phrase *by the victory* added to the participle *honored*.

A participial phrase can also be placed at the beginning of a sentence. The phrase is usually followed by a comma.

EXAMPLE   **Honored by the victory**, the well-known coach led the team.

See Practice 7.1H
See Practice 7.1I
See Practice 7.1J

PRACTICE 7.1G ▷ Identifying Present and Past Participles

Read the sentences. Then, write the participle in each sentence, and label it *present participle* or *past participle*.

EXAMPLE   Hurricane Katrina was a devastating storm.

ANSWER   *devastating* — *present participle*

1. A chirping bird woke me early this morning.

2. Weeping, the child pointed to the small bruise on her knee.

3. Late and worried, the driver checked the time over and over.

4. The grinning hockey player jumped in triumph.

5. The oatmeal, hardening quickly in the pot, would be difficult to remove.

6. The toaster produced burnt toast every morning.

7. The bustling commuters poured out of the subway and raced to their jobs.

8. During her visit to Grandma, my sister fixed a broken chair.

9. There was a moment of silent shock, followed by a great deal of noisy panic.

10. The shovel, lost in the snow, reappeared after the thaw.

PRACTICE 7.1H ▷ Distinguishing Verbs and Participles

Read the sentences. Then, write *verb* or *participle* for the underlined word in each sentence.

EXAMPLE   Trusty Toys is a growing business.

ANSWER   *participle*

11. The tired worker took a break.

12. Luis and I are going to the movies tomorrow.

13. Julie is a member of the planning committee.

14. We have been working on our science project.

15. Waiting patiently in the cold, the students chatted together at the bus stop.

16. We should be finished in half an hour.

17. Corey was carefully lifting the heavy suitcase.

18. The winners were not all chosen today.

19. I took three books out of the library, including an Indian cookbook.

20. When was the car's gas tank last filled?

SPEAKING APPLICATION

With a partner, take turns telling about a bad storm. Use two present participles and two past participles. Your partner should listen for and name the participles that you use, and say whether they are present or past participles.

WRITING APPLICATION

Write four sentences about preparing or eating food. In your first sentence, use a present participle. In your second, use the same word as a verb. In your third sentence, use a past participle. In your fourth, use the same word as a verb.

PRACTICE 7.1I Identifying Participial Phrases

Read the sentences. Then, write the participial phrase in each sentence. Underline the participle.

EXAMPLE Running swiftly, Cara won the race.

ANSWER *Running swiftly*

1. Working rapidly, the artist sketched my portrait.
2. The plumber's fee, calculated by the hour, was quite high.
3. Concentrating on his homework, Cal did not hear the phone.
4. The man leaning on the fence is my uncle.
5. The cost, paid in advance, included sales tax.
6. I liked the flowers growing in the garden.
7. The star sang ten songs, including my favorite.
8. Speaking clearly, Anna repeated her request.
9. The senator, elected five years ago, is up for reelection next year.
10. Running down the field, James shouted for his teammate to pass the ball.

PRACTICE 7.1J Combining Sentences Using Participial Phrases

Read the sentences. Combine each pair of sentences by using a participial phrase.

EXAMPLE The tree was very old. It towered over the others.

ANSWER *The tree, towering over the others, was very old.*

11. Ali jogged down the street. Ali met a friend.
12. The child squirmed in front the camera. He had his picture taken.
13. Bob was completely exhausted. He slept for hours.
14. I enjoyed the book. It was written by Maya Angelou.
15. The police officer interviewed witnesses. He obtained valuable information.
16. The case was argued in court. It finally ended in a guilty verdict.
17. The drama club staged a new one-act play. It was chosen from dozens of entries.
18. Zoe was nervous about her audition. She barely ate any of her lunch.
19. The treasure chest held jewels and gold coins. It was found after many years.
20. The hikers were lost in the woods. They were tired and hungry.

SPEAKING APPLICATION

With a partner, take turns describing a race or a contest. Use at least three participial phrases. Your partner should listen for and name the three participial phrases that you use.

WRITING APPLICATION

Tell how to do something by writing four or five short sentences. Then, combine two of the sentences by using a participial phrase. Underline the participial phrase.

Gerunds

Like present participles, **gerunds** end in *-ing*. While present participles are used as adjectives, gerunds can be used as subjects, direct objects, predicate nouns, and objects of prepositions.

> **A gerund is a form of a verb that acts as a noun.**

USE OF GERUNDS IN SENTENCES	
Subject	Replacing the car's interior was a great idea!
Direct Object	Alexis enjoys reading .
Predicate Noun	Her favorite activity is cooking .
Object of a Preposition	Joe never gets tired of driving .

Gerund Phrases

Gerunds can also be part of a phrase.

> **A gerund phrase is a gerund with modifiers or a complement, all acting together as a noun.**

This chart shows how gerunds are expanded to form gerund phrases.

FORMING GERUND PHRASES	
Gerund With Adjectives	The loud, shrill ringing continued all day.
Gerund With Direct Object	Listening to classical music has inspired many musicians.
Gerund With Prepositional Phrase	She helped the conductor by playing her instrument .
Gerund With Adverb and Prepositional Phrase	The conductor amazed the spectators by perfectly directing the orchestra and the chorus .

See Practice 7.1K
See Practice 7.1L

Infinitives

Infinitives are verb forms that are used as nouns, adjectives, and adverbs. Like participles and gerunds, they can be combined with other words to form phrases.

RULE 7.1.10

> An **infinitive** is a verb form that can be used as a noun, an adjective, or an adverb. The word *to* usually appears before the verb.

EXAMPLES

It is necessary **to drive**.

He is the one **to call**.

To be healthy can be difficult sometimes.

Infinitive Phrases

RULE 7.1.11

> An **infinitive phrase** is an infinitive with modifiers or a complement, all acting together as a single part of speech.

EXAMPLES

It is important **to drive carefully**.

It is not polite **to beep your horn in traffic**.

They want **to tell you to drive slower**.

An **infinitive phrase** can be used in a sentence as a noun, an adjective, or an adverb. As a noun, an infinitive phrase can function as a subject, an object, or an appositive.

USES OF INFINITIVES	
Used as a Subject	To drive carefully is vital.
Used as an Object	He tried to drive carefully.
Used as an Appositive	His mother's suggestion, to drive carefully, saved him.
Used as an Adjective	It was his goal to drive carefully.
Used as an Adverb	It isn't always easy to drive carefully when you're running late.

See Practice 7.1M
See Practice 7.1N

PRACTICE 7.1K > Identifying Gerund Phrases

Read the sentences. Then, write the gerund phrase from each sentence, and underline the gerund. Remember to include all modifiers with the phrase.

EXAMPLE   Writing a book was her lifelong dream.

ANSWER   *Writing a book*

1. Driving too fast is very dangerous.

2. Last night I started reading a new book.

3. You can learn a lot by asking questions.

4. Diving into the pool always gives me a thrill.

5. We will raise money by washing cars.

6. Tonight Mom plans on cooking beans and rice.

7. I love sleeping late in the morning.

8. Is learning a foreign language more difficult for older people?

9. The ringing of the telephone woke me up.

10. Today, using a computer is a vital skill for many jobs.

PRACTICE 7.1L > Writing Gerunds and Gerund Phrases

Read the sentences. Then, rewrite each sentence, completing it with a gerund or a gerund phrase.

EXAMPLE   _____ is Jody's favorite activity.

ANSWER   *Playing basketball is Jody's favorite activity.*

11. _____ is a popular sport.

12. For me, the best way to stay healthy is _____.

13. On cold winter days I enjoy _____.

14. That actor is famous for _____.

15. _____ interrupted the mayor's speech.

16. You can win friends by _____.

17. _____ is a good way to begin a sentence.

18. _____ can keep me busy for hours.

19. The idea of _____ is growing more and more appealing.

20. Sculpture is the art of _____.

SPEAKING APPLICATION

With a partner, take turns talking about summer activities. Use at least three gerunds or gerund phrases. Your partner should listen for and name the three gerunds or gerund phrases that you use.

WRITING APPLICATION

Write three sentences about your hobbies. Use a gerund or a gerund phrase in each sentence. Underline each gerund or gerund phrase.

Identifying Infinitives and Infinitive Phrases

Read the sentences. Then, write the infinitive phrase from each sentence, and underline the infinitive. Also write *noun, adjective,* or *adverb* to describe each infinitive phrase.

EXAMPLE   Stephen tried to work faster.

ANSWER   *to work faster* — noun

1. Celia's dream is to visit Paris.
2. Now is the time to begin the test.
3. To skip a meal is never a good practice.
4. One way to travel through Australia is by train.
5. I hope to win the spelling bee.
6. The best place to go swimming is Sandy Creek.
7. We waited in the rain to hear the speaker.
8. The actress's goal, to win an Oscar, seemed further away than ever.
9. Many of us went to the airport to complain about noise from the planes.
10. Jake was sorry to lose the souvenir bookmark.

Writing Infinitives and Infinitive Phrases

Read the sentences. Then, rewrite each sentence, completing it with an infinitive or an infinitive phrase.

EXAMPLE   There are five questions _____.

ANSWER   *There are five questions to answer.*

11. My plan for the future is _____.
12. _____ is a wonderful opportunity.
13. Some people think golf is not much fun _____.
14. The instructions _____ are not complicated.
15. The goal of the conference is _____.
16. My homeroom teacher asked me _____.
17. The simplest way _____ is on foot.
18. The salesclerk was happy _____.
19. A good pitcher knows how _____.
20. The mayor's promise, _____, brought hope to the residents.

SPEAKING APPLICATION

With a partner, take turns telling about a skill that you want to learn. Use at least three infinitives or infinitive phrases. Your partner should listen for and name the three infinitives or infinitive phrases that you use.

WRITING APPLICATION

Write three sentences about volunteer activities in your community. Use an infinitive or an infinitive phrase in each sentence. Underline each infinitive or infinitive phrase.

7.2 Clauses

Clauses are the basic structural unit of a sentence.

RULE 7.2.1

A clause is a group of words with its own subject and verb.

There are two basic kinds of clauses, **main** or **independent clauses** and **subordinate clauses**.

RULE 7.2.2

A main or independent clause has a subject and a verb and can stand by itself as a complete sentence.

As you can see in the examples below, a main clause can be long or short. All main clauses express a complete thought and can stand by themselves as complete sentences.

EXAMPLES

The **window** **rattled**.
     subject   verb

Later that week, **she** **began** using the bike.
     subject   verb

RULE 7.2.3

A subordinate clause, also known as a dependent clause, has a subject and a verb but cannot stand by itself as a complete sentence. It is only part of a sentence.

SUBORDINATE CLAUSES

after **she** **told** her story
   subject verb

while the **audience** **listened**
     subject   verb

After reading a subordinate clause, you will still need more information to have a complete sentence.

Subordinate clauses begin with **subordinating conjunctions**
or **relative pronouns.**

Some subordinate clauses begin with **subordinating
conjunctions,** such as *if, since, when, although, after, because,*
and *while*. Others begin with **relative pronouns,** such as *who,
which,* or *that*. These words are clues that the clause may not
be able to stand alone. Notice how the addition of subordinating
words changes the meaning of the main clauses in the examples
below.

| COMPARING TWO KINDS OF CLAUSES ||
MAIN	SUBORDINATE
They sing this evening.	*when* they sing this evening
This park has a sandpit.	*because* this park has a sandpit
I planted the roses.	the roses *that* I planted

In order to form a complete thought, a subordinate clause must be
combined with a main clause.

EXAMPLES **After she presented her data** , Tara felt
subordinate clause   main clause

relieved.

The committee applauded **after Tara presented**
main clause   subordinate clause

her data .

It was Jake **who was asked to present first** .
main clause   subordinate clause

When she arrives tonight , Hannah needs to
subordinate clause   main clause

unpack her suitcase.

See Practice 7.2A

See Practice 7.2B

PRACTICE 7.2A > Identifying Main and Subordinate Clauses

Read the sentences. Then, write the main and subordinate clauses in each sentence, and label them *main clause* or *subordinate clause*.

EXAMPLE   When I left, May was still singing.

ANSWER   *When I left* — *subordinate clause*
May was still singing — *main clause*

1. Before I moved to Iowa, I had never seen snow.

2. Grandma brings a pie whenever she visits.

3. Unless I am mistaken, that woman is Mrs. Lee.

4. He is a great teacher whom I respect very much.

5. Kenneth was relieved when he finished the test.

6. Wait behind the line until the train comes to a complete stop.

7. New Amsterdam, which became New York, was originally a Dutch colonial settlement.

8. If you walk on that road after dark, be careful of potholes.

9. The pants that you bought are too long.

10. Did the person whose entry won first prize ever pick up the award?

PRACTICE 7.2B > Identifying and Using Main and Subordinate Clauses

Read the clauses. Write *main clause* or *subordinate clause* for each clause. Then, expand each subordinate clause into a complete sentence by adding a main clause.

EXAMPLE   After we ate.

ANSWER   *subordinate clause*
After we ate, we went for a walk.

11. I enjoy old television shows.

12. If you send a text message.

13. Everyone clapped and whistled.

14. Whenever we eat spaghetti.

15. Unless we leave by four o'clock.

16. That book is a real page turner.

17. Whom I have known since kindergarten.

18. Although I waited for Kay for hours near the park entrance.

19. There was no answer.

20. Study the map carefully.

SPEAKING APPLICATION

With a partner, take turns telling about your weekend plans. Each statement you make should contain one main clause and one subordinate clause. Your partner should listen for and name the clauses.

WRITING APPLICATION

Write three sentences about traveling by car, bus, train, or plane. Each sentence should contain one main clause and one subordinate clause. Underline each main clause, and double underline each subordinate clause.

Adjectival Clauses

A subordinate clause will sometimes act as an adjective in a sentence. An adjectival clause or adjective clause is a dependent clause and can not stand on its own.

> An **adjectival clause** or **adjective clause** is a subordinate clause that modifies a noun or a pronoun.

Like one-word adjectives and adjectival phrases, **adjectival clauses** tell *what kind* or *which one*.

WHAT KIND?

EXAMPLES   apples **that are juicy and sweet**

WHICH ONE?

the town **where I am from**

Recognizing Adjectival Clauses

Most adjectival clauses begin with the words *that, which, who, whom,* and *whose*. Sometimes an adjectival clause begins with a subordinating conjunction, such as *since, where,* or *when*. In the chart below, the adjectival clauses are hightlighted in pink.

ADJECTIVAL CLAUSES
The manager whom I asked for help met me in her office. (*Which* manager?)
The beach party, which was planned a month ago, is this weekend. (*Which* beach party?)
In the few months since she started training, Tina has become an accomplished lifeguard. (*Which* months?)
The dog is in the pantry closet where I hid the treats. (*Which* closet?)
We visited the museum that shows animals from long ago. (*Which* museum?)
The museum whose exhibits include dinosaurs is located in the center of town. (*Which* museum?)

See Practice 7.2C

Combining Sentences With Adjectival Clauses

Two sentences can be combined into one sentence by changing one of them into an adjectival clause. Sometimes you will need to add a relative pronoun or subordinating conjunction to make the sentence read correctly. In the sentences below, the adjectival clauses are highlighted in pink.

TWO SENTENCES	COMBINED WITH AN ADJECTIVAL CLAUSE
My best friend has written songs based on her life. My friend is a musician.	My best friend, who has written songs based on her life, is a musician.
We visited Wild Animal World. Wild Animal World is my favorite animal park.	We visited Wild Animal World, which is my favorite animal park.
We decided to eat at the rest area. They usually offer the best prices there.	We decided to eat at the rest area, where the best prices are usually offered.
Laura visited her sister. Laura's sister lives on a beach in Florida.	Laura visited her sister, who lives on a beach in Florida.
Delmar goes to karate class on Main Street. He goes to class every week.	Every week, Delmar goes to his karate class, which is on Main Street.

See Practice 7.2D

PRACTICE 7.2C Identifying Adjectival Clauses

Read the sentences. Then, write the adjectival clause in each sentence. One sentence has two adjectival clauses.

EXAMPLE   The employee whom I phoned was not at her desk.

ANSWER   *whom I phoned*

1. The chorus, which meets on Tuesdays and Thursdays, is accepting new members.

2. Aunt Clarice, who was living in Ohio, just moved to Florida.

3. The new student, whom I met in science class, moved here from Atlanta.

4. The wallet that I bought is larger than my last one.

5. The street where I live is not far from here.

6. Someone whose voice is so good should sing in public.

7. Do you remember the day when we last saw each other?

8. What is the name of that excellent relief pitcher who plays for the Cubs?

9. One week after we began the school term, we had already taken two tests.

10. In the time since Sarah left, four people whom she knows arrived at the party and asked for her.

PRACTICE 7.2D Combining Sentences Using Adjectival Clauses

Read the sentences. Combine the pairs of sentences by changing one of them into an adjectival clause.

EXAMPLE   Eudora Welty was a famous writer. She lived in Mississippi.

ANSWER   *Eudora Welty, who lived in Mississippi, was a famous writer.*

11. My sister made me a pair of gloves. She knits beautifully.

12. A beret is a type of cap. It is worn at an angle.

13. The Memorial Day parade lasts for about two hours. It begins on High Street.

14. Barack Obama was born in Hawaii. He became president of the United States in 2009.

15. Newfoundland is Canada's easternmost province. It borders the Atlantic Ocean.

16. The tornado destroyed many homes. It swept through town last night.

17. We visited Gettysburg. That is where President Lincoln gave his famous address.

18. Felice is fluent in three languages. Her name means "happy."

19. My pen pal lives in Peru. I have never met her.

20. Was 1992 a leap year? That is when I was born.

SPEAKING APPLICATION

With a partner, take turns describing a place you have visited. Use at least three adjectival clauses. Your partner should listen for and name the three adjectival clauses that you use.

WRITING APPLICATION

Write three sentences about famous people in history. Use an adjectival clause in each sentence. Underline each adjectival clause.

Adverbial Clauses

Subordinate clauses can also be used as adverbs. Adverbial clauses or adverb clauses are dependent clauses.

> **An adverbial clause or adverb clause is a subordinate clause that modifies a verb, an adjective, or an adverb.**

7.2.6 RULE

Adverbial clauses can answer any of the following questions about the words they modify: *Where? When? In what manner? To what extent? Under what conditions?* or *Why?*

ADVERBIAL CLAUSES	
Modifying Verbs	Put the groceries wherever you find room. (Put *where?*)
	The service will begin when the speaker enters. (Will begin *when?*)
	Jan spoke as if she were joking. (Spoke *in what manner?*)
	I will have tea if you do too. (Will *have under what conditions?*)
Modifying an Adjective	I am happy because I have been shopping all day. (Happy *why?*)
Modifying an Adverb	He knows more than the other officers do. (More *to what extent?*)

Recognizing Adverbial Clauses

> **A subordinating conjunction introduces an adverbial clause.**

7.2.7 RULE

A **subordinating conjunction** always introduces an adverbial clause. In a sentence, the conjunction will usually appear in one of two places—either at the beginning, when the adverbial clause begins the sentence, or in the middle, connecting the independent clause to the subordinate clause. In the examples on the next page, the subordinating conjunctions are highlighted in purple.

EXAMPLES **Because** you came home early, I will prepare lunch.

I will prepare lunch **because** you came home early.

Whenever you go to Claire's house, I expect you to call.

I expect you to call **whenever** you go to Claire's house.

Common Subordinating Conjunctions

Here are the most common subordinating conjunctions. Knowing them can help you recognize adverbial clauses.

COMMON SUBORDINATING CONJUNCTIONS		
after	even though	unless
although	if	until
as	in order that	when
as if	since	whenever
as long as	so that	where
because	than	wherever
before	though	while

Elliptical Adverbial Clauses

In certain adverbial clauses, words are left out. These clauses are said to be elliptical.

In an elliptical adverbial clause, the verb or the subject and verb are understood rather than stated.

Many elliptical adverbial clauses are introduced by one of two subordinating conjunctions, *as* or *than*. In the following examples, the understood words have been added in parentheses. The first elliptical adverbial clause is missing a verb; the second is missing a subject and a verb.

EXAMPLES My cousin can eat as much **as I** (can eat).

I like this play more **than** (I liked) **that one**.

See Practice 7.2E

See Practice 7.2F

PRACTICE 7.2E ▷ Identifying Adverbial Clauses and Recognizing Elliptical Adverbial Clauses

Read the sentences. Then, write the adverbial clauses. For any of the adverbial clauses that are elliptical, add the understood words in parentheses.

EXAMPLE   My cousin can swim better than I.

ANSWER   *than I (can swim)*

1. I coughed because something tickled my throat.

2. If the weather gets warmer, I will walk to the supermarket.

3. Vic always does stretches before he runs.

4. Whenever I hurry, I make mistakes.

5. Because he broke the law, the man was arrested.

6. Manuel was upset when I arrived late for practice.

7. Although Maria is not a close friend, I always enjoy her company.

8. We left much later than our neighbors.

9. Let's stay at the mall until the last bus leaves.

10. Your guess is as good as mine.

PRACTICE 7.2F ▷ Combining Sentences With Adverbial Clauses

Read the sentences. Combine each pair of sentences by changing one of them into an adverbial clause. Use an appropriate subordinating conjunction, and drop or change words as necessary.

EXAMPLE   Charlotte should win the game. Someone else may outscore her.

ANSWER   *Charlotte should win the game unless someone else outscores her.*

11. I brushed my teeth. Then I went to bed.

12. I would love a new bike. However, I cannot afford one.

13. Gregory will mow the lawn. Only rain will prevent him.

14. The chef used potholders. She did not want to burn her hands.

15. You go to the party. Then I will go too.

16. Chet did the laundry. Later, he ironed his shirts.

17. I checked all the television channels. I finally found an old movie.

18. Terry likes children. She volunteers at the day-care center.

19. The bell rings. The dog barks every time.

20. I held the pieces of fabric in place. At the same time, my sister sewed them together.

SPEAKING APPLICATION

With a partner, take turns describing an animal's behavior. Use at least three adverbial clauses. Your partner should listen for and name the three adverbial clauses that you use.

WRITING APPLICATION

Write a short paragraph about a recent news event. Use an adverbial clause in three of your sentences. Underline the adverbial clauses.

7.3 Classifying Sentences by Structure

All sentences can be classified according to the number and kinds of clauses they contain.

The Simple Sentence

The **simple sentence** is the most common type of sentence structure.

> A **simple sentence** consists of a single independent clause.

Simple sentences vary in length. Some are quite short; others can be several lines long. All simple sentences, however, contain just one subject and one verb. They may also contain adjectives, adverbs, complements, and phrases in different combinations.

Simple sentences can also have various compound parts. They can have a compound subject, a compound verb, or both. Sometimes, they will also have other compound elements, such as a compound direct object or a compound phrase.

All of the following sentences are simple sentences.

TYPES OF SIMPLE SENTENCES	
With One Subject and Verb	The hail fell .
With a Compound Subject	Hail and rain are common.
With a Compound Verb	The floor squeaked and groaned .
With a Compound Subject and Compound Verb	My mother and sister bought the balloons and decorated the room for the party.
With a Compound Direct Object	She opened the gift box and the letter . direct object direct object
With a Compound Prepositional Phrase	You can walk from the subway or from the bus . prep phrase prep phrase

A simple sentence never has a subordinate clause, and it never has more than one main or independent clause.

The Compound Sentence

A **compound sentence** is made up of more than one simple sentence.

> A **compound sentence** consists of two or more main or independent clauses.

7.3.2 RULE

In most compound sentences, the main or independent clauses are joined by a comma and a coordinating conjunction (*and, but, for, nor, or, so,* or *yet*). They may also be connected with a semicolon (;) or a colon (:).

EXAMPLES   **Linda** **ran** a two-day computer seminar **,** **and** ten **managers** **agreed** to speak.

All of the managers **taught** on the first day **;** **two** were **missing** the second day.

See Practice 7.3A
See Practice 7.3B

Notice in both of the preceding examples that there are two separate and complete main clauses, each with its own subject and verb. Like simple sentences, compound sentences never contain subordinate clauses.

The Complex Sentence

Complex sentences contain subordinate clauses, which can be either adjectival clauses or adverbial clauses.

> A **complex sentence** consists of one main or independent clause and one or more subordinate clauses.

7.3.3 RULE

In a complex sentence, the independent clause is often called the **main clause.** The main clause has its own subject and verb, as does each subordinate clause.

In a complex sentence, the main clause can stand alone as a simple sentence. The subordinate clause cannot stand alone as a sentence.

July 4, 1776, is the day **that America won its**
          main clause   subordinate clause

independence .

Because this day is so important , **many towns**
             subordinate clause

have parades and picnics .
          main clause

In some complex sentences, the main clause is split by a subordinate clause that acts as an adjective.

EXAMPLE   **Many people** , **who have the day**

off , **participate in games and events** .

The two parts of the main clause form one main clause:
Many people participate in games and events.

See Practice 7.3C
See Practice 7.3D

The Compound-Complex Sentence

A **compound-complex sentence,** as the name indicates, contains the elements of both a compound sentence and a complex sentence.

RULE
7.3.4

> A **compound-complex sentence** consists of two or more main or independent clauses and one or more subordinate clauses.

EXAMPLE   **As Joan was leaving for vacation** ,
                subordinate clause

she remembered to take her ticket , but
          main clause

she forgot her passport **that she had renewed**
        main clause   subordinate clause

the day before .

> **PRACTICE 7.3A** **Distinguishing Simple and Compound Sentences**

Read the sentences. Then, write *simple* or *compound* for each sentence.

EXAMPLE   The zoo gives a student discount, but the museum charges full price.

ANSWER   *compound*

1. The state repaved the highways last year.

2. Sharon and Kayla met at summer camp.

3. I downloaded a song for my sister, but she already had it.

4. The school has a new science lab, and plans for the new auditorium are moving ahead.

5. Either Hugh or Josie will introduce the guest speaker to the class.

6. Please bring sunscreen, towels, and beach chairs.

7. Mom spotted Pell Road and turned right.

8. Terry used binoculars, yet he still could barely see the stage from the fourth balcony.

9. I ate eggs for breakfast; I want something else for lunch.

10. Speak quietly, or you will frighten the kittens.

> **PRACTICE 7.3B** **Combining Simple Sentences to Form Compound Sentences**

Read the sentences. Combine the pairs of simple sentences to form compound sentences.

EXAMPLE   Comedies are fine. I prefer action movies.

ANSWER   *Comedies are fine, but I prefer action movies.*

11. My sister sings well. I cannot carry a tune.

12. Our team may win. The other team may beat us.

13. Sue washed the car. Her brother did the laundry.

14. The map is a little dirty. Someone spilled coffee on it.

15. The train arrived at noon. Several passengers got on and off.

16. My study habits have improved. I expect better test scores.

17. The book is rather long. I finished it fairly quickly.

18. I invited Juan to my house. We studied for the test together.

19. The cruise ship stopped first in Juneau. The next stop was Skagway.

20. Louise's dog is a purebred border collie. Mine is a mutt.

SPEAKING APPLICATION

With a partner, take turns telling about a household chore. Use two simple sentences and two compound sentences. Your partner should listen for and identify the simple sentences and the compound sentences.

WRITING APPLICATION

Write four sentences about an event in American history. Use two simple sentences and two compound sentences. Underline the subject and verb in each simple sentence and the subjects and verbs in the clauses of each compound sentence.

PRACTICE 7.3C Recognizing Complex Sentences

Read the sentences. Then, label each sentence *complex* or *not complex.*

EXAMPLE Gloria bought pens, pencils, and paper at the store.

ANSWER *not complex*

1. Tomorrow is my sister's birthday, but her party is on Saturday.

2. While officials assessed the storm damage, the governor declared a state of emergency.

3. Clara brought a housewarming gift to her new neighbor.

4. Bruce put his backpack on the floor during lunch, and he forgot it when he left.

5. When the plumber arrived, Fran showed him the leaking pipe.

6. If you visit the eye doctor, you will take a vision test.

7. I have a large collection of comics; my brother's collection is even bigger.

8. The screenplay was finalized, and the filming began.

9. The athlete from the Ukraine is the one who earned the gold medal.

10. The real estate agent who sold us our house has now retired.

PRACTICE 7.3D Distinguishing Compound and Complex Sentences

Read the sentences. Then, label each sentence *compound* or *complex*.*

EXAMPLE The building that burned was a shoe store.

ANSWER *complex*

11. I visit the library often, but I never go by bus.

12. As soon as I got home, I took a shower.

13. The small shop, which was open only on weekends, sold meat and fish.

14. My dad speaks five different languages, yet he doesn't travel much anymore.

15. The airport metal detector went off because I was still wearing my watch.

16. Sam joined the hockey team, and he became the star player.

17. My grandfather cannot hear well if there is background noise.

18. Will Jody be ready when the taxi arrives?

19. I like mysteries; Juan prefers science fiction.

20. Answer quickly, before you forget the question.

SPEAKING APPLICATION

With a partner, take turns telling about a visit to the dentist. Use at least two complex sentences. Your partner should listen for and identify the complex sentences.

WRITING APPLICATION

Write four sentences about a family tradition. Use two compound sentences and two complex sentences.

CHAPTER 8

EFFECTIVE SENTENCES

Use sentences of different lengths and complexity to make your writing more dynamic.

WRITE GUY *Jeff Anderson, M.Ed.*

WHAT DO YOU NOTICE?

Focus on the variety of sentences as you zoom in on these sentences from Act II of *Diary of Anne Frank* by Frances Goodrich and Albert Hackett.

MENTOR TEXT

> Our stomachs are so empty that they rumble and make strange noises, all in different keys. Mr. Van Daan's is deep and low, like a bass fiddle. Mine is high, whistling like a flute.

Now, ask yourself the following questions:

- How and why does the author use sentences of different lengths?
- Why might the author have decided not to combine the second and third sentences?

The author begins with a longer sentence and follows with two shorter sentences. Sentences of different lengths create more variety so that the writing flows. The author may have decided to keep the second and third sentences separated in order to make two distinct points.

Grammar for Writers Writers create flow by using a combination of short and long, simple and complex sentences. If you find too many of one kind of sentence in a text block, look for ways to break them up or combine them for variety.

How can I combine these sentences?

I have an extra *and and* or you can use.

8.1 Classifying the Four Functions of a Sentence

Sentences can be classified according to what they do. Some sentences present facts or information in a direct way, while others pose questions to the reader or listener. Still others present orders or directions. A fourth type of sentence expresses strong emotion.

These four types of sentences are called **declarative, interrogative, imperative,** and **exclamatory.** As well as having a different purpose, each type of sentence is constructed in a different way.

The type of sentence you are writing determines the punctuation mark you use to end the sentence. The three end marks are the **period (.),** the **question mark (?),** and the **exclamation mark (!).**

The **declarative sentence** is the most common type of sentence. It is used to state, or "declare," facts.

RULE 8.1.1

A **declarative sentence** states, or declares, an idea and ends with a period.

DECLARATIVE   Space travel is very exciting.

Astronauts train for many years before they can fly into space.

Although it is a dangerous career choice, many people apply to the astronaut training program at NASA.

Interrogative means "asking." An **interrogative sentence** is a question. Interrogative sentences often begin with *who, what, when, why, how,* or *how many.* They end with a question mark.

An **interrogative sentence** asks a question and ends with a question mark.

8.1.2 RULE

INTERROGATIVE When is the student council election?

Who is running for president?

When will the candidates give their speeches?

An **imperative sentence** gives an order, or command, or a direction and ends with either a period or an exclamation mark.

8.1.3 RULE

EL8

The word *imperative* comes from the Latin word that means "commanding." **Imperative sentences** are commands or directions. Most imperative sentences start with a verb. In this type of sentence, the subject is understood to be *you.*

IMPERATIVE Be careful, the floor is slippery.

Watch where you step!

Notice the punctuation at the end of these examples. In the first sentence, the period suggests that a mild command is being given in an ordinary tone of voice. The exclamation mark at the end of the second sentence suggests a strong command, one given in a loud voice.

An **exclamatory sentence** conveys strong emotion and ends with an exclamation mark.

8.1.4 RULE

Exclaim means "to shout out." **Exclamatory sentences** are used to "shout out" emotions such as happiness, fear, delight, or anger.

See Practice 8.1A
See Practice 8.1B
See Practice 8.1C
See Practice 8.1D

EXCLAMATORY What a mess this room is!

I need the key now!

Identifying Four Types of Sentences

Read the sentences. Then, identify each type of sentence by writing *declarative*, *interrogative*, *imperative*, or *exclamatory*.

EXAMPLE   What did you do in science lab?

ANSWER   *interrogative*

1. Please turn down the volume on your radio.

2. Ginger is a spice popular in Asian cooking.

3. What a dilemma we faced!

4. Which famous American appears on the dollar bill?

5. Lucille Ball was a talented comic performer.

6. How many times has she visited Miami?

7. Stir a cup of water into the mixture.

8. This apple tastes great!

9. I heard thunder in the distance.

10. Don't call before nine in the morning.

Punctuating Four Types of Sentences

Read the sentences. Then, rewrite each sentence, adding the correct end punctuation.

EXAMPLE   Have you had a flu shot this year

ANSWER   *Have you had a flu shot this year?*

11. What a foolish error

12. Please bring a pencil for the test

13. From 1929 until World War II, America suffered through the Great Depression

14. Paula works as a nurse at the health clinic

15. How beautiful Santa Barbara is

16. Clean your room, please

17. What brand of shampoo do you usually use

18. I accept your facts but cannot agree with all your conclusions

19. How will you pay for the meal

20. I asked Don if he knew who the winner was

SPEAKING APPLICATION

With a partner, take turns telling about a beautiful place. Use each of the four types of sentences. Your partner should identify the four types of sentences that you used.

WRITING APPLICATION

Write four sentences about an activity you enjoy. Each sentence should be a different type—declarative, interrogative, imperative, or exclamatory. Be sure to use appropriate end punctuation.

PRACTICE 8.1C › Writing Four Types of Sentences

Read the topics. For each topic, write the type of sentence specified in parentheses. Be sure to use the appropriate end punctuation.

EXAMPLE   beautiful scenery (exclamatory)

ANSWER   *What a gorgeous sunset!*

1. a future plan (interrogative)
2. a request to a repair worker (imperative)
3. a movie review (exclamatory)
4. a fact from history (declarative)
5. something that is lost (interrogative)
6. a television newscaster (declarative)
7. a way to save money (imperative)
8. a gift you received (exclamatory)
9. a direction to a child (imperative)
10. a mysterious object (interrogative)

PRACTICE 8.1D › Revising Four Types of Sentences

Read the sentences. Rewrite each sentence, changing it to the type of sentence specified in parentheses. Be sure to use the appropriate end punctuation.

EXAMPLE   I sat under the tree. (imperative)

ANSWER   *Don't sit under the tree.*

11. The dog was lost. (interrogative)
12. You can look up the meaning in a dictionary. (imperative)
13. Skiing is exciting. (exclamatory)
14. Is the forest a place of mystery? (declarative)
15. Don't go to the movies today. (interrogative)
16. What a strange noise that was! (declarative)
17. Can I wear jeans to the interview? (imperative)
18. She is a computer genius. (exclamatory)
19. Use the smaller fork for the salad. (declarative)
20. How memorable his speech was! (interrogative)

SPEAKING APPLICATION

With a partner, take turns changing each other's sentence types. Say four sentences that illustrate one of each of the four sentence types. Your partner should change each one to another sentence type. Sentences can be on the subject of your choice.

WRITING APPLICATION

Write four sentences—one declarative, one interrogative, one imperative, and one exclamatory—all about the same natural wonder. Then, turn each sentence into a different type. Be sure to use appropriate end punctuation.

8.2 Combining Sentences

Good writing should include sentences of varying lengths and complexity to create a flow of ideas. One way to achieve sentence variety is to combine sentences to express two or more related ideas or pieces of information in a single sentence.

Look at the example below. Then, look at how the ideas are combined in different ways.

EXAMPLE   I trained for soccer. I trained for tennis.

COMBINED   I trained for soccer and tennis.

                      I trained for tennis after I trained for soccer.

Combining Sentence Parts

RULE 8.2.1 — Sentences can be combined by using a **compound subject,** a **compound verb,** or a **compound object.**

EXAMPLE   The sprints are exhausting to run.
                The marathon is exhausting to run.

COMPOUND SUBJECT   The **sprints** and the **marathon** are exhausting to run.

EXAMPLE   Our team trained hard.
                Our team won the championship.

COMPOUND VERB   Our team **trained** hard and **won** the championship.

EXAMPLE   Short races require a quick start.
                Short races require explosive speed.

COMPOUND OBJECT   Short races require a quick **start** and explosive **speed** .

Joining Clauses

A **compound sentence** consists of two or more main or independent clauses. (See Chapter 7 for more information about clauses.) Use a compound sentence when combining related ideas of equal weight.

To create a compound sentence, join two main clauses with a comma and a coordinating conjunction. Common conjunctions include *and, but, nor, for, so, or,* and *yet*. You can also link the two sentences with a semicolon (;) if they are closely related.

> Sentences can be combined by joining two main clauses to create a **compound sentence**.

 8.2.2 RULE

EXAMPLE	We went to the planetarium. We saw the planets and the stars.
COMPOUND SENTENCE	We went to the planetarium, and we saw the planets and the stars.
EXAMPLE	Sam enjoyed watching the sky. Mari enjoyed looking for constellations.
COMPOUND SENTENCE	Sam enjoyed watching the sky, and Mari enjoyed looking for constellations.
EXAMPLE	Lee assembled the telescope. Walt turned off the lights in the house.
COMPOUND SENTENCE	Lee assembled the telescope; Walt turned off the lights in the house.
EXAMPLE	Ming knows all of the phases of the moon. Jake knows how the moon affects the tides.
COMPOUND SENTENCE	Ming knows all of the phases of the moon, and Jake knows how the moon affects the tides.

See Practice 8.2A
See Practice 8.2B

RULE
8.2.3

> Sentences can be combined by changing one of them into a
> **subordinate clause.**

A **complex sentence** consists of one **main** or **independent
clause** and one or more **subordinate clauses.** (See Chapter 7
for more information about clauses.) Combine sentences into
a complex sentence to emphasize that one of the ideas in the
sentence depends on the other. A subordinating conjunction will
help readers understand the relationship. Common subordinating
conjunctions are *after, although, because, before, since,* and
unless. Generally no punctuation is required when a main and
a subordinate clause are combined. When the subordinate
clause comes first, a comma is needed. (See Chapter 13 for more
information on punctuation.)

EXAMPLE   We were frightened. All of the lights went off.

COMBINED   We were frightened because all of the lights

went off.

See Practice 8.2C

RULE
8.2.4

> Sentences can be combined by changing one of them into a
> **phrase.**

When combining sentences in which one of the sentences simply
adds details, change one of the sentences into a **phrase.**

EXAMPLE   The space shuttle will be launched tomorrow.

It will study asteroids that are close to Earth.

COMBINED   The space shuttle will be launched tomorrow to

study asteroids that are close to Earth.

EXAMPLE   The space shuttle will launch from Cape Canaveral.

It will lift off at noon.

COMBINED   The space shuttle will launch from Cape Canaveral

at noon.

See Practice 8.2D

PRACTICE 8.2A **Combining Sentences Using Compound Subjects, Verbs, and Objects**

Read the sentences. Combine the sentences in each group into a single sentence. Identify each combination as *compound subject, compound verb,* or *compound object.*

EXAMPLE   Sara likes movies. Jo likes them too.

ANSWER   *Sara and Jo like movies.* — compound subject

1. The farmer irrigated his crops. He also weeded them.

2. Margo studies ballet. Olga studies ballet.

3. I put ketchup on my hamburger. I put mustard on it too.

4. Sam phoned me last night. Jewel phoned me last night. April also phoned me last night.

5. Claude likes crosswords. He likes word jumbles. He likes most other word games too.

6. Sam plays soccer. I do too.

7. Yesterday Alexis called. She invited me to her house.

8. We may take a train. We may take a bus. We may take a car.

9. They serve a good breakfast. They serve a bad lunch.

10. Every morning, Liz exercises on her treadmill. Then she swims at the town pool.

PRACTICE 8.2B **Combining Sentences Using Main Clauses**

Read the sentences. Combine each pair into a compound sentence, using the coordinating conjunction in parentheses. Be sure to use the correct punctuation for compound sentences.

EXAMPLE   The supermarket is open. The pharmacy is closed. (but)

ANSWER   *The supermarket is open, but the pharmacy is closed.*

11. We arrived in Milwaukee at noon. Aunt Grace met us at the airport. (and)

12. Many gold seekers went to California by water. Some went overland. (but)

13. The desert is very dry. It gets little rainfall. (;)

14. Bring a towel. Don't forget sunscreen. (and)

15. The earphones may have a loose wire. The entire MP3 player may be broken. (or)

16. My family has a dog. We do not have a cat. (but)

17. The visitors felt special. The governor had greeted them by name. (for)

18. Will you be going downtown? Are you staying home? (or)

19. None of the boys will admit it. Someone sent me this unsigned Valentine card. (yet)

20. Lozenges did not cure my cough. Cough medicine did not make it better. (nor)

SPEAKING APPLICATION

Tell a partner about something you might do after school. Your partner should listen for and identify compound subjects, verbs, or objects.

WRITING APPLICATION

Use sentences 11, 12, and 13 as models, and write three pairs of sentences about a shopping trip. Then, combine each pair by using an appropriate connector.

PRACTICE 8.2C ▷ **Combining Sentences Using Subordinate Clauses**

Read the sentences. Combine each pair by changing one sentence into a subordinate clause, using the subordinating conjunction in parentheses. Be sure to use the correct punctuation for complex sentences.

EXAMPLE   Louise's shoes were too tight. Louise got blisters. (because)

ANSWER   *Because her shoes were too tight, Louise got blisters.*

1. The company changed its logo. Its products were repackaged with the new design. (after)

2. Thunder startled the horse. The horse nearly threw off its rider. (because)

3. Leo edited the school paper. Rita became the new editor. (until)

4. Ariana sang. Simon played the piano. (as)

5. Mr. Lowell mowed the lawn. Then he painted the house. (before)

6. My favorite team is in the playoffs. They will be more exciting for me this year. (since)

7. I went to northern Arizona. There I saw the Grand Canyon. (where)

8. Helen Keller could not hear or see. Anne Sullivan taught her to speak. (although)

9. In the 1890s, women began wearing loose pants. Bicycle riding became a fad. (when)

10. Hopefully, the library can raise the money. The new wing can be built. (if)

PRACTICE 8.2D ▷ **Combining Sentences Using Phrases**

Read the sentences. Combine each pair of sentences by changing one into a phrase.

EXAMPLE   Sharla served small sandwiches. They had no crusts.

ANSWER   *Sharla served small sandwiches without crusts.*

11. I read a book. It was about Alaska.

12. I am learning about ecology. That is the study of the environment.

13. The geese flew through the air. The geese maintained a V-shaped formation.

14. Please turn off your cellphone. Do it before entering the museum.

15. Mom and I will play a board game. We will play after dinner.

16. Sheila went to the bank. She made a deposit.

17. My uncle grows zucchini in his vegetable garden. Zucchini is a type of summer squash.

18. Mom ate breakfast. Then Mom left for work.

19. Ralph made an emergency call. The fire department responded promptly.

20. Amy Tan was born in 1952. She grew up in California.

SPEAKING APPLICATION

Tell a partner about something you are studying, using items 11 and 12 as models. Your partner should combine each pair of sentences.

WRITING APPLICATION

Use items 1, 2, and 3 as models, and write three pairs of sentences about a game you like to play. Then, combine each pair by using a subordinating conjunction.

8.3 Varying Sentences

When you vary the length and form of the sentences you write, you are able to create a rhythm, achieve an effect, or emphasize the connections between ideas.

There are several ways you can introduce variety into the sentences you write.

> **Varying the length of sentences makes writing lively and interesting to read.**

8.3.1 RULE

Varying Sentence Length

Reading too many long sentences in a row can be just as uninteresting as reading too many short sentences in a row. When you want to emphasize a point or surprise a reader, insert a short, direct sentence to interrupt the flow of several long sentences.

EXAMPLE

In the 1830s, model railroading was not a hobby. However, during that decade the first miniature railroad was built. This first railroad contained a locomotive, several passenger cars, and some track. It was not created for entertainment; it was a model for a locomotive that was being planned. **That first model served its purpose well.**

You can also break some longer sentences into shorter sentences. If the longer sentence contains two or more ideas, you can break up the ideas into separate sentences. However, if a longer sentence contains only one main idea, you should not break it apart.

LONGER SENTENCE

Mathias Baldwin created the first model railroad to help him design a new type of locomotive.

TWO SENTENCES

Mathias Baldwin created the first model railroad. This miniature helped him design a new locomotive.

See Practice 8.3A

Varying Sentence Beginnings

Another way to create variety is by changing from the usual subject–verb order in a sentence.

> **RULE 8.3.2**
>
> Sentence beginnings can also be varied by reversing the traditional subject–verb order or starting the sentence with an adverb or a phrase.

EXAMPLES

The **equipment** **is** **here**.
subject   verb   adverb

Here **is** the **equipment**.
adverb   verb   subject

The **cleats** **dug** **into the dirt**.
subject   verb   prepositional phrase

Into the dirt **dug** the **cleats**.
prepositional phrase   verb   subject

We **ran** the new **pattern** **quickly**.
subject verb   direct object   adverb

Quickly, **we** **ran** the new **pattern**.
adverb   subject verb   direct object

Another way to vary your sentences is to begin them in different ways. For instance, you can start sentences with different parts of speech.

See Practice 8.3B

WAYS TO VARY SENTENCE BEGINNINGS	
Start with a noun.	**Lab experiments**, surprisingly, are fun to conduct.
Start with an adverb.	**Surprisingly**, lab experiments are fun to conduct.
Start with an infinitive.	**To conduct lab experiments**, surprisingly, is fun.
Start with a gerund.	**Conducting lab experiments is**, surprisingly, fun.
Start with a prepositional phrase.	**For an interested student**, lab experiments are fun to conduct.

PRACTICE 8.3A ▷ Varying Sentence Length

Read the sentences. Rewrite each long compound sentence as two or more shorter sentences.

EXAMPLE   Salmon hatch in rivers, and they swim to the ocean, but they return to the rivers to breed.

ANSWER   *Salmon hatch in rivers. They swim to the ocean, but they return to the rivers to breed.*

1. The waiter brought a bowl of soup, and I ate it, and it was delicious.

2. I spilled juice on my computer keyboard, and now it does not work well, and the letters stick.

3. The tennis star served, and her opponent hit the ball back over the net, but it was a foul.

4. San Diego is a beautiful city, and it has a fine climate, and it also has a wonderful zoo.

5. Maida goes hiking with her brother, and they often hike in the national parks, but they have also hiked the Appalachian Trail.

PRACTICE 8.3B ▷ Varying Sentence Beginnings

Read the sentences. Rewrite each sentence, changing the beginning as specified in parentheses. If there are two sentences, combine them, using one of the sentences to help you create the specified beginning.

EXAMPLE   Gary and I went out for pizza. (begin with a prepositional phrase).

ANSWER   *After school, Gary and I went out for pizza.*

6. I caught a fish. That was surprising. (Begin with an adverb.)

7. Red-winged blackbirds flew toward the lake. (Begin with a prepositional phrase.)

8. Completing the crossword puzzle is my goal. (Begin with an infinitive.)

9. The dancer leaped into the air. (Change the subject-verb order.)

10. My favorite activity is playing baseball. (Begin with a gerund.)

SPEAKING APPLICATION

With a partner, take turns telling about packing a suitcase. Your partner should make suggestions about how to improve your sentences by varying sentence length.

WRITING APPLICATION

Write five sentences about a famous explorer or inventor. Vary your sentence beginnings. Include at least one sentence in which you change the subject-verb order.

8.4 Avoiding Sentence Problems

Recognizing problems with sentences will help you avoid and fix any problems in your writing.

Correcting Fragments

Some groups of words—even though they have a capital letter at the beginning and a period at the end—are not complete sentences. They are **fragments.**

RULE 8.4.1

> A **fragment** is a group of words that does not express a complete thought.

A fragment can be a group of words that includes a possible subject but no verb. A fragment could also be a group of words that includes a possible verb but no subject. It can even be a group of words that contains no subject and no verb. Fragments can be turned into complete sentences by adding a subject, a verb, or both.

FRAGMENTS	COMPLETE SENTENCES
heard the bell	**I** heard the bell. (A subject is added.)
the classroom door	The classroom door **is** closed. (A verb is added.)
in that hall	My **locker** **is** in that hall. (A subject and verb are added.)

See Practice 8.4A

Correcting Phrase Fragments A **phrase fragment** cannot stand alone because it does not have both a subject and a verb.

RULE 8.4.2

> A **phrase fragment** should not be capitalized and punctuated as if it were a sentence.

A phrase fragment can be corrected in one of two ways:
(1) by adding it to a nearby sentence or (2) by adding whatever is needed to make it a complete sentence.

<table>
<tr><td>PHRASE FRAGMENT</td><td>The explorers left for the Arctic.
on the morning of March 4</td></tr>
<tr><td>ADDED TO OTHER SENTENCE</td><td>The explorers left for the Arctic **on the morning of March 4** .</td></tr>
<tr><td>PHRASE FRAGMENT</td><td>They had packed heavy clothing. **along with weatherproof equipment**</td></tr>
<tr><td>COMPLETE SENTENCES</td><td>They had packed heavy clothing. They had also packed **weatherproof equipment** .</td></tr>
</table>

CHANGING PHRASE FRAGMENTS INTO SENTENCES	
PHRASE FRAGMENT	**COMPLETE SENTENCE**
in the early evening	The flight arrived **in the early evening** .
happy to be home	The travelers were **happy to be home** .
to pick up their luggage	They waited **to pick up their luggage** .

See Practice 8.4B

Correcting Clause Fragments

All clauses have subjects and verbs, but some cannot stand alone as sentences.

> **A subordinate clause** should not be capitalized and punctuated as if it were a sentence.

8.4.3 RULE

Subordinate clauses do not express complete thoughts. Although a subordinate adjective or adverb clause has a subject and a verb, it cannot stand by itself as a sentence. (See Chapter 7 for more information about subordinate clauses and the words that begin them.)

Like phrase fragments, **clause fragments** can usually be corrected in either of two ways: (1) by attaching the fragment to a nearby sentence or (2) by adding whatever words are needed to turn the fragment into a sentence.

CLAUSE FRAGMENT	Jane found the necklace. **that she had lost in gym class**
COMPLETE SENTENCE	Jane found the necklace **that she had lost in gym class** .
CLAUSE FRAGMENT	It was lying on a book. **which was underneath the bench near her locker**
COMPLETE SENTENCE	It was lying on a book, **which was underneath the bench near her locker** .
CLAUSE FRAGMENT	The clasp had broken. **that had held the chain together**
COMPLETE SENTENCE	The clasp **that had held the chain together** had broken.

To change a clause fragment into a sentence by the second method, you must add an independent clause to the fragment.

CHANGING CLAUSE FRAGMENTS INTO SENTENCES	
CLAUSE FRAGMENT	COMPLETE SENTENCE
that was overdue	I returned the library book **that was overdue** . The library book **that was overdue** has been returned.
when I got there	The library was almost ready to close **when I got there** . **When I got there** , the library was almost ready to close.
why I was so late	I couldn't figure out **why I was so late** .

See Practice 8.4C

See Practice 8.4D

PRACTICE 8.4A **Recognizing Fragments**

Read the groups of words. Then, write whether each group of words is a *sentence* or a *fragment*.

EXAMPLE   A child reaching for a toy.

ANSWER   *fragment*

1. At the very end of the street.
2. Did they arrive?
3. This highway has no rest stops.
4. A reporter holding a microphone.
5. When we left for Mexico City.
6. Please join us.
7. To say my lines without breaking into laughter.
8. The city with the best restaurants in America.
9. A guard helping the children across the street.
10. We're lost.

PRACTICE 8.4B **Changing Phrase Fragments Into Sentences**

Read the phrase fragments. Then, use each fragment in a sentence.

EXAMPLE   below the ceiling

ANSWER   *Below the ceiling is a shelf with plates on display.*

11. before ten o'clock
12. exhausted by the ordeal
13. a famous inventor
14. to reach school on time
15. between my friend and me
16. should have been informed
17. exercising often
18. buying a new sweater
19. a farmer harvesting his crops
20. a good movie to watch on DVD

SPEAKING APPLICATION

With a partner, take turns creating fragments. Your partner should listen to the fragment and turn it into a sentence.

WRITING APPLICATION

Choose two fragments in Practice 8.4B and write two new sentences.

PRACTICE 8.4C Changing Clause Fragments Into Sentences

Read the clause fragments. Then, use each fragment in a sentence.

EXAMPLE   since I heard from her yesterday

ANSWER   *Since I heard from her yesterday, I don't expect Delia to phone today.*

1. if you know the answer
2. before you arrived
3. because I love fruit
4. which you cannot afford to buy
5. since no one can ride that horse
6. after we leave the locker room
7. whom I trust most in the world
8. as long as you keep your promise
9. that I tried hardest to master
10. whose house is closest to mine

PRACTICE 8.4D Changing Fragments Into Sentences

Read the groups of words. If a group of words is a fragment, use it in a sentence. If a group of words is already a sentence, write *sentence*.

EXAMPLE   A new pencil with an eraser.

ANSWER   *I want a new pencil with an eraser.*

11. Around the corner from the deli.
12. Don't give up without a fight.
13. Dreaming of a career as a lawyer.
14. When the cable guy came to the door.
15. The house by the side of the road.
16. A tree fell.
17. The hedge that needs trimming.
18. To put money aside and save it for a rainy day.
19. Are you ready?
20. Unless you think that you can do better.

SPEAKING APPLICATION

With a partner, take turns using fragments 1, 2, and 3 in new sentences.

WRITING APPLICATION

Write two sentences and two fragments about a fictional character. Then, exchange papers with a partner. Identify the two fragments that your partner wrote, and turn them into sentences.

Run-on Sentences

A fragment is an incomplete sentence. A **run-on,** on the other hand, is two or more complete sentences that are punctuated as though they were one sentence.

> **A run-on is two or more complete sentences that are not properly joined or separated.**

8.4.4

RULE

Run-ons are usually the result of carelessness. Check your sentences carefully to see where one sentence ends and the next one begins.

Two Kinds of Run-ons

There are two kinds of run-ons. The first one is made up of two sentences that are run together without any punctuation between them. This is called a **fused sentence.**

The second type of run-on consists of two or more sentences separated by only a comma. This type of run-on is called a **comma splice.**

FUSED SENTENCES	Jimmy ran for the bus he was late.
	I use the gym at school often I like the basketball court.
COMMA SPLICE	I like new cars with sunrooms, they are fun on summer days.
	The new field at the park has lots of rocks, someone needs to get rid of them.

See Practice 8.4E

A good way to distinguish between a run-on and a sentence is to read the words aloud. Your ear will tell you whether you have one or two complete thoughts and whether you need to make a complete break between the thoughts.

Three Ways to Correct Run-ons

There are three ways to correct run-on sentences. You can use end marks, commas and coordinating conjunctions, or semicolons.

Using End Marks
Periods, question marks, and exclamation marks are useful to fix run-on sentences.

RULE

8.4.5

> **Use an end mark to separate a run-on sentence into two sentences.**

Sometimes the best way to correct a run-on is to use an end mark to split the run-on into two shorter but complete sentences. End marks help your reader pause and group your ideas more effectively.

RUN-ON   Last Saturday I saw a new movie, it was really exciting.

CORRECTED   Last Saturday I saw a new movie. It was really exciting.

RUN-ON   Where are you going I can't keep up.

CORRECTED   Where are you going? I can't keep up.

RUN-ON   What did you say I can't hear you.

CORRECTED   What did you say? I can't hear you.

RUN-ON   Where are the new basketballs they were here yesterday.

CORRECTED   Where are the new basketballs? They were here yesterday.

Using Commas and Coordinating Conjunctions
Sometimes the two parts of a run-on are related and should be combined into a compound sentence.

> **Use a comma and a coordinating conjunction** to combine two independent clauses into a compound sentence.

To separate the clauses properly, use both a comma and a coordinating conjunction. The most common coordinating conjunctions are *and, but, or, for, nor,* and *yet.* Before you separate a sentence into parts, though, be sure each part expresses a complete thought.

RUN-ON   Jim's football uniform is too tight, he needs money to buy a larger size.

CORRECTED   Jim's football uniform is too tight, and he needs money to buy a larger size

RUN-ON   He has grown several inches since last year, his shoes still fit.

CORRECTED   He has grown several inches since last year, but his shoes still fit.

Using Semicolons
You can sometimes use a semicolon to connect the two parts of a run-on into a correct sentence.

> **Use a semicolon** to connect two closely related ideas into one sentence.

Use a semicolon only when the ideas in both parts of the sentence are closely related.

RUN-ON   My geometry class is scheduled for 1:00, my biology class is scheduled for 1:50.

CORRECTED   My geometry class is scheduled for 1:00; my biology class is scheduled for 1:50.

See Practice 8.4F

PRACTICE 8.4E > **Recognizing Run-ons**

Read the groups of words. Then, write whether each group is a *sentence* or a *run-on*.

EXAMPLE   I went to the post office, I bought stamps.

ANSWER   *run-on*

1. The speech was too long I had to cut it.

2. The hurricane hit the small island, it was quite severe.

3. Well after midnight, I was still awake.

4. I would like to visit Greenland to see the northern lights.

5. The Pacific Ocean was named by Ferdinand Magellan, pacific means "peaceful."

6. Viv lives in a fairy tale she always expects a happy ending.

7. I rode my bicycle to Turner Park, where the music festival was held.

8. Jackson is the capital of Mississippi, it is named for President Andrew Jackson.

9. Kites flew in the sky they were so colorful.

10. Has the mail carrier come, or is she late?

PRACTICE 8.4F > **Correcting Run-ons**

Read the sentences. Rewrite each run-on sentence to correct the problem.

EXAMPLE   Alice went on the school trip, Sylvia did not.

ANSWER   *Alice went on the school trip, but Sylvia did not.*

11. I visited the dentist I had my teeth cleaned.

12. Miranda has a sapphire ring, it is very lovely.

13. New Hampshire was one of the original Thirteen Colonies, Vermont was not.

14. I like baked chicken I had it for dinner.

15. You can go to the six o'clock show, you can go to the eight o'clock show.

16. Agatha Christie wrote mysteries they had clever plots.

17. Vincent Van Gogh was a wonderful painter, his work includes many self-portraits.

18. The washing machine is leaking I cannot find what is wrong with it.

19. Digital cameras can take fine pictures, you can discard the bad ones.

20. The Marfa lights are a mystery, no one knows what causes them.

SPEAKING APPLICATION

Use run-on sentences 11, 12, and 13 as models, and tell your partner about local news. Ask your partner to correct each of your run-on sentences.

WRITING APPLICATION

Write two sentences and two run-ons describing a room in your house. Then, exchange papers with a partner. Identify the two run-ons that your partner wrote, and rewrite them as correct sentences.

Properly Placing Modifiers

If a phrase or clause acting as an adjective or adverb is not placed near the word it modifies, it may seem to modify a different word. Then the sentence may seem unclear or odd.

> **A modifier** should be placed as close as possible to the word it describes.

A modifier placed too far away from the word it describes is called a **misplaced modifier.**

MISPLACED MODIFIER

The soccer club practiced **with new uniforms**.

The misplaced phrase *with new uniforms* makes it seem as though the practice had new uniforms.

PROPERLY PLACED MODIFIER

The soccer club **with new uniforms** practiced.

Below is a different type of misplaced modifier that is sometimes called a **dangling modifier.** A dangling modifier at the beginning of a sentence causes the sentence to be unclear.

DANGLING MODIFIER

Sitting on the sidelines, the sun felt hot on our faces.

In this sentence, *sitting on the sidelines* should modify a person or people. Instead, it incorrectly modifies *sun.*

CORRECTED

Sitting on the sidelines, we felt the hot sun on our faces.

See Practice 8.4G
See Practice 8.4H

PRACTICE 8.4G Revising to Correct Misplaced Modifiers

Read the sentences. Then, rewrite each sentence to correct the underlined misplaced modifier.

EXAMPLE   <u>Rushing for the bus</u>, my lunch was forgotten.

ANSWER   *Rushing for the bus, I forgot my lunch.*

1. <u>Visiting my cousin on Elm Street</u>, my bicycle got a flat tire.

2. The delegates discussed world peace and human rights <u>at the United Nations</u>.

3. I saw a bird through my binoculars <u>that I had never seen before</u>.

4. Gordon will post that photo of Union Station <u>in the morning</u>.

5. Sherry bought a gift for her uncle <u>that she thought would be useful</u>.

6. I visited Minnesota and saw a famous radio show there <u>with Mary</u>.

7. Our car got stuck in the middle of the street <u>when it stalled</u>.

8. <u>At an early age</u>, my parents taught me good manners.

9. You need to enter the contest <u>to win a prize</u>.

10. <u>Making lots of noise</u>, bears hopefully would be scared away from our campsite.

PRACTICE 8.4H Recognizing and Correcting Misplaced Modifiers

Read the sentences. If a sentence has a misplaced modifier, rewrite the sentence so the modifier is properly placed. If a sentence is correct, write *correct*.

EXAMPLE   The dog lost the bone it liked to chew in the alley.

ANSWER   *In the alley, the dog lost the bone it liked to chew.*

11. The child played on the beach with her shovel and pail.

12. Pam wore a gray hat on her head that was clearly too small.

13. To get a rebate, you must mail in a form.

14. She stubbed her toe on the table leg wearing sandals.

15. Changing into a bathing suit, I went for a swim.

16. I found twenty dollars in my pocket that I thought I had lost.

17. In Hollywood, we spotted two movie stars riding around in our old car.

18. Our teacher described traveling through the jungle in our geography class.

19. At the museum I saw the self-portrait of Picasso with my sister.

20. Arriving in the dark, finding the motel gave us trouble.

SPEAKING APPLICATION

With a partner, take turns describing a favorite place. Your partner should identify any misplaced modifiers.

WRITING APPLICATION

Write three sentences about the clothing you are wearing. Include a misplaced modifier in each sentence. Then, exchange papers with a partner. Your partner should correct the misplaced modifiers.

Avoiding Double Negatives

Negative words, such as *nothing* and *not*, are used to deny or to say *no*. Some people mistakenly use **double negatives**—two negative words—when only one is needed.

> **Avoid writing sentences that contain double negatives.**

8.4.9 **RULE**

In the following examples, negative words are highlighted. The first sentence in each example contains double negatives. The corrected sentences show two ways to correct each double-negative sentence.

DOUBLE NEGATIVES	Mack **didn't** tell **no one** about the party.
CORRECTED SENTENCES	Mack **didn't** tell anyone about the party.
	Mack told **no one** about the party.

DOUBLE NEGATIVES	It seems we **won't** **never** have good weather.
CORRECTED SENTENCES	It seems we will **never** have good weather.
	It seems we **won't** ever have good weather.

DOUBLE NEGATIVES	My sweater **doesn't** fit **no** more.
CORRECTED SENTENCES	My sweater **doesn't** fit any more.
	My sweater **no** longer fits.

DOUBLE NEGATIVES	**Aren't** you taking **nothing** with you?
CORRECTED SENTENCES	**Aren't** you taking anything with you?
	Are you taking **nothing** with you?

DOUBLE NEGATIVES	We **haven't no** new books here.
CORRECTED SENTENCES	We **haven't** any new books here.
	We have **no** new books here.

See Practice 8.4I
See Practice 8.4J

PRACTICE 8.4I Using Negatives Correctly

Read the sentences. Then, write the word in parentheses that makes each sentence negative without creating a double negative.

EXAMPLE   I haven't (ever, never) been to Italy.

ANSWER   *ever*

1. I (will, won't) never be taller than my brother.
2. We (do, don't) want anything to spoil the day.
3. He will not do (anything, nothing) to correct the problem.
4. Why hasn't (anybody, nobody) answered yet?
5. Since she moved to Hawaii, my cousin doesn't (ever, never) get home for Thanksgiving.
6. I cannot see (anyone, no one) in this fog.
7. Dean (should, shouldn't) never have gone out in such cold weather.
8. Aren't there (any, no) scrambled eggs left?
9. She is going (anywhere, nowhere) without me.
10. I couldn't read (any, none) of the small print without my glasses.

PRACTICE 8.4J Revising to Correct Double Negatives

Read the sentences. Then, rewrite each sentence to correct the double negative.

EXAMPLE   I haven't seen none of those movies.

ANSWER   *I haven't seen any of those movies.*
   OR
   I have seen none of those movies.

11. I can't do nothing about it.
12. There isn't nobody who can replace you.
13. I wouldn't have let no one bother you.
14. There weren't no birds in the nest.
15. Wasn't he never going to stop talking?
16. She didn't eat none of the mashed potatoes.
17. Be sure to tell no one nothing.
18. When I left, I still hadn't seen none of the parade.
19. You ought not to give him nothing.
20. The manager never gave nobody the job.

SPEAKING APPLICATION

With a partner, take turns telling where and when not to use a cellphone. Your partner should identify any double negatives and help correct them.

WRITING APPLICATION

With a partner, write three sentences telling a child how to behave. Include a double negative in each sentence. Then, exchange papers and correct your partner's double negatives.

Avoiding Common Usage Problems

This section contains fifteen common usage problems in alphabetical order. Some are expressions that you should avoid in both your speaking and your writing. Others are words that are often confused because of similar spellings or meanings.

(1) accept, except   Do not confuse the spelling of these words. *Accept*, a verb, means "to take what is offered" or "to agree to." *Except*, a preposition, means "leaving out" or "other than."

VERB   Brian **accepted** a part in the play.

PREPOSITION   No one **except** me passed the test.

(2) advice, advise   Do not confuse the spelling of these related words. *Advice*, a noun, means "an opinion." *Advise*, a verb, means "to give an opinion."

NOUN   I took her **advice** to join a club.

VERB   I **advise** new students to join clubs.

(3) affect, effect   *Affect*, a verb, means "to influence" or "to cause a change in." *Effect*, usually a noun, means "result."

VERB   A late start will **affect** your time in a race.

NOUN   What **effect** did the late start have on your race time?

(4) at   Do not use *at* after *where*.

INCORRECT   **Where** is my lunch **at**?

CORRECT   **Where** is my lunch?

(5) because   Do not use *because* after *the reason*. Eliminate one or the other.

INCORRECT   The **reason** he won is **because** he was fast.

CORRECT   He won **because** he was fast.

                The **reason** he won is **that** he was fast.

(6) beside, besides These two prepositions have different meanings and cannot be interchanged. *Beside* means "at the side of" or "close to." *Besides* means "in addition to."

EXAMPLES   My brother and I sit **beside** each other.

No one **besides** us sits on this side of the table.

(7) different from, different than *Different from* is preferred over *different than*.

EXAMPLE   My uniform is **different from** my brother's.

(8) farther, further *Farther* is used to refer to distance. *Further* means "additional" or "to a greater degree or extent."

EXAMPLES   The store is **farther** than the next corner.

After he sang, we needed no **further** auditions.

(9) in, into *In* refers to position. *Into* suggests motion.

POSITION   The groceries are **in** the refrigerator.

MOTION   I put the carrots **into** the vegetable drawer.

(10) kind of, sort of Do not use *kind of* or *sort of* to mean "rather" or "somewhat."

INCORRECT   My mountain bike is **sort of** new.

CORRECT   My mountain bike is **rather** new.

(11) like *Like*, a preposition, means "similar to" or "in the same way as." It should be followed by an object. Do not use *like* before a subject and a verb. Use *as* or *that* instead.

PREPOSITION   The house across the street looks **like** ours.

INCORRECT   This radio doesn't work **like** it should.

CORRECT   This radio doesn't work **as** it should.

(12) that, which, who   *That* and *which* refer to things. *Who* refers only to people.

THINGS	There is the book **that** I wanted.
PEOPLE	Where are the people **who** signed up for the trip?

(13) their, there, they're   Do not confuse the spelling of these three words. *Their,* a possessive adjective, always modifies a noun. *There* is usually used as a sentence starter or as an adverb. *They're* is a contraction of *they are.*

POSSESSIVE ADJECTIVE	The girls wanted to try on **their** uniforms.
SENTENCE STARTER	**There** are cardinals on the new shirts.
ADVERB	The new baseballs are over **there** .
CONTRACTION	**They're** waiting to go to the field.

(14) to, too, two   Do not confuse the spelling of these words. *To* plus a noun creates a prepositional phrase. *To* plus a verb creates an infinitive. *Too* is an adverb and modifies adjectives and other adverbs. *Two* is a number.

PREPOSITION	**to** the station	**to** Dallas
INFINITIVE	**to** understand	**to** receive
ADVERB	**too** strangely	**too** quickly
NUMBER	**two** notebooks	**two** newspapers

(15) when, where, why   Do not use *when, where,* or *why* directly after a linking verb such as *is.* Reword the sentence.

INCORRECT	To win the race is **why** we trained hard.
CORRECT	We trained hard to win the race.
INCORRECT	In the morning is **when** I like to run.
CORRECT	I like to run in the morning.

See Practice 8.4K
See Practice 8.4L
See Practice 8.4M
See Practice 8.4N

Read the sentences. Then, write the word in parentheses that best completes each sentence.

EXAMPLE   Let's talk (farther, further) about our plans next week.

ANSWER   *further*

1. Everyone (accept, except) me brought a bathing suit to the barbecue.

2. (Their, They're) trying as hard as they can.

3. My best friend gives me good (advice, advise).

4. What (affect, effect) did the weather have on your plans?

5. Your outfit is quite (different from, different than) what you usually wear.

6. I tried to find the television remote but I don't know where (it is, it's at).

7. Will someone (beside, besides) me prepare food for the party?

8. The reason I left early is (because, that) I needed to finish my homework.

9. Pablo was (to, too) exhausted to keep running.

10. She is the politician with (which, whom) I most agree.

Read the sentences. If the underlined word is used correctly, write *correct*. If the word is incorrect, write the correct word.

EXAMPLE   I sat <u>besides</u> the lake in the park.

ANSWER   *beside*

11. <u>There</u> clever remarks made us laugh.

12. Is someone <u>besides</u> Jane going to help me?

13. I walked <u>in</u> the classroom and took my seat.

14. Does music in stores have any <u>effect</u> on shopping habits?

15. The airport was crowded, just <u>like</u> I expected.

16. When I went to the bowling alley, my younger sister went <u>to</u>.

17. Is Saturn <u>farther</u> from the sun than Jupiter?

18. Will your sister <u>except</u> Carl's invitation and go to the party?

19. The reason I struggle with my locker is <u>because</u> my locker door is always getting stuck.

20. What does your doctor <u>advise</u> that you do to get rid of your cold?

SPEAKING APPLICATION

With a partner, take turns talking about runners in a race. Use four sentences, each with a different one of these words: *beside*, *besides*, *farther*, and *further*. Your partner should listen to make sure that you use the four words correctly.

WRITING APPLICATION

With a partner, write four incomplete sentences about a club or a team. In parentheses, give the same choices to complete the sentences as those in Practice 8.4K, sentences 1–4. Then, exchange papers and indicate the correct words to complete your partner's sentences.

PRACTICE 8.4M Recognizing and Correcting Usage Problems

Read the sentences. Then, if a sentence has a usage problem, rewrite it to correct the problem. If a sentence is correct, write *correct*.

EXAMPLE   Jake was to tired to finish the race.

ANSWER   *Jake was too tired to finish the race.*

1. Their are nine justices on the Supreme Court.
2. The biography is sort of interesting.
3. The students went in the computer room.
4. Noon is when we usually eat lunch.
5. The wallpaper looks just as it should look.
6. Please advice me of the problems you encountered.
7. Mom doesn't know where the dog could be at.
8. I have answered all the survey questions except the last one.
9. Our school newspaper is different from other school newspapers.
10. The reason I did poorly on the test is because I did not study enough.

PRACTICE 8.4N Avoiding Usage Problems

Read the pairs of words. For each pair of words, write two sentences that are related in meaning.

EXAMPLE   their, there

ANSWER   *The children have their hearts set on visiting an amusement park.*
They should have fun there.

11. accept, except
12. advice, advise
13. affect, effect
14. beside, besides
15. farther, further
16. in, into
17. like, as
18. their, they're
19. too, two
20. which, who

SPEAKING APPLICATION

With a partner, choose two of the fifteen common usage problems. Explain the rules in your own words to your partner, and give two examples to illustrate.

WRITING APPLICATION

With a partner, write four sentences, each using a different word from the fifteen common usage problems. Then, exchange papers, and make sure your partner has avoided the common usage problems. Correct any errors you find.

PRACTICE 1 Using Complete Subjects and Predicates

Each item below contains only a complete subject or a complete predicate. Rewrite each item, making a sentence by adding the missing part indicated in parentheses.

1. The police officer (add a predicate).
2. (add a subject) splashed through the puddles.
3. The new shopping mall (add a predicate).
4. Is (add a subject) dangerous?
5. The star reporter (add a predicate).
6. (add a subject) walked to school.
7. The large ship (add a predicate).
8. (add a subject) smelled wonderful.
9. The pitcher and the catcher (add a predicate).
10. (add a subject) hurried into the building.

PRACTICE 2 Using Direct Objects

Rewrite each incomplete sentence, supplying a direct object where indicated in parentheses. You may also include the article *a, an,* or *the* or another modifier along with the direct object.

1. Babies require (direct object).
2. I dislike loud (direct object).
3. The chef is making (direct object).
4. In the waiting room, I saw (direct object).
5. Myra decorated (direct object) with sprinkles.
6. Bryce put (direct object) on the shelf.
7. She asked (direct object) and (direct object) for assistance.
8. Val amuses (direct object) with her chatter.
9. The captain showed us (direct object).
10. What causes (direct object) to appear?

PRACTICE 3 Identifying Indirect Objects

Read the sentences. Then, write the indirect object in each sentence. If there is no indirect object, write *none*.

1. The ticket agent sold him a ticket.
2. The teacher gave the class a test.
3. My sister sewed herself a new skirt.
4. Edith shoveled snow for more than an hour.
5. Don't confuse me with too much information.
6. The opera star sang us the new aria.
7. Marnie offered her friend sound advice.
8. I wish you a good time on your travels.
9. The doctor gave the patient more medicine.
10. Who will toss the seals some fish to eat?

PRACTICE 4 Identifying Subject Complements

Read the sentences. Then, write the subject complement in each sentence. Also indicate whether it is a *predicate noun,* a *predicate pronoun,* or a *predicate adjective.*

1. The children look happy.
2. The singer with the loudest voice is you.
3. She will be the new star of the show.
4. The flight seemed very turbulent.
5. The puppy is energetic.
6. Louisa May Alcott was a writer.
7. Of all the team's players, the best one is he.
8. Please do not be so noisy at this hour.
9. That loud leopard print is really something.
10. Is Rover a good watchdog?

Using Prepositional Phrases

Read the sentences. Then, rewrite each sentence, supplying the type of prepositional phrase indicated in parentheses.

1. Al bought the DVD. (Add an adjective phrase.)
2. The cat sat patiently. (Add an adverb phrase.)
3. The sound was eerie. (Add an adjective phrase.)
4. Ina brought lemonade. (Add an adverb phrase.)
5. A stranger arrived. (Add an adjective phrase and an adverb phrase.)

PRACTICE 6 **Identifying Appositive, Participial, Gerund, and Infinitive Phrases**

Read the sentences. Then, write whether the underlined phrase in each sentence is an *appositive phrase*, a *participial phrase*, a *gerund phrase*, or an *infinitive phrase*.

1. <u>Delighted by the puppet show,</u> the children clapped wildly.
2. The Truscotts hope <u>to visit in May</u>.
3. Lance enjoys <u>paddling his canoe up the river</u>.
4. The aardvark, <u>an ant-eating mammal</u>, is found in South Africa.
5. I stood on tiptoe <u>to reach the highest shelf</u>.
6. The acrobat <u>dangling from the rope</u> is one of the Flying Four.
7. Edgar Allan Poe, <u>the author of "The Raven,"</u> is also known as the father of the detective story.
8. <u>Listening to quiet music</u> often helps calm people's nerves.
9. <u>Trying not to disturb other library users,</u> David spoke in a whisper.
10. The spacecraft aims <u>to explore Mars</u>.

PRACTICE 7 **Recognizing Main and Subordinate Clauses**

Read the sentences. Then, write and label the *main clause* and the *subordinate clause* in each sentence.

1. When the teacher asked a question, Sharon raised her hand.
2. The beautician, whose shop is always full, was cutting a customer's hair.
3. I will finish my report on time unless my computer breaks again.
4. A crowd of people waited in the rain for a bus that never came.
5. The straps on your purse ripped because you stuffed too many things into it.

PRACTICE 8 **Combining Sentences With Subordinate Clauses**

Read the sentences. Combine each pair of sentences by turning one into a subordinate clause. Then, underline the subordinate clause, and indicate whether it is an *adjectival clause* or an *adverbial clause*.

1. The weather is very chilly. You had better wear a warm hat.
2. My dad travels all over the world. He is an airline pilot.
3. I thumbed through the magazine. I finally found the article about the best DVD players.
4. The escalator is quite long. It goes from the basement to the second floor.
5. My cousin Barbara will perform at the birthday party. She is a trained clown.

Continued on next page ▶

Cumulative Review Chapters 6–8

PRACTICE 9 > Writing Sentences

For each item, write the indicated type of sentence using the words provided.

1. Write a compound sentence using *the librarian* as one of the subjects.

2. Write a declarative sentence using *the kite* as the subject.

3. Write a complex sentence using *has starred* as one of the verbs.

4. Write an exclamatory sentence using the word *enormous*.

5. Write an imperative sentence using *remove* as the verb.

PRACTICE 10 > Combining Sentences

Read the sentences. Combine each pair of sentences by using compound structures. Indicate whether your sentence contains a *compound subject*, a *compound verb*, or a *compound object*, or whether it is a *compound sentence*.

1. Connor is playing soccer. Pierre is playing soccer too.

2. The gardener planted a tree. She also planted some lilies.

3. The chef added the ingredients. He then mixed the ingredients.

4. Darlene may have lost her umbrella at the movie theater. She may have lost it at the restaurant.

5. The children wanted a new ballfield. The town could not afford one.

PRACTICE 11 > Revising to Correct Fragments and Run-ons

Read each group of words. If it is a fragment, use it in a sentence. If it a run-on, correct the run-on. If it is a sentence that needs no correction, write *correct*.

1. I sat on a park bench the day was so peaceful.

2. A strange creature sitting on a toadstool.

3. Unless the delivery comes by noon.

4. The youngster was pedaling her tricycle.

5. We saw Sandy, she didn't see us.

PRACTICE 12 > Revising to Correct Common Usage Problems

Read the sentences. Then, rewrite each sentence to correct misplaced modifiers, double negatives, and other usage problems.

1. Kay couldn't read none of the letters in the bottom row of the eye doctor's chart.

2. Going without enough sleep effects people's health.

3. I answered every question accept the last.

4. Do we need farther discussion of the issue, or shall we vote?

5. Dressed in sandals and shorts, the rain came as a surprise to me.

6. The reason she could not speak her lines is because her costar made her laugh.

7. There to late to enter their dogs in the dog show.

8. Beside being a wonderful cook, Grandma gives me good advise.

9. Astronomy is where you study the stars, the planets, and other objects in space.

10. A visiting park ranger made a speech describing acid rain in our science class.

CHAPTER 9

USING VERBS

Use the correct tenses of verbs to establish clear, consistent timing of actions in your writing.

WRITE GUY *Jeff Anderson, M.Ed.*

WHAT DO YOU NOTICE?

Think about verbs as you zoom in on these sentences from the story "Flowers for Algernon" by Daniel Keyes.

MENTOR TEXT

> With all due respect for both of these fine scientists, I am well aware of their limitations. If there is an answer, I'll have to find it out for myself.

Now, ask yourself the following questions:

- What does the verb tense in the first sentence tell about the time of the action?
- How does the verb tense change in the second sentence?

In the first sentence, the verb *am* is the present tense of the verb *be*. Therefore, the narrator is speaking about something happening currently. In the second sentence, you can tell the narrator is thinking of doing something in the future because he uses the helping verb *will,* which is embedded in the contraction *I'll.*

Grammar for Writers Writers use verb tenses to show a time of action or state of being in the past, present, or future. Help your writing flow smoothly by changing tenses to show the order of actions and keeping tenses consistent when actions happen at the same time.

My muscles were tense after the race.

But now that's all in the past!

9.1 The Four Principal Parts of Verbs

Verbs have different tenses to express time. The tense of the verb *walk* in the sentence "They *walk* very fast" expresses action in the present. In "They *walked* too far from home," the tense of the verb shows that the action happened in the past. In "They *will walk* home from school," the verb expresses action in the future. These forms of verbs are known as **tenses.**

A verb's **tense** shows the time of the action or state of being that is being described. To use the tenses of a verb correctly, you must know the **principal parts** of the verb.

EL5

EL6

RULE

9.1.1

A verb has four **principal parts: the present**, the **present participle**, the **past**, and the **past participle.**

THE FOUR PRINCIPAL PARTS OF *SERVE*			
PRESENT	PRESENT PARTICIPLE	PAST	PAST PARTICIPLE
serve	(am) serving	served	(have) served

The first principal part, called the present, is the form of a verb that is listed in a dictionary. The present participle and the past participle must be combined with helping verbs before they can be used as verbs in sentences. The result will always be a verb phrase.

EXAMPLES

He **serves** the community.

Bill **was serving** his neighbors yesterday.

He **served** his community today.

He **has served** throughout his life.

The way the past and past participle of a verb are formed shows whether the verb is **regular** or **irregular.**

Using Regular Verbs

Most verbs are **regular**, which means that their past and past participle forms follow a standard, predictable pattern.

> The past and past participle of a **regular verb** are formed by adding **-ed** or **-d** to the present form.

9.1.2 RULE

To form the past and past participle of a regular verb such as *chirp* or *hover*, you simply add -*ed* to the present. With regular verbs that already end in *e*—verbs such as *move* and *charge*—you simply add -*d* to the present.

PRINCIPAL PARTS OF REGULAR VERBS			
PRESENT	PRESENT PARTICIPLE	PAST	PAST PARTICIPLE
call	(am) calling	called	(have) called
change	(am) changing	changed	(have) changed
charge	(am) charging	charged	(have) charged
chirp	(am) chirping	chirped	(have) chirped
contain	(am) containing	contained	(have) contained
describe	(am) describing	described	(have) described
fix	(am) fixing	fixed	(have) fixed
hover	(am) hovering	hovered	(have) hovered
jump	(am) jumping	jumped	(have) jumped
lift	(am) lifting	lifted	(have) lifted
look	(am) looking	looked	(have) looked
move	(am) moving	moved	(have) moved
play	(am) playing	played	(have) played
save	(am) saving	saved	(have) saved
serve	(am) serving	served	(have) served
ski	(am) skiing	skied	(have) skied
talk	(am) talking	talked	(have) talked
type	(am) typing	typed	(have) typed
visit	(am) visiting	visited	(have) visited
walk	(am) walking	walked	(have) walked

See Practice 9.1A
See Practice 9.1B

The Four Principal Parts of Verbs

Read the sentences. Then, label each underlined verb *present*, *present participle*, *past*, or *past participle*.

EXAMPLE   I watched the football game.

ANSWER   *past*

1. I usually type on the computer instead of writing.
2. We have listened to public radio for years.
3. I am trying to be a good friend.
4. I really like the new school uniforms.
5. I was waiting for you for a long time.
6. Ali planned my surprise party down to the smallest detail.
7. I had expected a longer meeting.
8. Mr. Jameson coaches the Little League team.
9. The band will be playing at Town Hall.
10. Maura has often visited her aunt in Florida.

Read the verbs. Then, write and label the four principal parts of each verb. Use a form of the helping verb *be* with the present participle and a form of the helping verb *have* with the past participle.

EXAMPLE   explain

ANSWER   *explain* — present
            am explaining — present participle
            explained — past
            has explained — past participle

11. discuss
12. suggest
13. agree
14. remain
15. attempt
16. pause
17. exercise
18. practice
19. play
20. cry

SPEAKING APPLICATION

With a partner, describe in four sentences an activity that you enjoy. In each sentence, use a different principal part of the same verb. Your partner should listen for and identify which principal part you used in each sentence.

WRITING APPLICATION

Write four sentences about someone you have known for a long time. In each sentence, use a different one of the four principal parts of verbs. Label the verbs *present*, *present participle*, *past*, and *past participle*.

Using Irregular Verbs

While most verbs are regular, many very common verbs are **irregular**—their past and past participle forms do not follow a predictable pattern.

> The past and past participle of an **irregular verb** are not formed by adding *-ed* or *-d* to the present tense form.

9.1.3 RULE

IRREGULAR VERBS WITH THE SAME PAST AND PAST PARTICIPLE			
PRESENT	PRESENT PARTICIPLE	PAST	PAST PARTICIPLE
bring	(am) bringing	brought	(have) brought
build	(am) building	built	(have) built
buy	(am) buying	bought	(have) bought
catch	(am) catching	caught	(have) caught
fight	(am) fighting	fought	(have) fought
find	(am) finding	found	(have) found
get	(am) getting	got	(have) got *or* (have) gotten
hold	(am) holding	held	(have) held
lay	(am) laying	laid	(have) laid
lead	(am) leading	led	(have) led
lose	(am) losing	lost	(have) lost
pay	(am) paying	paid	(have) paid
say	(am) saying	said	(have) said
sit	(am) sitting	sat	(have) sat
sleep	(am) sleeping	slept	(have) slept
spin	(am) spinning	spun	(have) spun
stand	(am) standing	stood	(have) stood
stick	(am) sticking	stuck	(have) stuck
swing	(am) swinging	swung	(have) swung
teach	(am) teaching	taught	(have) taught
win	(am) winning	won	(have) won

Check a dictionary whenever you are in doubt about the correct form of an irregular verb.

IRREGULAR VERBS WITH THE SAME PRESENT, PAST, AND PAST PARTICIPLE			
PRESENT	PRESENT PARTICIPLE	PAST	PAST PARTICIPLE
bid	(am) bidding	bid	(have) bid
burst	(am) bursting	burst	(have) burst
cost	(am) costing	cost	(have) cost
hurt	(am) hurting	hurt	(have) hurt
put	(am) putting	put	(have) put
set	(am) setting	set	(have) set

IRREGULAR VERBS THAT CHANGE IN OTHER WAYS			
PRESENT	PRESENT PARTICIPLE	PAST	PAST PARTICIPLE
arise	(am) arising	arose	(have) arisen
be	(am) being	was	(have) been
bear	(am) bearing	bore	(have) borne
beat	(am) beating	beat	(have) beaten
begin	(am) beginning	began	(have) begun
blow	(am) blowing	blew	(have) blown
break	(am) breaking	broke	(have) broken
choose	(am) choosing	chose	(have) chosen
come	(am) coming	came	(have) come
do	(am) doing	did	(have) done
draw	(am) drawing	drew	(have) drawn
drink	(am) drinking	drank	(have) drunk
drive	(am) driving	drove	(have) driven
eat	(am) eating	ate	(have) eaten
fall	(am) falling	fell	(have) fallen
fly	(am) flying	flew	(have) flown
forget	(am) forgetting	forgot	(have) forgotten
freeze	(am) freezing	froze	(have) frozen

IRREGULAR VERBS THAT CHANGE IN OTHER WAYS (CONTINUED)			
PRESENT	PRESENT PARTICIPLE	PAST	PAST PARTICIPLE
give	(am) giving	gave	(have) given
go	(am) going	went	(have) gone
grow	(am) growing	grew	(have) grown
know	(am) knowing	knew	(have) known
lie	(am) lying	lay	(have) lain
ride	(am) riding	rode	(have) ridden
ring	(am) ringing	rang	(have) rung
rise	(am) rising	rose	(have) risen
run	(am) running	ran	(have) run
see	(am) seeing	saw	(have) seen
shake	(am) shaking	shook	(have) shaken
sing	(am) singing	sang	(have) sung
sink	(am) sinking	sank	(have) sunk
speak	(am) speaking	spoke	(have) spoken
spring	(am) springing	sprang	(have) sprung
strive	(am) striving	strove	(have) striven
swear	(am) swearing	swore	(have) sworn
swim	(am) swimming	swam	(have) swum
take	(am) taking	took	(have) taken
tear	(am) tearing	tore	(have) torn
throw	(am) throwing	threw	(have) thrown
wear	(am) wearing	wore	(have) worn
weave	(am) weaving	wove	(have) woven
write	(am) writing	wrote	(have) written

See Practice 9.1C
See Practice 9.1D
See Practice 9.1E
See Practice 9.1F

As you can see, there are many irregular verbs. For most of these verbs, you should memorize the different forms. Whenever you are not sure of which form of an irregular verb to use, check a dictionary.

Read the verbs. Then, write and label the four principal parts of each verb. Use a form of the helping verb *be* with the present participle and a form of the helping verb *have* with the past participle.

EXAMPLE   know

ANSWER   *know* — present
          am knowing — present participle
          knew — past
          has known — past participle

1. write

2. hurt

3. burst

4. drink

5. teach

6. sink

7. swim

8. swing

9. lay

10. rise

Read the sentences. Then, choose and write the form of the verb in parentheses that correctly completes each sentence.

EXAMPLE   I have (shook, shaken) the bottle.

ANSWER   *shaken*

11. George (did, done) as much as he could.

12. Yesterday I (ran, run) five miles.

13. I have (spoke, spoken) to him on several occasions.

14. The visitor (rang, rung) the doorbell.

15. The trucker had (drove, driven) hundreds of miles.

16. The fog has finally (rose, risen).

17. She had (began, begun) the project.

18. Have you ever (swam, swum) in an Olympic-sized pool?

19. The owl (came, come) back to our tree.

20. Has the library board (chose, chosen) the new director yet?

SPEAKING APPLICATION

With a partner, share four sentences about going to a restaurant. In each sentence, use a different principal part of the same irregular verb. Your partner should listen for and identify which principal part you used in each sentence.

WRITING APPLICATION

Write two pairs of sentences about school last year. Use only two irregular verbs, one in each pair. One sentence in each pair should use the past form of the verb; the other should use the past participle. Be sure you use the irregular verb forms correctly.

PRACTICE 9.1E > Using Irregular Verbs

Read the sentences. Rewrite each sentence, using the form of the verb in parentheses that correctly completes the sentence.

EXAMPLE   Yesterday Sarah (fall) off her chair.

ANSWER   *Yesterday Sarah fell off her chair.*

1. Last week our teacher (speak) about the effects of the American Revolution.
2. We had (ride) to Audubon Park on the ferry.
3. Yesterday May (sit) at the piano for hours.
4. The new cars have (got) more fuel efficient.
5. The top (spin) for nearly five minutes and finally stopped.
6. At the rally, the politician (shake) my hand.
7. Until this year, Zach had never (fly) in a plane.
8. Have burglars (break) into that apartment?
9. Last week's lunch (cost) less than this week's.
10. Has the ice on the lake (freeze)?

PRACTICE 9.1F > Revising for Irregular Verbs

Read the sentences. Then, if the underlined verb is in the correct form, write *correct*. If it is not, rewrite the sentence with the correct verb form.

EXAMPLE   I <u>drunk</u> a glass of pineapple juice.

ANSWER   *I drank a glass of pineapple juice.*

11. Have you <u>saw</u> this movie?
12. He <u>run</u> over the track at top speed.
13. The doctor has <u>spoke</u> with her patient.
14. My feet <u>sank</u> into the sand.
15. Finally the race <u>begun</u>.
16. Teresa <u>wore</u> long golden earrings.
17. The colony had <u>rose</u> in rebellion.
18. Church bells <u>rung</u> all over London.
19. The dog <u>sprang</u> up at the sound.
20. She had <u>wrote</u> me about the change in plans.

SPEAKING APPLICATION

With a partner, take turns telling about things that have happened in the past month at school. Use at least four irregular verbs, two of them after a form of the helping verb *have*. Your partner should listen for the irregular verbs and make sure they are used correctly.

WRITING APPLICATION

Write four sentences about things you did last summer. In each sentence, use a different irregular verb, two of them after a form of the helping verb *have*.

9.2 The Six Tenses of Verbs

In English, verbs have six **tenses**: the **present**, the **past**, the **future**, the **present perfect**, the **past perfect**, and the **future perfect**.

EL6

RULE 9.2.1

The **tense** of a verb shows the time of the action or state of being.

Every tense has both **basic** forms and **progressive** forms.

Identifying the Basic Forms of the Six Tenses

The chart below shows the **basic** forms of the six tenses, using *stick* as an example. The first column gives the name of each tense. The second column gives the basic form of *stick* in all six tenses. The third column gives the principal part needed to form each tense. Only three of the four principal parts are used in the basic forms: the present, the past, and the past participle.

BASIC FORMS OF THE SIX TENSES OF *STICK*		
TENSE	BASIC FORM	PRINCIPAL PART USED
Present	I stick.	Present
Past	I stuck.	Past
Future	I will stick.	Present
Present Perfect	I have stuck.	Past Participle
Past Perfect	I had stuck.	Past Participle
Future Perfect	I will have stuck.	Past Participle

Study the chart carefully. First, learn the names of the tenses. Then, learn the principal parts needed to form them. Notice also that the last four tenses need helping verbs.

As you have already learned, some verbs form their tenses in a regular, predictable pattern. Other verbs use an irregular pattern. *Stick* is an example of an irregular verb.

See Practice 9.2A

Conjugating the Basic Forms of Verbs

A helpful way to become familiar with all the forms of a verb is by **conjugating** it.

> A **conjugation** is a list of the singular and plural forms of a verb in a particular tense.

Each tense in a conjugation has six forms that fit with first-, second-, and third-person forms of the personal pronouns. These forms may change for each personal pronoun, and they may change for each tense.

To conjugate any verb, begin by listing its principal parts. For example, the principal parts of the verb *go* are *go, going, went,* and *gone.* The following chart shows the conjugation of all the basic forms of *go* in all six tenses. Notice that the forms of the helping verbs may also change for each personal pronoun and tense.

CONJUGATION OF THE BASIC FORMS OF *GO*		
TENSE	SINGULAR	PLURAL
Present	I go. You go. He, she, or it goes.	We go. You go. They go.
Past	I went. You went. He, she, or it went.	We went. You went. They went.
Future	I will go. You will go. He, she, or it will go.	We will go. You will go. They will go.
Present Perfect	I have gone. You have gone. He, she, or it has gone.	We have gone. You have gone. They have gone.
Past Perfect	I had gone. You had gone. He, she, or it had gone.	We had gone. You had gone. They had gone.
Future Perfect	I will have gone. You will have gone. He, she, or it will have gone.	We will have gone. You will have gone. They will have gone.

See Practice 9.2B

Conjugating *Be*

The verb *be* is an important verb to know how to conjugate. It is both the most common and the most irregular verb in the English language. You have already seen how to use forms of *be* with the perfect tenses. You will also use the basic forms of *be* when you conjugate the progressive forms of verbs later in this section.

EL6

PRINCIPAL PARTS OF *BE*			
PRESENT	PRESENT PARTICIPLE	PAST	PAST PARTICIPLE
be	being	was	been

Once you know the principal parts of *be*, you can conjugate all of the basic forms of *be*.

CONJUGATION OF THE BASIC FORMS OF *BE*		
TENSE	SINGULAR	PLURAL
Present	I am. You are. He, she, or it is.	We are. You are. They are.
Past	I was. You were. He, she, or it was.	We were. You were. They were.
Future	I will be. You will be. He, she, or it will be.	We will be. You will be. They will be.
Present Perfect	I have been. You have been. He, she, or it has been.	We have been. You have been. They have been.
Past Perfect	I had been. You had been. He, she, or it had been.	We had been. You had been. They had been.
Future Perfect	I will have been. You will have been. He, she, or it will have been.	We will have been. You will have been. They will have been.

See Practice 9.2C

See Practice 9.2D

PRACTICE 9.2A Identifying Present, Past, and Future Tenses of Verbs

Read the sentences. Then, label each underlined verb *present, past,* or *future.*

EXAMPLE   I <u>answered</u> the telephone.

ANSWER   *past*

1. The lighthouse <u>stands</u> in the harbor.
2. A helicopter <u>will fly</u> them to the hospital.
3. We <u>rushed</u> past the scene of the accident.
4. A fence <u>surrounds</u> the Coast Guard station.
5. Emily <u>caught</u> her skirt in the car door.
6. Carl <u>threw</u> the basketball to a teammate.
7. <u>Will</u> you <u>remain</u> behind?
8. The children <u>hurt</u> themselves yesterday.
9. I <u>will</u> not <u>be</u> responsible for your mistakes.
10. The surgeon <u>set</u> the scalpel on the table.

PRACTICE 9.2B Identifying Perfect Tenses of Verbs

Read the sentences. Then, write the verb in each sentence, and label it *present perfect, past perfect,* or *future perfect.*

EXAMPLE   I will have finished summer school by next Friday.

ANSWER   *will have finished* — *future perfect*

11. The players have practiced every day after school.
12. Chuck has memorized the names on the list.
13. I have gone to the jazz festival many times.
14. By Monday, I will have attended three graduation parties.
15. The acting company has completed rehearsal.
16. By 5 P.M. I had finished my homework.
17. By 11:30 A.M. I will have finished the exam.
18. I had never considered a different route.
19. By midnight, you will probably have heard spooky noises in the attic.
20. Have you put the dog out?

SPEAKING APPLICATION

With a partner, say one sentence each about your past, present, and future. Use a different tense in each sentence. Your partner should listen for and name the tenses that you use.

WRITING APPLICATION

Use the perfect tenses in sentences 13, 14, and 18 and write three sentences with other verbs in the perfect tense.

PRACTICE 9.2C > **Forming Verb Tenses**

Read the sentences, which are all in the present tense. Then, rewrite each sentence, changing it to the tense indicated in parentheses.

EXAMPLE   I go to the store every day. (past)

ANSWER   *I went to the store every day.*

1. I collect both stamps and coins. (present perfect)

2. We stay at the lodge during the summer. (future)

3. I wait in the ticket line for hours. (future perfect)

4. He clips quite a few discount coupons from the newspaper. (past perfect)

5. We usually eat breakfast late on Sundays. (past)

6. Josephine teaches many kids how to swim. (present perfect)

7. I see Irma on Friday. (future perfect)

8. A football player catches a pass. (past)

9. The museum is not busy today. (future)

10. The farmer always grows corn. (past perfect)

PRACTICE 9.2D > **Using Verb Tenses Correctly**

Read the sentences. Then, write the verb in parentheses that correctly completes each sentence.

EXAMPLE   I (live, lived) in Wyoming last year.

ANSWER   *lived*

11. That musician (performed, has performed) at our school last month.

12. I (had spoken, speak) to her before last Thanksgiving.

13. I (phoned, will phone) you next Tuesday.

14. Next week the principal (has told, will tell) the students about the plans for the new gym.

15. Until this year, she always (has helped, will help) the school.

16. By tomorrow the electric company (had repaired, will have repaired) the grid.

17. Before now, the lake never (has frozen, freezes).

18. I usually (enjoy, will have enjoyed) her music.

19. By the end of the year, the rock band (has visited, will have visited) all fifty states.

20. All human beings (need, needed) oxygen for survival.

SPEAKING APPLICATION

With a partner, take turns talking about the actions of a small child. Use three sentences, each with a different verb and verb tense. Your partner should restate each sentence by changing the verb tense.

WRITING APPLICATION

Write six sentences about a job or career. In each sentence, use the same verb in a different tense. Label the verb tense in each sentence.

Recognizing the Progressive Tense of Verbs

The six tenses of *go* and *be* in their basic forms were shown in the charts earlier in this section. Each of these tenses also has a progressive tense or form. The progressive form describes an event that is in progress. In contrast, the basic forms of a verb describe events that have a definite beginning and end.

EL6

> The **progressive tense,** or form, of a verb shows an action or condition that is ongoing.

9.2.3 RULE

All six of the progressive tenses of a verb are made using just one principal part: the present participle. This is the principal part that ends in *-ing*. Then, the correct form of *be* is added to create the progressive tense or form.

Progressive Tenses of *Jog*

PROGRESSIVE TENSE = be + present participle

PRESENT　　I **am jogging** around the track.
　　　　　　　　　be　present participle

PAST　　　　I **was jogging** around the track.
　　　　　　　　　be　present participle

FUTURE　　 I **will be jogging** around the track.
　　　　　　　　　　be　　present participle

PRESENT PERFECT　　I **have been jogging** around the track since
　　　　　　　　　　　　　　be　　　present participle

　　　　　　　　five A.M.

PAST PERFECT　　I **had been jogging** around the track, but now
　　　　　　　　　　　　be　　present participle

　　　　　　　I am running too.

FUTURE PERFECT　　I **will have been jogging** around the track since
　　　　　　　　　　　　　　be　　　　　present participle

　　　　　　　early this morning.

Conjugating Progressive Tenses

To create the progressive tenses or forms of a verb, you must know the basic forms of *be*.

RULE 9.2.4

> To conjugate the **progressive** forms of a verb, add the present participle of the verb to a conjugation of the basic forms of *be*.

A complete conjugation of the basic forms of *be* is shown earlier in this section. Compare that conjugation with the following conjugation of the progressive forms of *run*. You will notice that, even though the present participle form of the verb does not change, the form of the helping verb does change. It is the form of *be* that tells you whether the action or condition is taking place in the past, present, or future.

CONJUGATION OF THE PROGRESSIVE FORMS OF *RUN*		
TENSE	SINGULAR	PLURAL
Present Progressive	I am running. You are running. He, she, or it is running.	We are running. You are running. They are running.
Past Progressive	I was running. You were running. He, she, or it was running.	We were running. You were running. They were running.
Future Progressive	I will be running. You will be running. He, she, or it will be running.	We will be running. You will be running. They will be running.
Present Perfect Progressive	I have been running. You have been running. He, she, or it has been running.	We have been running. You have been running. They have been running.
Past Perfect Progressive	I had been running. You had been running. He, she, or it had been running.	We had been running. You had been running. They had been running.
Future Perfect Progressive	I will have been running. You will have been running. He, she, or it will have been running.	We will have been running. You will have been running. They will have been running.

See Practice 9.2E

See Practice 9.2F

PRACTICE 9.2E ⟩ **Identifying the Progressive Tenses of Verbs**

Read the sentences. Then, write whether the underlined verb tense in each sentence is *present progressive, past progressive, future progressive, present perfect progressive, past perfect progressive,* or *future perfect progressive.*

EXAMPLE   She <u>has been working</u> all day.

ANSWER   *present perfect progressive*

1. Leticia <u>was studying</u> for the midterm.

2. The morning show <u>will be discussing</u> new movies after the commercial break.

3. I <u>have been shopping</u> there for years.

4. The mechanic <u>is repairing</u> our car.

5. The storyteller <u>had been recounting</u> an interesting tale.

6. Bruce <u>has been telling</u> me all about his adventure.

7. It <u>had been snowing</u> for days.

8. They <u>were explaining</u> the answer to us.

9. By Friday, we <u>will have been living</u> in the new house for six weeks.

10. <u>Are</u> you <u>babysitting</u> tonight?

PRACTICE 9.2F ⟩ **Using Progressive Tenses of Verbs**

Read the sentences. Then, rewrite each one as a complete sentence using the tense of the verb in parentheses.

EXAMPLE   Jay _____ home. (*go,* past progressive)

ANSWER   *Jay was going home.*

11. The birds _____ south. (*fly,* present progressive)

12. The columnist _____ for the magazine for two decades. (*write,* present perfect progressive)

13. They _____ company for dinner. (*expect,* past progressive)

14. Up until then, the mail carrier _____ his route. (*walk,* past perfect progressive)

15. I _____ at least one box. (*carry,* future progressive)

16. Before the incident, Uncle Tom _____ a trip to Tampa. (*plan,* past perfect progressive)

17. On their next anniversary, they _____ here for twenty years. (*come,* future perfect progressive)

18. I _____ my name on the list. (*put,* present progressive)

19. By tomorrow, you _____ for your presentation for a week. (*prepare,* future perfect progressive)

20. Jolene _____ foolish again. (*be,* past progressive)

SPEAKING APPLICATION

Tell a partner about events that have happened in the last week and events that will happen next week. Your partner should listen for and identify the verbs you use in a progressive tense.

WRITING APPLICATION

Write six sentences about a traveling circus. Use a different progressive verb tense in each sentence. Then, exchange papers with a partner. Identify the progressive tenses that your partner has used, and check that they are used correctly.

Identifying Active and Passive Voice

Just as verbs change tense to show time, they may also change form to show whether or not the subject of the verb is performing an action.

RULE 9.2.5

> The **voice** of a verb shows whether or not the subject is performing the action.

In English, most verbs have two **voices: active,** to show that the subject is performing an action, and **passive,** to show that the subject is having an action performed on it.

RULE 9.2.6

> A verb is in the **active voice** when its subject performs the action.

ACTIVE VOICE

Bob **edited** the paper.

Bill **presented** the project for the group.

In each example above, the subject performs the action, so the verb is said to be in the active voice.

RULE 9.2.7

EL6

> A verb is in the **passive voice** when its subject does not perform the action.

PASSIVE VOICE

The paper **is being edited** by Bob.

The project **was presented** by Bill.

In each example above, the person doing the action becomes the object of the preposition *by* and is no longer the subject. Both subjects—*paper* and *project*—are receivers rather than performers of the action. When the subject is acted upon, the verb is said to be in the passive voice.

See Practice 9.2G

Forming the Tenses of Passive Verbs

A passive verb always has two parts.

> **A passive verb** is always a verb phrase made from a form of *be* plus a past participle.

9.2.8 RULE

The following chart shows a conjugation of the passive forms of the verb *determine* with the pronoun *it*.

CONJUGATION OF THE PASSIVE FORMS OF *DETERMINE*	
TENSE	PASSIVE FORM
Present	It is determined.
Past	It was determined.
Future	It will be determined.
Present Perfect	It has been determined.
Past Perfect	It had been determined.
Future Perfect	It will have been determined.

While there are uses for the passive voice, most writing is more lively when it is in the active voice. Think about how to change each sentence below to the active voice. Follow the pattern in the first two examples.

PASSIVE It **is determined** that she is late.

ACTIVE We **have determined** that she is late.

PASSIVE It **was determined** that she is late.

ACTIVE We **determined** that she is late.

PASSIVE It **will be determined** that she is late.

It **has been determined** that she is late.

It **had been determined** that she was late.

It **will have been determined** that she is late.

Using Active and Passive Voices

Each of the two voices has its proper use in English.

9.2.9 Use the **active voice** whenever possible.

Sentences with active verbs are less wordy and more forceful than those with passive verbs. Compare, for example, the following sentences. Notice the different number of words each sentence needs to report the same information.

ACTIVE   The teacher **presented** a new project.

PASSIVE   A new project **was presented** by the teacher.

Although you should aim to use the active voice in most of your writing, there will be times when you will need to use the passive voice.

9.2.10 Use the **passive voice** to emphasize the receiver of an action rather than the performer of an action.

EL6

In the following example, the receiver of the action is the subject *orchestra*. It is the *conductor* (the direct object) who is actually performing the action.

EMPHASIS   The orchestra **was directed** by the conductor.
ON RECEIVER

The passive voice should also be used when there is no performer of the action.

9.2.11 Use the **passive voice** to point out the receiver of an action when the performer is unknown or not named in the sentence.

PERFORMER   The sculpture **was created** sometime
UNKNOWN   in the last century.

See Practice 9.2H

PRACTICE 9.2G ▷ **Distinguishing Active and Passive Voice**

Read the sentences. Then, write *AV* if the underlined verb is in active voice or *PV* if the verb is in passive voice.

EXAMPLE   A new meeting *was called.*

ANSWER   *PV*

1. Those elm trees <u>were planted</u> by my father.

2. They <u>welcomed</u> the foreign-exchange students.

3. I <u>was comforted</u> by your kind words.

4. The leftovers <u>were heated</u> in the microwave.

5. Roy <u>took</u> our picture by the White House fence.

6. This momentous occasion <u>will be recorded</u> for future generations.

7. The house <u>was covered</u> with moss.

8. She <u>printed</u> the directions for us.

9. A new mayor <u>was elected</u> last November.

10. Clarice <u>was running</u> down the street.

PRACTICE 9.2H ▷ **Revising to Use Active Voice**

Read the sentences. Then, rewrite each sentence that is in passive voice so that it is in active voice. If a sentence is already in active voice, write *active.*

EXAMPLE   The dinner was cooked by me.

ANSWER   *I cooked the dinner.*

11. This poem was written by Langston Hughes.

12. The designer gown was worn by the model.

13. This garden is shared by several neighbors.

14. She lives in a town by the Mexican border.

15. All the bowling pins were knocked down by Harvey's ball.

16. The Plymouth colony was established by the Pilgrims in 1620.

17. Cassandra was baking a cake.

18. I am informed by Sean about the new schedule.

19. Several questions have been asked by me.

20. Will Lola be chosen by the casting director?

SPEAKING APPLICATION

With a partner, take turns describing an old house or another old building. Use at least two sentences in the active voice and two in the passive voice. Your partner should listen for and name the active and passive verbs that you use.

WRITING APPLICATION

Write an announcement for an activity at your school. Use four sentences, two in the active voice and two in the passive voice.

Moods of Verbs

Verbs in English also use **mood** to describe the status of an action.

> There are three moods for English verbs: the **indicative mood,** the **subjunctive mood**, and the **imperative mood.**

The **indicative mood** indicates, or states, something. It is also used to ask questions. The **subjunctive mood** describes a wish or a condition that may be contrary to fact.

INDICATIVE MOOD	SUBJUNCTIVE MOOD
Ben **is** in my meeting.	I wish he **were** here for the meeting.
John **has** a new car.	If he **had brought** his car to school, we could have driven together.
I **would like** to run the meeting.	If I **were running** the meeting, I would let everyone speak.

The subjunctive mood can be used to describe situations that are unlikely to happen or not possible. It is often used in clauses that begin with *if* or *that.* In these cases, use the plural form of the verb.

EXAMPLES

If I **were** he, I would drive home before it got dark.
(I am not he, so the situation is not possible.)

Sally wishes that she **were joining** the team today.
(She is not joining until next month, so the situation is not possible.)

The **imperative** mood states a request or command and always uses the present tense. A mild imperative is followed by a period; a strong imperative is followed by an exclamation point.

EL8

EXAMPLES

Write me when you arrive. Please **don't** forget.

Be careful, that glass is broken!

Notice that the subject, *you,* is understood but omitted.

See Practice 9.2I
See Practice 9.2J

PRACTICE 9.2I ➤ Identifying Moods of Verbs

Read the sentences. Then, write *indicative, subjunctive, or imperative* for the mood of the underlined verb in each sentence.

EXAMPLE   I wish I <u>were</u> an astronaut.

ANSWER   *subjunctive*

1. The country singer <u>wore</u> a sequined suit.
2. <u>Tear</u> this open on the dotted line.
3. If you <u>had watched</u> the game, you would have seen me hit a home run.
4. If Shelley <u>were</u> here at the party, we would have had more fun.
5. Please <u>stay</u> behind the yellow line.
6. In the summer, they often <u>go</u> to the beach.
7. Don't <u>put</u> your elbows on the table.
8. I prefer that she <u>wait</u> until tomorrow.
9. What <u>were</u> those strange creatures?
10. I wish my grandfather <u>were</u> here today.

PRACTICE 9.2J ➤ Writing Sentences to Express Mood

Read the verbs. Write sentences using the different moods of verbs as indicated below.

EXAMPLE   were (subjunctive)

ANSWER   *If I were you, I'd be careful with that vase.*

11. asked (indicative)
12. were (subjunctive)
13. speak (imperative)
14. visit (indicative)
15. explain (indicative)
16. worked (indicative)
17. wait (imperative)
18. had attended (subjunctive)
19. give (imperative)
20. were (subjunctive)

SPEAKING APPLICATION

With a partner, take turns telling about something you wished for as a child. Use at least one verb in each of the three moods. Your partner should listen for and identify the moods of your verbs.

WRITING APPLICATION

Use sentences 1, 2, and 4 as models, and write three sentences in which you use the same mood as in the sentences.

9.3 Troublesome Verbs

The following verbs cause problems for many speakers and writers of English. Some of the problems involve using the principal parts of certain verbs. Others involve learning to distinguish between the meanings of certain confusing pairs of verbs.

(1) *ain't* *Ain't* is not considered standard English. Avoid using it in speaking and in writing.

INCORRECT   She **ain't** the first to complete this project.

CORRECT   She **isn't** the first to complete this project.

(2) *did, done* Remember that *done* is a past participle and can be used as a verb only with a helping verb such as *have* or *has*. Instead of using *done* without a helping verb, use *did*.

INCORRECT   I already **done** the assignment for school.

CORRECT   I already **did** the assignment for school.

    I **have** already **done** the assignment for school.

See Practice 9.3A

(3) *dragged, drug* *Drag* is a regular verb. Its principal parts are *drag, dragging, dragged,* and *dragged*. *Drug* is never correct as the past or past participle of *drag*.

INCORRECT   The letter carrier **drug** the package up the stairs.

CORRECT   The letter carrier **dragged** the package up the stairs.

(4) *gone, went* *Gone* is the past participle of *go* and can be used as a verb only with a helping verb such as *have* or *has*. *Went* is the past of *go* and is never used with a helping verb.

INCORRECT   Mike and Tom **gone** to the concert.

    We **should have went** along with them.

CORRECT   The group **went** (or **has gone**) to the concert.

    Mike and Tom **should have gone** to the concert.

(5) *have, of* The words *have* and *of* often sound very similar. Be careful not to write *of* when you mean the helping verb *have* or its contraction *'ve.*

INCORRECT   Amber should **of** walked home.

CORRECT   Amber should **have** (or **should've**) walked home.

(6) *lay, lie* These verbs look and sound almost alike and have similar meanings. The first step in distinguishing between *lay* and *lie* is to memorize the principal parts of both verbs.

PRINCIPAL PARTS			
lay	laying	laid	laid
lie	lying	lay	lain

Lay usually means "to put (something) down" or "to place (something)." It is almost always followed by a direct object. *Lie* means "to rest in a reclining position" or "to be situated." This verb is used to show the position of a person, place, or thing. *Lie* is never followed by a direct object.

EXAMPLES   The soldier **lays** his mess kit on the ground.

                 The children must **lie** down at rest time.

Pay special attention to the past tense of *lay* and *lie*. *Lay* is the past tense of *lie*. The past tense of *lay* is *laid.*

PRESENT TENSE OF *LAY*   I **lay** the book on the shelf.

PAST TENSE OF *LAY*   The athlete **laid** his sneakers on the bench.

PAST TENSE OF *LIE*   The tourist **lay** down in his room.

See Practice 9.3B

(7) *leave, let* *Leave* means "to allow to remain." *Let* means "to permit." Do not reverse the meanings.

INCORRECT   **Leave** me to cook quietly. **Let** the recipe alone.

CORRECT   **Let** me cook quietly. **Leave** the recipe alone.

(8) _raise, rise_ _Raise_ can mean "to lift (something) upward," "to build (something)," or "to increase (something)." It is usually followed by a direct object. _Rise_ is not usually followed by a direct object. This verb means "to get up," "to go up," or "to be increased."

EXAMPLES   **Raise** the sail to begin the journey.

The kite must **rise** into the sky.

(9) _saw, seen_ _Seen_ is a past participle and can be used as a verb only with a helping verb such as _have_ or _has_.

INCORRECT   I **seen** the sun this morning.

CORRECT   I **saw** the sun this morning.

(10) _says, said_ A common mistake in reporting what someone said is to use _says_ (present tense) rather than _said_ (past tense).

INCORRECT   The chef **says** , "I need it now."

CORRECT   The chef **said** , "I need it now."

(11) _set, sit_ The first step in learning to distinguish between _set_ and _sit_ is to become thoroughly familiar with their principal parts.

PRINCIPAL PARTS

set	setting	set	set
sit	sitting	sat	sat

Set means "to put (something) in a certain place or position." It is usually followed by a direct object. _Sit_ usually means "to be seated" or "to rest." It is usually not followed by a direct object.

EXAMPLES   He **set** the hammer on the workbench.

We **have set** the tools safely in the box.

Kris **sat** in the director's chair.

The kitten **has sat** on the fence since it ate.

See Practice 9.3C
See Practice 9.3D

PRACTICE 9.3A Using *Did* and *Done*

Read the sentences. Then, for each sentence, if *did* or *done* is used correctly, write *correct*. If it is not, write *incorrect*.

EXAMPLE   She done well on the test.

ANSWER   *incorrect*

1. Lara done her homework on time.

2. The volunteers did a lot in the community.

3. My parents have did a lot of work on the house.

4. I haven't done a thing about it.

5. Michael has did his report already.

6. Andrea's done her hair in a new style.

7. I'm not done with you yet.

8. When she finally done the backward somersault, everyone applauded.

9. She'd did a lot for the recycling program.

10. The steak was very well done.

PRACTICE 9.3B Using *Lay* and *Lie*

Read the sentences. Then, choose and write the correct form of the verb from the pair in parentheses.

EXAMPLE   Yesterday I (lay, laid) in bed until nearly ten o'clock.

ANSWER   *lay*

11. Please ask the cook to (lay, lie) a slice of tomato on my grilled cheese sandwich.

12. My pen was (laying, lying) right there.

13. Last night Mom (laid, lay) the new tablecloth on the dining-room table.

14. I am (laying, lying) the tissues right by my bed.

15. The accountant has (laid, lain) the tax forms on his desk.

16. Sometimes Shane (lays, lies) too long in the sun.

17. It has (lay, lain) there for several months.

18. Where have I (laid, lay) my keys?

19. (Lay, Lie) down and go to sleep.

20. The fox (laid, lay) in wait for the chickens.

SPEAKING APPLICATION

With a partner, take turns telling about something a friend did. Use *did* and *done* two times each. Your partner should listen for the words *did* and *done* and make sure they are used correctly.

WRITING APPLICATION

Write six sentences, each using a different principal part of the verbs *lay* and *lie*. You may use the sentences in Practice 9.3B as models.

PRACTICE 9.3C > Using *Set* and *Sit*

Read the sentences. Then, choose and write the correct form of the verb from the pair in parentheses.

EXAMPLE   She (set, sat) down on the sofa.

ANSWER   *sat*

1. Jack (set, sat) the book on the shelf.
2. We (set, sit) down to a tasty meal every night.
3. I (set, sat) the mouse pad near the keyboard.
4. The workers have finally (set, sat) down for a lunch break.
5. Mae and Jimmy have been (setting, sitting) on the porch for hours.
6. She often (sets, sits) and reads by the creek.
7. Please (set, sit) it down on that chair.
8. Two minutes before show time, everyone had finally (set, sat) down in their seats.
9. The new patio furniture is (setting, sitting) beside the pool.
10. I'm (setting, sitting) on top of the world.

PRACTICE 9.3D > Using Troublesome Verbs

Read the sentences. If the underlined verb is used correctly, write *correct*. If it is not, rewrite the sentence using the correct verb.

EXAMPLE   She could <u>of</u> done a better job.

ANSWER   *She could have done a better job.*

11. You should have <u>went</u> with them.
12. They <u>ain't</u> ready yet.
13. My grandmother <u>sat</u> her knitting on the couch.
14. The soldiers <u>raised</u> the flag.
15. Please <u>let</u> your sister alone.
16. I <u>drug</u> the cart across the lawn.
17. I <u>seen</u> a long road stretching ahead.
18. My sister sighed loudly, and she <u>says</u>, "I would love to have a million dollars!"
19. I <u>did</u> my German homework.
20. I <u>could've</u> done better on the test.

SPEAKING APPLICATION

With a partner, take turns telling about things you do in a kitchen or dining room. Use at least two forms of *sit* and two forms of *set*. Your partner should listen for the forms of *sit* and *set* and make sure that they are used correctly.

WRITING APPLICATION

Write five sentences in which you use these words correctly: *done, went, seen, raise, said.*

USING PRONOUNS

Match nouns and personal pronouns correctly in your writing to create meaningful sentences.

CHAPTER 10

WRITE GUY *Jeff Anderson, M.Ed.*

WHAT DO YOU NOTICE?

Take note of personal pronouns as you zoom in on these sentences from *An American Childhood* by Annie Dillard.

MENTOR TEXT

> The things in the world did not necessarily cause my overwhelming feelings; the feelings were inside me, beneath my skin, behind my ribs, within my skull. They were even, to some extent, under my control.

Now, ask yourself the following questions:

- How is the personal pronoun *my* used in both clauses in the first sentence?
- How is the personal pronoun *they* used in the second sentence?

In both clauses of the first sentence, *my* is used before nouns (*feelings, skin, ribs,* and *skull*) to show that these things belong to the narrator. *My* is in the possessive case. In the second sentence, *they* is used to refer to the narrator's feelings, which are the subject of the second sentence. *They* is in the nominative case.

Grammar for Writers Selecting the correct case of a personal pronoun allows a writer to express ideas clearly. Use the appropriate personal pronoun cases in your writing to present details accurately.

A pronoun wouldn't wait in line for something, would it?

No, it would just take someone else's place.

10.1 Recognizing Cases of Personal Pronouns

In Chapter 1, you learned that personal pronouns can be arranged in three groups: first person, second person, and third person. Pronouns can also be grouped by their **cases.**

> English has three cases: **nominative, objective,** and **possessive.**

The chart below shows the personal pronouns grouped according to the three cases. The case shows whether a pronoun is being used as a subject, an object, or a possessive.

THE THREE CASES OF PERSONAL PRONOUNS	
NOMINATIVE CASE	**USE IN A SENTENCE**
I, we, you, he, she, it, they	subject of a verb predicate pronoun
OBJECTIVE CASE	**USE IN A SENTENCE**
me, us, you, him, her, it, them	indirect object object of a preposition direct object
POSSESSIVE CASE	**USE IN A SENTENCE**
my, mine, our, ours, your, yours, his, her, hers, its, their, theirs	to show ownership

SUBJECT OF A VERB	**She** wanted badly to read the book.
PREDICATE PRONOUN	The author is **he**.
INDIRECT OBJECT	Please give **me** the telephone.
OBJECT OF A PREPOSITION	Please show the letter to **me**.
DIRECT OBJECT	A tennis ball hit **her** on the head.
TO SHOW OWNERSHIP	That is **my** pencil, not **yours**.

See Practice 10.1A

See Practice 10.1B

PRACTICE 10.1A Identifying Cases of Personal Pronouns

Read the sentences. Then, identify the case of each underlined personal pronoun by writing *nominative*, *objective*, or *possessive*.

EXAMPLE   <u>They</u> told Mr. Finch the news.

ANSWER   *nominative*

1. <u>She</u> designed the team's Web site.
2. Please tell <u>me</u> the location of the nearest post office.
3. <u>Our</u> skit was the funniest of all.
4. Are these slippers <u>yours</u>?
5. At the beach, other friends met <u>them</u>.
6. The leader of the group is <u>he</u>.
7. For <u>us</u>, eating dinner at seven is very late.
8. It was <u>I</u> who answered the phone.
9. <u>Mine</u> is the wool hat with the black dots.
10. The book looks as if <u>it</u> has been read often.

PRACTICE 10.1B Identifying Pronoun Cases and Uses

Read the sentences. Write the case of each underlined pronoun. Then, label it *subject of a verb*, *predicate pronoun*, *direct object*, *indirect object*, or *object of a preposition*.

EXAMPLE   <u>He</u> liked the new teacher.

ANSWER   *nominative, subject of a verb*

11. Luis rode with <u>her</u> on the Ferris wheel.
12. <u>We</u> would like a better sound system.
13. Kayla told <u>him</u> about the homework assignment.
14. Serena saw <u>them</u> in the school yard.
15. Yesterday <u>he</u> and Samantha went to the fitness center.
16. <u>Hers</u> is the pale blue house on the corner.
17. The small canoe is <u>theirs</u>.
18. I used to have a pet caterpillar, but <u>it</u> turned into a butterfly.
19. The winners were Max and <u>I</u>.
20. With <u>it</u> comes a money-back guarantee.

SPEAKING APPLICATION

With a partner, talk about students on a school bus. Use several personal pronouns in different cases. Your partner should listen for and name the personal pronouns and their cases.

WRITING APPLICATION

Write five sentences about students in science class. Underline your pronouns and identify the case of each.

The Nominative Case

Personal pronouns in the nominative case have two uses.

RULE 10.1.2

> **Use the nominative case for (1) the subject of a verb and (2) a predicate pronoun.**

Note that predicate pronouns follow linking verbs. Pronouns that follow linking verbs should be in the nominative case. The linking verbs are highlighted in orange in the examples below.

SUBJECTS

He hopes to be in the play.

Excitedly, **they** dressed for the show.

PREDICATE PRONOUNS

It **was** **I** who called the meeting.

The best spellers **are** **she** and Joan.

Checking for Errors in the Nominative Case
People seldom forget to use the nominative case for a pronoun that is used by itself as a subject. Problems sometimes arise, however, when the pronoun is part of a compound subject.

INCORRECT

Jessie and **me** played catch.

CORRECT

Jessie and **I** played catch.

To make sure you are using the correct case of the pronoun in a compound subject, isolate the pronoun and the verb in the sentence. *Me played catch* is obviously wrong, so the nominative case *I* should be used instead.

If the sentence is in verb–subject order, rearrange it into subject–verb order, and then isolate the pronoun and verb.

INCORRECT

Are you and **her** going bowling?

REARRANGED

You and **?** are going bowling.

CORRECT

Are you and **she** going bowling?

See Practice 10.1C

The Objective Case

Personal pronouns in the objective case have three uses.

> Use the **objective** case for (1) a direct object, (2) an indirect object, and (3) the object of a preposition.

DIRECT OBJECT	Frank's reaction to the news upset **me**.
	The teacher lectured **her**.
INDIRECT OBJECT	Tell **him** about the results.
	My father gave **me** directions to the mall.
OBJECT OF PREPOSITION	Our sister voted for **her**.
	The children gathered around **me**.

Checking for Errors in the Objective Case

As with the nominative case, people seldom forget to use the objective case for a pronoun that is used by itself as a direct object, indirect object, or object of a preposition. Problems may arise, however, when the pronoun is part of a compound object.

INCORRECT	The children gathered around Sal and **I**.
CORRECT	The children gathered around Sal and **me**.

To make sure you are using the correct case of the pronoun in a compound object, use only the pronoun with the rest of the sentence. *The children gathered around I* is obviously wrong, so the objective case *me* should be used instead.

If the sentence is in verb–subject order, rearrange it into subject–verb order.

INCORRECT	Did my father give Glen and **she** a drink?
REARRANGED	My father gave Glen and **?** a drink.
CORRECT	Did my father give Glen and **her** a drink?

See Practice 10.1D

The Possessive Case

Personal pronouns in the possessive case show ownership of one sort or another.

RULE 10.1.4

> Use the **possessive** case of personal pronouns before nouns to show possession. In addition, certain personal pronouns may also be used by themselves to indicate possession.

BEFORE NOUNS

The team won **its** tournament.

Andrew carried **my** package.

BY THEMSELVES

Is this calculator **yours** or **mine**?

Hers was the longest story.

Checking for Errors in the Possessive Case

Personal pronouns in the possessive case are never written with an apostrophe because they already show ownership. Keep this in mind, especially with possessive pronouns that end in *s*.

INCORRECT These drinks are **our's**, not **their's**.

CORRECT These drinks are **ours**, not **theirs**.

When the pronoun *it* is followed by an apostrophe and an *s*, the word becomes *it's,* which is a contraction of *it is*. The possessive pronoun *its* does not have an apostrophe.

CONTRACTION **It's** going to be a long day.

POSSESSIVE PRONOUN The team loves **its** practices.

To check if you need the contraction *it's* or the possessive pronoun *its*, substitute *it is* and reread the sentence.

INCORRECT My shoe has lost **it's** heel.

CORRECT My shoe has lost **its** heel.

See Practice 10.1E
See Practice 10.1F

PRACTICE 10.1C > Identifying Nominative Case Pronouns

Read the sentences. Write the correct pronoun from the choices in parentheses. Then, label the pronoun *subject of a verb* or *predicate pronoun*.

EXAMPLE   Marty and (I, me) ate lunch.

ANSWER   *I — subject of a verb*

1. Apparently (she, her) and Lucy were early.

2. The heads of the student body are Randolph and (I, me).

3. On our street, the Jacksons and (we, us) are the only ones with satellite television.

4. Either Doris or (he, him) will win the prize.

5. (They, them) and their friends chat a lot on their cellphones.

6. The first two people in line were Maurice and (she, her).

7. When the ship sailed into the harbor, (they, them) and the crew cheered.

8. I think the most helpful guidance counselors are Mrs. Kelvin and (he, him).

9. Did (we, us) or the Robinsons arrive first?

10. Before this summer, the best player had been Chester or (I, me).

PRACTICE 10.1D > Using Objective Case Pronouns

Read the sentences. Write an objective case pronoun to complete each sentence. Then, label each pronoun *direct object*, *indirect object*, or *object of a preposition*.

EXAMPLE   I gave Darlene and _____ a lift.

ANSWER   *him — indirect object*

11. I saw Fred and _____ at the recycling plant.

12. I offered Pam and _____ a helping hand.

13. Ask the baker or _____ for some hard rolls.

14. I am going to town with Saul and _____ .

15. Please give Dolores or _____ the message.

16. For my cousin and _____ , each football game is more exciting than the last.

17. Rona and I usually walk to school, but sometimes my brother drives _____ .

18. Since Mrs. Pai was so helpful, Mom brought Mr. Pai and _____ vegetables from our garden.

19. Did the lifeguard really save Howie and _____ from drowning?

20. I usually go with Paul or my two sisters, but today I am going without Paul or _____ .

SPEAKING APPLICATION

With a partner, talk about two people you know. Your partner should listen for nominative pronouns and make sure they are used correctly.

WRITING APPLICATION

Use sentences 12, 16, and 20 as models, and write three sentences about family members. Underline the objective pronouns you include in your sentences.

PRACTICE 10.1E > **Using Possessive Case Pronouns**

Read the sentences. Write the correct pronoun from the choices in parentheses.

EXAMPLE   The dog gnawed (its, it's) bone.

ANSWER   *its*

1. Those ballet slippers are (hers, her's).
2. One of (me, my) oldest shirts ripped in the wash.
3. The elephant ate (its, it's) dinner.
4. Is the camera (yours, your's)?
5. That van is (theirs, their's).
6. (Ours, Our's) was a happy ending.
7. That handkerchief is (his, his').
8. The company has changed (its, it's) name.
9. (My, Mine) enemy is plotting against me.
10. (Theirs, There's) is a lovely home.

PRACTICE 10.1F > **Revising to Correct Pronoun Errors**

Read the sentences. For each sentence with a pronoun error, write the incorrect pronoun. Then, rewrite the sentence with the correct pronoun. If a sentence has no pronoun error, write *correct*.

EXAMPLE   The agency gave the assignment to Brody and he.

ANSWER   *he; The agency gave the assignment to Brody and him.*

11. Her and Thomas are fraternal twins.
12. Please give us another chance.
13. The winners were Ava and I.
14. Mom took my sister and I to the dentist.
15. Owen, Emily, and me are all in the school play.
16. The last house on the left is ours.
17. Keep this secret strictly between you and I.
18. The hotel and it's restaurant were listed in the guidebook.
19. The students speaking in the school auditorium were Chloe and he.
20. Their's was a foolish decision.

SPEAKING APPLICATION

With a partner, talk about your classmates' clothing. Your partner should identify the possessive pronouns and make sure they are used correctly.

WRITING APPLICATION

Write five sentences about people's pets using possessive pronouns. Be sure to use the pronouns correctly. Then, exchange papers with a partner. Your partner should correct any pronoun errors.

Cases of *Who* and *Whom* The pronouns *who* and *whom*
are often confused. *Who* is a nominative case pronoun, and
whom is an objective case pronoun. *Who* and *whom* have two
common uses in sentences: They can be used in questions or
to begin subordinate clauses in complex sentences.

> **Use *who* for the subject of a verb. Use *whom* for (1) the direct
> object of a verb and (2) the object of a preposition.**

RULE 10.1.5

You will often find *who* used as the subject of a question. *Who*
may also be used as the subject of a subordinate clause in a
complex sentence.

SUBJECT OF A QUESTION	**Who** ran the fastest?
SUBJECT OF A SUBORDINATE CLAUSE	I admire the student **who** ran the fastest.

The following examples show *whom* used in questions.

DIRECT OBJECT	**Whom** did she meet at the park?
OBJECT OF PREPOSITION	From **whom** are you getting new skates?

Questions that include *whom* are generally in inverted word
order, with the verb appearing before the subject. If you reword
the first example in subject–verb word order, you will see
that *whom* is the direct object of the verb *did meet: She did
meet whom?* In the second example, *whom* is the object of the
preposition *from: You are getting the new skates from whom?*

Subordinate clauses that begin with *whom* will always be in
verb–subject word order. To check the case of the pronoun,
reword the clause into subject–verb word order.

VERB–SUBJECT ORDER	From **whom** had she received the tickets?
SUBJECT–VERB ORDER	She had received the tickets from **whom**?

See Practice 10.1G
See Practice 10.1H

PRACTICE 10.1G **Identifying the Correct Use of** *Who* **and** *Whom*

Read the sentences. Write the pronoun in parentheses that correctly completes each sentence.

EXAMPLE   I saw (who, whom) you took to the dance.

ANSWER   *whom*

1. (Who, Whom) received the most praise?

2. With (who, whom) did you walk home?

3. Nora is the cheerleader (who, whom) stands behind the others.

4. (Who, Whom) have they chosen for team captain?

5. I know the reporter (who, whom) the newspaper sent to the school cafeteria.

6. The mayor is the elected official in (who, whom) the citizens place the most trust.

7. (Who, Whom) in the play has Drew replaced?

8. Please tell me (who, whom) you would choose as the best speaker.

9. You recommended (who, whom) for the committee?

10. I do not know (who, whom) she is.

PRACTICE 10.1H **Revising to Correct** *Who* **and** *Whom*

Read the sentences. Then, if a sentence uses *who* or *whom* incorrectly, rewrite the sentence with the correct pronoun form. If a sentence has no pronoun error, write *correct*.

EXAMPLE   Who did you meet at the store?

ANSWER   *Whom did you meet at the store?*

11. Who in this crowd ever keeps quiet?

12. Who did she take to the playground?

13. Gail is the one in who I place my faith.

14. I ran into Valerie, whom you saw yesterday.

15. My brother, who needs new gloves, could also use a new winter hat.

16. To who were you talking on the telephone?

17. Of the two, whom is the most efficient?

18. Whom among us has ever been on television?

19. This movie was directed by whom?

20. Please tell me who that is.

SPEAKING APPLICATION

With a partner, take turns asking and answering questions about famous singers. Use *who* or *whom* in each question and answer. Your partner should listen for the pronouns and make sure they are used correctly.

WRITING APPLICATION

Write six sentences about the suspects in a mystery you read or in a movie you saw. Use *who* in three of the sentences and *whom* in the other three. Then, exchange papers with a partner. Your partner should check to make sure you've used the pronouns correctly.

CHAPTER 11

MAKING WORDS AGREE

Present ideas clearly in your writing by making each subject and verb agree and by matching each pronoun to its antecedent, the word or words for which the pronoun stands.

WRITE GUY *Jeff Anderson, M.Ed.*

WHAT DO YOU NOTICE?

Pick out pronouns as you zoom in on this sentence from the story "The Adventure of the Speckled Band" by Arthur Conan Doyle.

MENTOR TEXT

"The metallic clang heard by Miss Stoner was obviously caused by her stepfather hastily closing the door of his safe upon its terrible occupant."

Now, ask yourself the following questions:

- How does the pronoun *her* agree with its antecedent?
- Whose safe was hastily closed? How do you know?

The antecedent of *her* is *Miss Stoner. Her* agrees with *Miss Stoner* because it is a singular, feminine pronoun, and *Miss Stoner* is a singular, feminine noun. The possessive pronoun *his* shows that the safe belongs to her stepfather.

Grammar for Writers Creating agreement in number and gender between pronouns and their antecedents is one way writers achieve clarity. An antecedent may be a noun, a group of words, or another pronoun, so keep each situation in mind as you write.

Your subject and my verb can work together.

Just as long as they agree.

11.1 Subject-Verb Agreement

For a sentence to be correct, its subject and verb must match each other, or agree. Subject–verb agreement has one main rule.

The subject and verb in a sentence must agree in number.

In grammar, the concept of **number** is simple. The number of a word can be either **singular** or **plural.** A singular word indicates *one*. A plural word indicates *more than one*. In English, only nouns, pronouns, and verbs have number.

Singular and Plural Subjects

Most of the time, it is easy to tell whether a simple subject, such as a noun or pronoun, is singular or plural. That is because most nouns are made plural by adding *-s* or *-es* to their singular form.

EXAMPLES

friend	friend **s**
nation	nation **s**
leash	leash **es**
coach	coach **es**

Some nouns form plurals in irregular ways.

EXAMPLES

goose	**geese**
man	**men**
child	**children**
life	**lives**

Pronouns also have different forms to indicate singular and plural. For example, the pronouns *I*, *he*, *she*, *it*, and *this* are singular. *We*, *they*, and *these* are plural. *You*, *who*, and *some* can be either singular or plural.

Singular and Plural Verbs

Like nouns, verbs have singular and plural forms. Problems involving number in verbs normally involve the third-person forms in the present tense (*she wants, they want*) and certain forms of the verb *be* (*I am, he is* or *was, we are* or *were*).

The chart shows all the basic forms of several different verbs in the present tense.

SINGULAR AND PLURAL VERBS IN THE PRESENT TENSE		
SINGULAR		**PLURAL**
First and Second Person	**Third Person**	**First, Second, and Third Person**
(I, you) send	(he, she, it) sends	(we, you, they) send
(I, you) go	(he, she, it) goes	(we, you, they) go
(I, you) look	(he, she, it) looks	(we, you, they) look
(I, you) dance	(he, she, it) dances	(we, you, they) dance
(I, you) visit	(he, she, it) visits	(we, you, they) visit
(I, you) work	(he, she, it) works	(we, you, they) work
(I, you) run	(he, she, it) runs	(we, you, they) run
(I, you) discuss	(he, she, it) discusses	(we, you, they) discuss
(I, you) vote	(he, she, it) votes	(we, you, they) vote
(I, you) choose	(he, she, it) chooses	(we, you, they) choose
(I, you) learn	(he, she, it) learns	(we, you, they) learn

Notice that the form of the verb changes only in the third-person singular, when an *-s* or *-es* is added to the verb. Unlike nouns, which usually become plural when *-s* or *-es* is added, verbs with *-s* or *-es* added to them are singular.

The helping verb *be* may also indicate whether a verb is singular or plural. The following chart shows only those forms of the verb *be* that are always singular.

FORMS OF THE HELPING VERB *BE* THAT ARE ALWAYS SINGULAR			
am	is	was	has been

Making Verbs Agree With Singular and Plural Subjects

To check subject–verb agreement, determine the number of the subject. Then, make sure the verb has the same number.

SINGULAR SUBJECT AND VERB	**Megan likes** surfing. **She was** at the beach earlier today.
PLURAL SUBJECT AND VERB	**They like** surfing. **Surfers were** in the water yesterday.

> **RULE 11.1.2**
>
> **A prepositional phrase that comes between a subject and its verb does not affect subject–verb agreement.**

Often, a subject is separated from its verb by a prepositional phrase. In these cases, it is important to remember that the object of a preposition is never the subject of a sentence.

INCORRECT	The **arrival** of the students **have caused** much excitement at the ceremony.
CORRECT	The **arrival** of the students **has caused** much excitement at the ceremony.
INCORRECT	The **calls** of the bird **was heard** several blocks away.
CORRECT	The **calls** of the bird **were heard** several blocks away.

In the first example, the subject is *arrival,* not *students,* which is the object of the preposition *of.* Because *arrival* is singular, the singular verb *has caused* must be used. In the second example, the subject is the plural *calls,* not *bird;* therefore, it takes the plural verb *were heard.*

See Practice 11.1A
See Practice 11.1B

PRACTICE 11.1A Making Subjects and Verbs Agree

Read the sentences. Write the verb in parentheses that agrees with the subject. Then, label the subject *singular* or *plural*.

EXAMPLE   The mice (likes, like) cheese.

ANSWER   *like — plural*

1. The index (lists, list) items in alphabetical order.

2. The flag (ripples, ripple) in the wind.

3. Some birds (fly, flies) south in winter.

4. The businessmen (goes, go) to lunch at noon.

5. A box of crackers (sits, sit) on the shelf.

6. The people in our state (votes, vote) for governor next Tuesday.

7. The glow of streetlights and neon signs (makes, make) the nighttime skyline memorable.

8. The size of the pieces of the jigsaw puzzle (decreases, decrease) with the level of difficulty.

9. How many students (are, is) in your class?

10. The papers hidden in a secret drawer of her desk (is, are) missing.

PRACTICE 11.1B Revising for Subject-Verb Agreement

Read the sentences. Then, if a sentence has an error in subject-verb agreement, rewrite the sentence correctly. If a sentence has no error, write *correct*.

EXAMPLE   The lions in the cage roars loudly.

ANSWER   *The lions in the cage roar loudly.*

11. It often happens that way.

12. The women belongs to the fitness club.

13. The ballplayers on the bench look bored.

14. The sound of the drums hurt my ears.

15. The tourists on the walk of Old Alexandria like the historical buildings.

16. A sack of groceries are on the counter.

17. The houses across the street from the beach enjoy wonderful views.

18. The students in the library studies for their test.

19. The behavior of the bears in the park often surprise visitors.

20. Her plan to visit several countries in South America sound very interesting.

SPEAKING APPLICATION

With a partner, talk about items found in a cupboard, a pantry, or a kitchen. Use singular and plural subjects and present-tense verbs. Your partner should check that your subjects and verbs agree.

WRITING APPLICATION

Write five sentences about animals in a zoo. Underline your subjects once and verbs twice, and make sure the subjects and verbs agree.

Making Verbs Agree With Collective Nouns

Collective nouns—such as *assembly, audience, class, club,* and *committee*—name groups of people or things. Collective nouns are challenging as subjects because they can take either singular or plural verbs. The number of the verb depends on the meaning of the collective noun in the sentence.

RULE

11.1.3

> **Use a singular verb with a collective noun acting as a single unit. Use a plural verb when the individual members of the group are acting individually.**

SINGULAR	The **committee votes** on the new chair.
PLURAL	The **committee have split** their votes on the issue.
SINGULAR	The history **club plans** a debate.
PLURAL	The history **club were proud** of their debating skills.
SINGULAR	The **class plants** lettuce and cucumbers.
PLURAL	The **class have divided** the lettuce and tomato seeds among the members.
SINGULAR	The soccer **team marches** in the parade.
PLURAL	The soccer **team have scored** many goals.
SINGULAR	The **audience roars** after the performance.
PLURAL	The **audience have given** their reviews of the show.

See Practice 11.1C
See Practice 11.1D

PRACTICE 11.1C > Making Verbs Agree With Collective Nouns

Read the sentences. Then, write the verb in parentheses that agrees with the subject.

EXAMPLE   The chorus (sounds, sound) lovely.

ANSWER   *sounds*

1. The club (offers, offer) members many advantages.
2. The family often (eats, eat) dinner together.
3. The team (is, are) not likely to reach the finals.
4. The choir (harmonizes, harmonize) well with one another.
5. The class (talks, talk) among themselves.
6. A flock of sheep (needs, need) a shepherd.
7. At weekly meetings, the staff (suggests, suggest) all sorts of ideas to the boss.
8. The jury (discusses, discuss) the verdict.
9. At the end of each act, the audience (applauds, applaud).
10. (Does, do) the army recruit on campus?

PRACTICE 11.1D > Revising for Agreement Between Verbs and Collective Nouns

Read the sentences. Then, if a sentence has an error in subject-verb agreement, rewrite the sentence correctly. If a sentence has no error, write *correct*.

EXAMPLE   Our team need someone like you.

ANSWER   *Our team needs someone like you.*

11. The group quarrels among themselves.
12. The troop are seeking new members.
13. The crowd often swells to over a thousand.
14. The company provide jobs to the community.
15. The cast discuss the script with one another.
16. The faculty offers different opinions.
17. Sometimes the herd stampedes.
18. The ship's crew displays different talents.
19. The orchestra rehearse every morning.
20. The swarm descend on the beekeeper.

SPEAKING APPLICATION

With a partner, take turns discussing community organizations. Use at least three collective nouns, such as *club*, *staff*, and *team*. Your partner should listen for the collective nouns and make sure your verbs agree.

WRITING APPLICATION

Write three sentences in the present tense, using these collective nouns as subjects: *cast*, *group*, *company*.

Making Verbs Agree With Compound Subjects

A **compound subject** refers to two or more subjects that share a verb. Compound subjects are connected by conjunctions such as *and, or,* or *nor.*

EXAMPLES   The **museums** and **historical sites** in
                                          compound subject
            Chicago **attract** many visitors.
                        plural verb

            Either **Sally** or **Frank** **knows** the way to the
                    compound subject   singular
                                             verb
            historical museum.

            Neither the **Hancock Observatory** nor the **Art**
                         compound subject
            Institute **disappoints** tourists.
                          singular
                          verb

A number of rules can help you choose the right verb to use with a compound subject.

Compound Subjects Joined by *And*

RULE 11.1.4 When a compound subject is connected by *and,* the verb that follows is usually plural.

EXAMPLE   **El Paso** and **Dallas** **are** my favorite Texas cities.
           compound subject   plural verb

There is an exception to this rule: If the parts of a compound subject are thought of as one person or thing, the subject is singular and takes a singular verb.

EXAMPLES   **Franks and beans** **is** a popular meal when
            compound subject   singular
                                  verb
            camping.

            The **pad and paper** **is** on the table.
                compound subject   singular
                                   verb

Compound Subjects Joined by *Or* or *Nor*

> **When two singular subjects are joined by *or* or *nor*, use a singular verb. When two plural subjects are joined by *or* or *nor*, use a plural verb.**

11.1.5 RULE

SINGULAR   A **bicycle** or a **skateboard** **is** a good way to
compound subject   singular
verb
get to the park.

PLURAL   Neither **boys** nor **men** **like** to wear a tie.
compound subject   plural verb

In the first example, *or* joins two singular subjects. Although two things make up the compound subject, the subject does not take a plural verb. Either a bicycle or a skateboard is a good way to get to the park, not both of them.

> **When a compound subject is made up of one singular and one plural subject joined by *or* or *nor*, the verb agrees with the subject closer to it.**

11.1.6 RULE

EXAMPLES   Either the **monuments** or the **Alamo**
plural subject   singular subject

is interesting to see.
singular verb

Either the **Alamo** or the **monuments**
singular subject   plural subject

are interesting to see.
plural verb

See Practice 11.1E

Agreement in Inverted Sentences

In most sentences, the subject comes before the verb. Sometimes, however, this order is turned around, or **inverted.** In other sentences, the helping verb comes before the subject even though the main verb follows the subject.

> When a subject comes after the verb, the subject and verb still must agree with each other in number.

EXAMPLE   **Do** the cultural **attractions** in New York City
       plural verb   plural subject

    sound exciting to you?

Sentences Beginning With a Prepositional Phrase
In sentences that begin with a prepositional phrase, the object of the preposition may look like a subject, even though it is not.

EXAMPLE   Along the river **were** **throngs** of spectators.
             plural verb plural subject

In this example, the plural verb *were* agrees with the plural subject *throngs.* The singular noun *river* is the object of the preposition *along.*

Sentences Beginning With *There* or *Here*
Sentences beginning with *there* or *here* are almost always in inverted word order.

EXAMPLES   There **were** several **magazines** about sports.
           plural verb   plural subject

    Here **is** the latest **magazine** about sports.
    singular verb   singular subject

The contractions *there's* and *here's* both contain the singular verb *is*: *there is* and *here is*. Do not use these contractions with plural subjects.

INCORRECT   Here**'s** the **papers** for the class.

CORRECT   Here **are** the **papers** for the class.

Questions With Inverted Word Order
Many questions are also written in inverted word order.

EXAMPLE   Where **are** the **papers** for the class?
           plural verb   plural subject

See Practice 11.1F

PRACTICE 11.1E **Making Verbs Agree With Compound Subjects**

Read the sentences. Then, write the verb in parentheses that agrees with the subject.

EXAMPLE   Kay and Janine (sings, sing) well.

ANSWER   *sing*

1. Either Brad or Ann (takes, take) out the garbage every night.

2. Both chicken and chickpeas (supplies, supply) protein.

3. The rooms and hall (fills, fill) to capacity.

4. Peanut butter and jelly (is, are) traditional in our house.

5. Neither Zack nor Trish (plays, play) tennis.

6. Either the workers or their boss (takes, take) care of the delivery.

7. The doctor or her nurses (administers, administer) flu shots.

8. (Do, Does) Rick or Seth know the answer?

9. Neither the teacher nor his students (arrives, arrive) before nine o'clock.

10. Macaroni and cheese (is, are) the best comfort food.

PRACTICE 11.1F **Revising for Agreement Between Verbs and Compound Subjects**

Read the sentences. Then, if a sentence has an error in subject-verb agreement, rewrite the sentence correctly. If a sentence has no error, write *correct*.

EXAMPLE   Phil or Edie often help me.

ANSWER   *Phil or Edie often helps me.*

11. The toaster oven or the microwave often reheat leftovers.

12. The lion and the tiger come from two different continents.

13. Either Anna or Mark attends the meetings.

14. Both the magician and his assistant performs amazing tricks.

15. Neither the coach nor the players spoke to the reporter.

16. Ham and eggs is my favorite breakfast.

17. Either the editors or their publisher respond to readers' letters.

18. Neither Jackie nor Lance write for the magazine anymore.

19. The car and the bike is in the garage.

20. Either the art direction or the costumes was awarded an Oscar.

SPEAKING APPLICATION

With a partner, take turns discussing your favorite foods, using sentences 2 and 4 as models. Use four compound subjects with present-tense verbs. Your partner should listen for the compound subjects and decide if the verbs agree with them.

WRITING APPLICATION

Write four sentences about sports figures and their achievements. Use compound subjects with present-tense verbs. Underline the compound subjects and circle the verbs.

Verb Agreement With Indefinite Pronouns

Indefinite pronouns refer to people, places, or things in a general way.

> When an **indefinite pronoun** is the subject of a sentence, the verb must agree in number with the pronoun.

INDEFINITE PRONOUNS				
SINGULAR			PLURAL	SINGULAR OR PLURAL
anybody	everyone	nothing	both	all
anyone	everything	one	few	any
anything	much	other	many	more
each	neither	somebody	several	most
either	nobody	someone	others	none
everybody	no one	something		some

Indefinite Pronouns That Are Always Singular

Indefinite pronouns that are always singular take singular verbs. Do not be misled by a prepositional phrase that follows an indefinite pronoun. The singular verb agrees with the indefinite pronoun, not with the object of the preposition.

EXAMPLES

Each of the football team mascots **is** at
singular subject   singular verb
the game.

Either of the cars in the lot **is** in good condition.
singular subject   singular verb

Everyone in the back of the bus **was** singing
singular subject   singular verb
along.

Each of the girls **plays** on the tennis team.
singular subject   singular verb

Indefinite Pronouns That Are Always Plural

Indefinite pronouns that are always plural are used with plural verbs.

EXAMPLES   **Both** of my notebooks **are** in the car.
plural subject   plural verb

Many of the townspeople **are picnicking** in the
plural subject   plural verb

park today.

Several **have decided** to join the swim team.
plural subject   plural verb

Few **are planning** to be at home in July.
plural subject   plural verb

Indefinite Pronouns That May Be Either Singular or Plural

Many indefinite pronouns can take either a singular or a plural verb.

> The number of the indefinite pronoun is the same as the number of its **referent,** or the noun to which it refers.

11.1.9 RULE

The indefinite pronoun is singular if the referent is singular. If the referent is plural, the indefinite pronoun is plural.

SINGULAR   **Some** of the **cheese** **has** spoiled.

PLURAL   **Some** of the **eggs** **have** spoiled, too.

In the examples above, *some* is singular when it refers to *cheese*, but plural when it refers to *eggs*.

SINGULAR   **All** of the **money** we collected **is** missing.

PLURAL   **All** of these **cards** **are** for you.

See Practice 11.1G
See Practice 11.1H

In these examples, *all* is singular when it refers to *money*, but plural when it refers to *cards*.

PRACTICE 11.1G Making Verbs Agree With Indefinite Pronouns

Read the sentences. Then, write the verb in parentheses that agrees with the subject.

EXAMPLE   Both of them (looks, look) happy.

ANSWER   *look*

1. Several of the apples (tastes, taste) bad.
2. Some of the clocks (has, have) the wrong time.
3. More of the music (was, were) played.
4. Most of my questions (have, has) been answered.
5. Few of us (knows, know) the reason.
6. Each of the planets (orbits, orbit) the sun.
7. Neither of the mechanics (works, work) on weekends.
8. None of the residents (is, are) at home.
9. Everything in the closets and attics (was, were) old and dusty.
10. Most of the team members (does, do) different things on weekends.

PRACTICE 11.1H Revising for Agreement Between Verbs and Indefinite Pronouns

Read the sentences. Then, if a sentence has an error in subject-verb agreement, rewrite the sentence correctly. If a sentence has no error, write *correct*.

EXAMPLE   None of the dogs barks a lot.

ANSWER   *None of the dogs bark a lot.*

11. Both of the women play tennis often.
12. More of the workers needs new jobs.
13. Some of the food needs salt.
14. Everything stated in newspaper articles are not always true.
15. Few of the teachers uses the cafeteria.
16. Each of the suggestions have merit.
17. Any of your assistance is welcome.
18. The spices in this meal tastes wonderful.
19. Most of the meal was left over.
20. All of the class members likes to debate with one another.

SPEAKING APPLICATION

With a partner, talk about a board game or another game you have played. Use four indefinite pronouns as subjects with present-tense verbs. Your partner should listen for and confirm that your verbs agree with your subjects.

WRITING APPLICATION

Use sentences 15 and 20 as models, and write four sentences about the results of an imaginary survey. Use indefinite pronouns as subjects with present-tense verbs. Underline your subjects once and verbs twice, and make sure the subjects and verbs agree.

11.2 Agreement Between Pronouns and Antecedents

An **antecedent** is the word or words for which a pronoun stands. A pronoun's antecedent may be a noun, a group of words acting as a noun, or even another pronoun. As with subjects and verbs, pronouns should agree with their antecedents.

Making Personal Pronouns and Antecedents Agree

Person tells whether a pronoun refers to the person speaking (first person), the person spoken to (second person), or the person, place, or thing spoken about (third person). **Number** tells whether the pronoun is singular or plural. **Gender** tells whether a third-person-singular antecedent is masculine or feminine.

> **A personal pronoun must agree with its antecedent in person, number, and gender.**

RULE
11.2.1

EXAMPLE   I told **Talie** to bring a jacket with **her** .

In this example, the pronoun *her* is third person and singular. It agrees with its feminine antecedent, *Talie.*

Avoiding Shifts in Person
A personal pronoun must have the same person as its antecedent. Otherwise, the meaning of the sentence is unclear.

INCORRECT   The **students** know **we** must check the answers before handing in tests.
(Who must check the answers? *We* must.)

CORRECT   The **students** know **they** must check the answers before handing in tests.
(Who must check the answers? *The students* must.)

As you can see, a shift in the person of the personal pronoun can make it unclear who is going to check the answers.

Avoiding Problems With Number and Gender

Making pronouns and antecedents agree in number and gender can be difficult. Problems may arise when the antecedent is a collective noun, when the antecedent is a compound joined by *or* or *nor,* or when the gender of the antecedent is not known.

Making Pronouns Agree in Number With Collective Nouns
Collective nouns are challenging because they can take either singular or plural pronouns. The number of the pronoun depends on the meaning of the collective noun in the sentence.

> Use a singular pronoun to refer to a collective noun that names a group that is acting as a single unit. Use a plural pronoun to refer to a collective noun when the members or parts of a group are acting individually.

SINGULAR The **audience showed its** approval with applause.

PLURAL The **audience voted** for **their** favorite songs.

In the first example above, the audience is acting as a single unit when it applauds, so the singular pronoun, *its,* refers to *audience.* In the second example, each member of the audience is voting individually, so the plural pronoun, *their,* refers to *audience.*

Making Pronouns Agree in Number With Compound Nouns

> Use a singular personal pronoun to refer to two or more singular antecedents joined by *or* or *nor.* Use a plural pronoun with two or more singular antecedents joined by *and.*

Two or more singular antecedents joined by *or* or *nor* must have a singular pronoun, just as they must have a singular verb.

INCORRECT **Marco** or **John** will bring **their** sandwich.

CORRECT **Marco** or **John** will bring **his** sandwich.

CORRECT **Marco** and **John** will bring **their** sandwiches.

Avoiding Problems With Gender

When the gender of a third-person-singular antecedent is not known, you can make the pronoun agree with its antecedent in one of three ways:

(1) Use *he or she, him or her,* or *his or hers.*

(2) Rewrite the sentence so that the antecedent and pronoun are both plural.

(3) Rewrite the sentence to eliminate the pronoun.

Traditionally, the masculine pronouns *he* and *his* have been used to stand for both males and females. Today, using *he or she* and *him or her* is preferred. If any of these corrections seem awkward to you, rewrite the sentence.

Making Personal Pronouns and Indefinite Pronouns Agree

Indefinite pronouns are words such as *each, everybody, either,* and *one.* Pay special attention to the number of a personal pronoun when the antecedent is a singular indefinite pronoun.

> **Use a singular personal pronoun when its antecedent is a singular indefinite pronoun.**

11.2.4 RULE

Do not be misled by a prepositional phrase that follows an indefinite pronoun. The personal pronoun agrees with the indefinite pronoun, not with the object of the preposition.

INCORRECT	**One** of the birds has lost **their** feathers.
CORRECT	**One** of the birds has lost **its** feathers.
INCORRECT	**Everyone** in the group wanted to read **their** book report.
CORRECT	**Everyone** in the group wanted to read **his or her** book report.
CORRECT	**All** of the students in the group wanted to read **their** book reports.

See Practice 11.2A
See Practice 11.2B

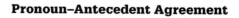

PRACTICE 11.2A ▷ **Making Pronouns and Antecedents Agree**

Read the sentences. Then, write the pronoun in parentheses that agrees with its antecedent.

EXAMPLE   Each of the girls wore (her, their) hair in braids.

ANSWER   *her*

1. Mr. Blair and his wife signed (his or her, their) names on the petition.

2. The table or the chair had (its, their) legs repaired.

3. Each of the scientists brought (his or her, their) own equipment.

4. Either Sol or Jed will gladly share (his, their) knowledge with others.

5. Everybody in the girls' club promised that (she, they) would attend the lecture.

6. Neither of the two boys showed (his, their) fear.

7. Ian attended a class where (you, he) learned how to use a computer.

8. "Brooke and I can vividly recall (her, our) childhood memories," Nadine said.

9. Everyone on the boy's track team is wearing (his, their) socks inside out for luck.

10. None of the children changed (his or her, their) behavior despite the scolding.

PRACTICE 11.2B ▷ **Revising for Pronoun-Antecedent Agreement**

Read the sentences. If a sentence has an error in pronoun-antecedent agreement, rewrite the sentence correctly. Then, circle the pronoun and underline its antecedent. If a sentence has no error, write *correct*.

EXAMPLE   Both admirals gave his orders firmly.

ANSWER   *Both admirals gave their orders firmly.*

11. Both Steve and Dan finished his homework before supper.

12. Several actresses had her problems with the script.

13. Neither Dora nor her sister lost her gloves.

14. Each of the young boys had difficulties using their plastic scissors.

15. Everyone needs time to change into their dressy clothes before the reception.

16. "Mom and I ate our meal together," Madison recalled.

17. The poodles had its toenails clipped.

18. Everybody in the pool agreed that they would stop swimming and have lunch.

19. Did the shirts lose its color in the wash?

20. Each student has their own book.

SPEAKING APPLICATION

With a partner, talk about students in gym class. Use several personal pronouns, including *her*, *his*, *its*, and *their*. Your partner should identify the personal pronouns and their antecedents, and decide whther they agree.

WRITING APPLICATION

Write six sentences about school supplies. Use compound subjects and indefinite pronouns as subjects, and refer to them with personal pronouns. Make sure the pronouns and antecedents agree.

USING MODIFIERS

Understanding how to use different forms of adjectives and adverbs as modifiers will help you add variety to your sentences.

CHAPTER 12

WRITE GUY *Jeff Anderson, M.Ed.*

WHAT DO YOU NOTICE?

Focus on modifiers as you zoom in on these sentences from the book *Harriet Tubman: Conductor on the Underground Railroad* by Ann Petry.

MENTOR TEXT

> Harriet felt safer now, though there were danger spots ahead. But the biggest part of her job was over.

Now, ask yourself the following questions:

- What was the author comparing Harriet's feeling to when she wrote that Harriet felt safer?
- What does the superlative adjective *biggest* suggest about the rest of Harriet's job?

The author was comparing Harriet's feelings in the present to her feelings in the past. To compare two things, the *-er* ending is added to most one- or two-syllable adjectives and adverbs. The ending *-est* is used to compare three or more things in the superlative form. *Biggest* is the superlative form of *big* and suggests that Harriet still has parts of her job to do.

Grammar for Writers When writers use modifiers to show forms of comparison, they can craft a complete picture for their readers.

I want to receive a higher score on my next test.

You should try for the highest score.

12.1 Comparisons Using Adjectives and Adverbs

You may recall that adjectives and adverbs are **modifiers.** Adjectives can modify nouns or pronouns. Adverbs can modify verbs, adjectives, or other adverbs. You can use modifiers to make comparisons.

Three Forms of Comparison

Modifiers change their form when they show comparison. These different forms are called **forms,** or **degrees, of comparison.**

> **Most adjectives and adverbs have three forms, or degrees, of comparison: positive, comparative, and superlative.**

The **positive degree** is used when no comparison is being made. This is the form of a word that is listed in a dictionary. The **comparative degree** is used when two items are being compared. The **superlative degree** is used when three or more items are being compared. When the superlative degree is used, the article *the* is often added.

DEGREE	ADJECTIVE	ADVERB
Positive	My brother has a **large** bedroom.	My dog runs **fast**.
Comparative	His bedroom is **larger** than mine.	My dog runs **faster** than Sam's dog.
Superlative	My sister has the **largest** bedroom in our home.	Of all the dogs in the neighborhood, my dog runs the **fastest**.

Like verbs, adjectives and adverbs change forms in different ways. Some adjectives and adverbs change in regular ways, or according to predictable patterns. As you can see in the chart above, *large* and *fast* form their comparative and superlative degrees regularly, by adding *-er* and *-est* to their positive form.

Regular Modifiers With One or Two Syllables

Most modifiers are **regular**—their degrees of comparison are formed in predictable ways.

> Use *-er* or *more* to form the comparative degree and use *-est* or *most* to form the superlative degree of most one- and two-syllable modifiers.

12.1.2
RULE

COMPARATIVE AND SUPERLATIVE DEGREES FORMED WITH *-ER* AND *-EST*		
POSITIVE	COMPARATIVE	SUPERLATIVE
deep	deeper	deepest
fast	faster	fastest
friendly	friendlier	friendliest
narrow	narrower	narrowest
sunny	sunnier	sunniest

Use *more* to form a modifier's comparative degree when adding *-er* sounds awkward. Use *most* to form a modifier's superlative degree when adding *-est* sounds awkward.

COMPARATIVE AND SUPERLATIVE DEGREES FORMED WITH *MORE* AND *MOST*		
POSITIVE	COMPARATIVE	SUPERLATIVE
careful	more careful	most careful
complete	more complete	most complete
handsome	more handsome	most handsome
often	more often	most often
quietly	more quietly	most quietly

More and *most* should not be used when the result sounds awkward, however. If you are not sure which form to use, check a dictionary. Most dictionaries list modifiers formed with *-er* and *-est*.

See Practice 12.1A

Regular Modifiers With Three or More Syllables

Modifiers for words with three or more syllables follow the same rules.

RULE

12.1.3

Use *more* and *most* to form the comparative and superlative degrees of all modifiers of three or more syllables. Do not use *-er* or *-est* with modifiers of more than two syllables.

DEGREES OF MODIFIERS WITH THREE OR MORE SYLLABLES		
POSTIVE	COMPARATIVE	SUPERLATIVE
expensive	more expensive	most expensive
flexible	more flexible	most flexible

Adverbs Ending in *-ly*

To modify most adverbs ending in *-ly*, use *more* or *most*.

RULE

12.1.4

Use *more* to form the comparative degree and *most* to form the superlative degree of most adverbs ending in *-ly*.

EXAMPLES   easily, more easily, most easily

peacefully, more peacefully, most peacefully

Using *Less* and *Least*

Less and *least* can show decreasing comparisons.

RULE

12.1.5

Use *less* with a modifier to form the decreasing comparative degree and *least* to form the decreasing superlative degree.

EXAMPLES   cautiously, less cautiously, least cautiously

effectively, less effectively, least effectively

See Practice 12.1B

PRACTICE 12.1A Forming Comparatives and Superlatives of One- and Two-Syllable Modifiers

Read the modifiers. Write the comparative and superlative forms of each modifier.

EXAMPLE   long

ANSWER   *longer, longest*

1. young
2. neat
3. fine
4. hot
5. cloudy
6. hungry
7. careful
8. precious
9. lovely
10. quickly

PRACTICE 12.1B Using Forms of Modifiers

Read the sentences. Then, write each sentence using the form of the modifier in parentheses.

EXAMPLE   Bianca is _____ than I am. (*young*, comparative)

ANSWER   *Bianca is younger than I am.*

11. This box is _____ than that one. (*large*, comparative)

12. Daniela is the _____ runner on the track team. (*swift*, superlative)

13. Which is the _____ item in the museum's gem collection? (*costly*, superlative)

14. The bus arrived _____ than we expected. (*soon*, comparative)

15. In my opinion, he is the _____ actor performing today. (*talented*, superlative)

16. It is even _____ here than it is on the river. (*foggy*, comparative)

17. She is the _____ of my advisers. (*intelligent*, superlative)

18. Charles is _____ in the evening than he is in the morning. (*tired*, comparative)

19. I spoke _____ than I should have. (*loudly*, comparative)

20. Of the three children, who is the _____ ? (*tall*, superlative)

SPEAKING APPLICATION

With a partner, talk about a favorite sports team. Use comparatives and superlatives of one- and two-syllable modifiers. Your partner should listen for the comparatives and superlatives and decide if they are formed correctly.

WRITING APPLICATION

Write four sentences stating your opinions about different places to live. Use two comparative and two superlative forms of modifiers.

Irregular Adjectives and Adverbs

A few adjectives and adverbs are irregular.

Memorize the comparative and superlative forms of adjectives and adverbs that have irregular spellings.

The chart lists the most common irregular modifiers.

DEGREES OF IRREGULAR ADJECTIVES AND ADVERBS		
POSITIVE	COMPARATIVE	SUPERLATIVE
bad (adjective)	worse	worst
badly (adverb)	worse	worst
far (distance)	farther	farthest
far (extent)	further	furthest
good (adjective)	better	best
well (adverb)	better	best
many	more	most
much	more	most

When you are unsure about how a modifier forms its degrees of comparison, check a dictionary.

See Practice 12.1C

Using Comparative and Superlative Degrees

Keep these rules in mind when you use the comparative and superlative degrees.

Use the comparative degree to compare *two* people, places, or things. Use the superlative degree to compare *three or more* people, places, or things.

Usually, you do not need to mention specific numbers when you are making a comparison. Other words in the sentence should help make the meaning clear whether you are comparing two items or three or more items.

EXAMPLES   The lifeguard felt **better** once all
swimmers were safely on the beach.

The lifeguard completed the rowing exercise
in her **best** time this week.

Pay particular attention to the modifiers you use when you are
comparing just two items. Do not use the superlative degree with
fewer than three items.

INCORRECT   Of the two teams, that one was the **best**.

CORRECT   Of the two teams, that one was **better**.

INCORRECT   His was the **fastest** of the two skateboards.

CORRECT   His was the **faster** of the two skateboards.

> Do not make **double comparisons.** Do not use both *-er* and
> *more* to form the comparative degree or both *-est* and *most* to
> form the superlative degree. Also, be sure not to use *-er*, *more*,
> and *most* with an irregular modifier.

RULE 12.1.8

INCORRECT   Laura finished the assignment the **most
fastest**.

CORRECT   Laura finished the assignment the **fastest**.

INCORRECT   The test was **more worse** than the one the
class took last month.

CORRECT   The test was **worse** than the one the class
took last month.

See Practice 12.1D

> **PRACTICE 12.1C** **Forming Comparatives and Superlatives of Irregular Adjectives and Adverbs**

Read the modifiers. Write the comparative and superlative forms of each modifier.

EXAMPLE   far (distance)

ANSWER   *farther, farthest*

1. much
2. well (adverb)
3. far (extent)
4. bad (adjective)
5. many
6. good (adjective)
7. badly (adverb)

> **PRACTICE 12.1D** **Using Comparatives and Superlatives of Irregular Adjectives and Adverbs**

Read the sentences. Then, write each sentence using the form of the modifier in parentheses.

EXAMPLE   The storm was _____ (*bad*, comparative) than predicted.

ANSWER   *The storm was worse than predicted.*

8. The school yard looks _____ than it did before Clean-up Day. (*good*, comparative)

9. He is the _____ dancer in the group. (*good*, superlative)

10. Jared scored the _____ points in last night's basketball game. (*many*, superlative)

11. My _____ friend is my dog. (*good,* superlative)

12. How much _____ is the diner? (*far*, comparative)

13. Milo spends _____ time on the phone than I do. (*much*, comparative)

14. Jamie is the _____ runner on our team. (*fast*, superlative)

15. Sienna did _____ than Cam on the midterm. (*well*, comparative)

16. You sing _____ than I do. (*badly*, comparative)

17. Is Neptune the _____ planet from the sun? (*far*, superlative)

SPEAKING APPLICATION

With a partner, talk about some of your favorite and least favorite things. Use comparative and superlative forms of any of the modifiers in Practice 12.1D.

WRITING APPLICATION

Write five sentences about an athletic competition, each containing a different irregular comparative or superlative modifier. Then, exchange papers with a partner. Your partner should identify the irregular modifiers and the positive forms from which they come.

Making Logical Comparisons

In most situations, you will have no problem forming the degrees of modifiers and using them correctly in sentences. Sometimes, however, you may find that the way you have phrased a sentence makes your comparison unclear. You will then need to think about the words you have chosen and revise your sentence, making sure that your comparison is logical.

> **When you make a comparison, be sure you are comparing things that have clear similarities.**

12.1.9 RULE

Balanced Comparisons

Most comparisons make a statement or ask a question about the way in which similar things are either alike or different.

EXAMPLE   Is the **Black Sea** **deeper** than the

Mediterranean Sea ?

(Both bodies of water have depths that can be measured and compared.)

Because the sentence compares depth to depth, the comparison is balanced. Problems can occur, however, when a sentence compares dissimilar things. For example, it would be illogical to compare the depth of one sea to the shape of another sea. Depth and shape are not similar things and cannot be compared meaningfully.

ILLOGICAL   The girls in his class are taller than her class.

(*Girls* and *class* cannot be logically compared.)

LOGICAL   The girls in his class are taller than the girls in

her class.

(Two sets of girls can be logically compared.)

> **Make sure that your sentences compare only similar items.**

12.1.10 RULE

An unbalanced comparison is usually the result of carelessness. The writer may have simply left something out. Read the following incorrect sentences carefully.

INCORRECT	**Cooking pasta** is **faster** than **rice** .
	The **crowd** on the north side of the field cheer **louder** than the **south side of the field** .

In the first sentence, cooking pasta is mistakenly compared to rice. In the second sentence, people are compared to a place. Both sentences can easily be corrected to make the comparisons balanced.

CORRECT	**Cooking pasta** is **faster** than **cooking rice** .
	The **crowd** on the north side of the field cheer **louder** than the **crowd** on the south side.

See Practice 12.1E

Other and *Else* in Comparisons
Another common error in writing comparisons is to compare something to itself.

RULE
12.1.11

> **When comparing one of a group to the rest of the group, make sure your sentence contains the word *other* or *else*.**

Adding *other* or *else* can make a comparison clear. For example, in the second sentence below, because *my school* is itself a school, it cannot logically be compared to any *school*. It must be compared to any *other school*.

PROBLEM SENTENCES	CORRECTED SENTENCES
Alia researched and presented her project before anyone.	Alia researched and presented her project before anyone else.
My school was built ten years before any school in the district.	My school was built ten years before any other school in the district.

See Practice 12.1F

PRACTICE 12.1E Making Balanced Comparisons

Read the sentences. Rewrite each sentence, correcting the unbalanced comparison.

EXAMPLE The temperature indoors is hotter than outdoors.

ANSWER *The temperature indoors is hotter than the temperature outdoors.*

1. The price of a new home is higher than a car.

2. The traffic at the airport is worse than the highway.

3. My science teacher's tests are harder than my English teacher.

4. The air in the city is more polluted than the country.

5. The recipe for this soup is easier to follow than this stew.

6. This year's festival was better attended than last year.

7. The magazine's readership is much larger than the newspaper.

8. Abby's hair is not as long as Maria.

9. The number of homes on Elm Street is greater than Maple Street.

10. The cold water from the tap in the kitchen is cleaner than the bathroom.

PRACTICE 12.1F Using *Other* and *Else* to Make Logical Comparisons

Read the sentences. Rewrite each sentence, adding *other* or *else* to make the comparisons logical.

EXAMPLE My sister dances better than anyone in the family.

ANSWER *My sister dances better than anyone else in the family.*

11. My dad cooks better than anyone in the family.

12. I enjoy football more than any sport.

13. News reporter Aaron Dovetree has worked here longer than anyone.

14. I like sweet potatoes better than any vegetable.

15. I arrived at the party before anyone.

16. Tom plays basketball better than anyone on the team.

17. This tree is taller than any tree in the park.

18. The president gets more press coverage than any politician.

19. Our social studies teacher gives harder tests than anyone on the teaching staff.

20. I find jazz more interesting than any music.

SPEAKING APPLICATION

With a partner, take turns making comparisons about different nations and their customs. Your partner should listen to the comparisons and make sure they are balanced and logical.

WRITING APPLICATION

Write four sentences describing a talented person you know. Make logical comparisons that use *other* and *else* correctly. Use *other* in two of the comparisons; use *else* in the other two.

12.2 Troublesome Adjectives and Adverbs

The common adjectives and adverbs listed below often cause problems in both speaking and writing.

(1) bad and badly *Bad* is an adjective. Use it after linking verbs, such as *are, appear, feel, look,* and *sound. Badly* is an adverb. Use it after action verbs, such as *act, behave, do,* and *perform.*

INCORRECT	Sandy felt **badly** for the losing team.
CORRECT	Sandy felt **bad** for the losing team.

INCORRECT	My car performed **bad** on the road test.
CORRECT	My car performed **badly** on the road test.

(2) good and well *Good* is an adjective. *Well* can be either an adjective or an adverb, depending on its meaning. A common mistake is the use of *good* after an action verb. Use the adverb *well* instead.

INCORRECT	My class danced **good** last evening.
	The report looks **well**.

CORRECT	My class danced **well** last evening.
	The report looks **good**.

As adjectives, *good* and *well* have slightly different meanings, which are often confused. *Well* usually refers simply to health.

EXAMPLES	Maria felt **good** after scoring the only goal.
	The campfire smells **good**.
	My grandmother does not feel **well**.

(3) *fewer and less* Use the adjective *fewer* to answer the question, "How many?" Use the adjective *less* to answer the question, "How much?"

HOW MANY	**fewer** pencils	**fewer** students
HOW MUCH	**less** work	**less** time

EL7

(4) *just* When used as an adverb, *just* often means "no more than." When *just* has this meaning, place it right before the word it logically modifies.

INCORRECT	Does she **just** want to try on **one dress**?
CORRECT	Does she want to try on **just** **one dress**?

(5) *only* The position of *only* in a sentence sometimes affects the sentence's entire meaning. Consider the meaning of these sentences.

EXAMPLES   **Only** Adam played the guitar.
(Nobody else played the guitar.)

Adam **only** played the guitar.
(Adam did nothing else with the guitar.)

Adam played **only** the guitar.
(Adam played the guitar and no other instrument.)

Mistakes involving *only* usually occur when its placement in a sentence makes the meaning unclear.

UNCLEAR	**Only** follow the rules from the coach.
BETTER	Follow the rules **only** from the coach.
	(not from anyone else)

See Practice 12.2A
See Practice 12.2B

Follow **only** the rules from the coach.
(nothing but the rules)

 **PRACTICE 12.2A** Using *Bad* and *Badly,* *Good* and *Well*

Read the sentences. Write the word in parentheses that correctly completes each sentence.

EXAMPLE   Emilia writes (good, well).

ANSWER   *well*

1. This chili tastes very (good, well).
2. I feel very (bad, badly) about what happened.
3. I hope to do (good, well) in the contest.
4. Oscar plays basketball (bad, badly).
5. The dancer moves (good, well) even when she is not dancing.
6. The music sounds (good, well).
7. She performed (bad, badly) on the test.
8. The new perfume smells really (good, well).
9. If you eat (bad, badly), your health may be affected.
10. I think the milk turned (bad, badly).

PRACTICE 12.2B Revising for Troublesome Modifiers

Read the sentences. Rewrite the sentences that contain errors in the use of modifiers. If a sentence has no error, write *correct*.

EXAMPLE   That restaurant only serves brunch on weekends.

ANSWER   *That restaurant serves brunch only on weekends.*

11. There were less people at the mall an hour ago.
12. Amelia paints landscapes really well.
13. Most students only attend school on weekdays.
14. Tommy behaves good for a two-year-old child.
15. That polluted lake smells really badly.
16. We should hurry or we'll have less time to study.
17. Nydia only bought that new coat yesterday.
18. Dad had fewer days off this year.
19. I went to the doctor because I did not feel well.
20. How bad did you do in the hockey tryouts?

SPEAKING APPLICATION

Use sentence 3 as a model, and tell a partner two things that you hope to do. Your partner should make sure you've used the modifiers correctly.

WRITING APPLICATION

Write seven sentences, each using a different one of these modifiers: *bad, badly, good, well, fewer, less,* and *only.* Then, exchange papers with a partner. Your partner should make sure you have used the modifiers correctly.

PRACTICE 1 ▷ Identifying Verb Tenses

Read the sentences. For each sentence, write whether the verb tense is *present, past, future, present perfect, past perfect,* or *future perfect.* Also indicate if the verb is *progressive.*

1. The band is practicing a new march.
2. Mr. Lisi has taught at our school for 10 years.
3. In June, Miriam will have been a postal worker for twenty years.
4. That wholesaler supplies all the restaurants in the area.
5. The public relations department will eventually respond to the complaint.
6. My mother attended a state university.
7. Susanna has been watching that television series for several years.
8. No team from our high school had ever won the state championships before.
9. A group of friends were traveling together.
10. The congressional committee hearing will be airing on television.

PRACTICE 2 ▷ Revising to Use Active Voice

Read the sentences. Then, rewrite each passive voice sentence so that it is in active voice. If a sentence is already in active voice, write *active*.

1. The patient was examined by the doctor.
2. That opera was composed by Giuseppe Verdi.
3. A generous donation to the hospital was made by Mrs. O'Connor.
4. The finest knitwear is designed by her company.
5. The cruise ship is heading for Key West.

PRACTICE 3 ▷ Using Verbs Correctly

Read the sentences. Then, rewrite the sentences to correct any incorrect verb forms. If a sentence has no errors, write *correct*.

1. Yesterday Mom lay the new quilt on the old couch.
2. We have never went to Alabama.
3. The head librarian has asked the town board for more funding for our local library.
4. Sit your package beside the door.
5. At the photo studio yesterday, the photographer says to me, "Smile for the camera."
6. Felicia finally done her science project.
7. The fans have chose a new team mascot for the Cougars.
8. I seen you in the line for concert tickets.
9. Somebody swum across the river yesterday.
10. A talented new performer has arose on the local music scene.

PRACTICE 4 ▷ Identifying Pronoun Cases and Uses

Read the sentences. Write whether each underlined pronoun is in the *nominative, objective,* or *possessive* case. Then, write whether it is used as a *subject,* a *predicate pronoun,* a *direct object,* an *indirect object,* or the *object of a preposition.*

1. I spoke with <u>her</u> before class.
2. The waiter brought <u>us</u> our order.
3. <u>Yours</u> is the silliest-looking hat I have ever seen.
4. Dad always helps <u>me</u> with my math homework.
5. The best singers in our family are Mom and <u>I</u>.

Continued on next page ▶

Cumulative Review   Chapters 9–12

PRACTICE 5 **Using Pronouns Correctly**

Read the sentences. Then, rewrite the sentences to correct any incorrect pronouns. If a sentence has no errors, write *correct*.

1. I hope the alligator has had it's dinner.
2. Mr. Newman and her traded news.
3. The oldest students in the class are Ray and me.
4. The neighbor gave my sister and I a lift.
5. Whom did you call for more information?
6. Friendship still exists between Shirley and he.
7. Lydia is the one who the teacher praised most.
8. The shed is our's, but the lawn mower is their's.
9. Where did you see Caroline and he?
10. I do not know whom their spokesperson is.

PRACTICE 6 **Revising for Subject–Verb Agreement**

Read the sentences. Then, rewrite the sentences to correct any errors in subject–verb agreement. If a sentence has no errors, write *correct*.

1. Neither Ruby nor I type very quickly.
2. A deck of cards sit on the card table.
3. Each of the spices taste distinctive.
4. The flock flies every which way.
5. None of the answers are correct.
6. Patrick and Maura enjoy Irish step dancing.
7. Bacon and eggs are my favorite breakfast.
8. The coach or his players yells at the umpire.
9. Are the singer or the composer very famous?
10. The team has won another game.

PRACTICE 7 **Revising for Pronoun–Antecedent Agreement**

Read the sentences. Then, rewrite the sentences to correct any errors in pronoun–antecedent agreement. If a sentence has no errors, write *correct*.

1. Each of the girls had their hair in pigtails.
2. They do a dance where you jump in the air.
3. None of the winners received his or her prize.
4. Either the snake or the lizard lost its skin.
5. Everyone kept their boots clean.
6. Several of the factories had closed its doors.
7. Becky and Ella wore braces on her teeth.
8. Neither Gary nor Frank wore their boots.
9. Some of the detectives solved his or her cases.
10. Did everybody have his or her homework?

PRACTICE 8 **Using Modifiers Correctly**

Read the sentences. Then, rewrite the sentences to correct any errors involving modifiers. If a sentence has no errors, write *correct*.

1. Andrea did good at the swim meet.
2. I will ask nothing farther of you.
3. He feels more well but will still visit the doctor.
4. In winter, less fans attend his concerts.
5. Of all the snowstorms, this is the baddest.
6. The ballet company only performs on Fridays.
7. Brian is taller than I am.
8. The music sounds really well.
9. Sheepdogs are more loyal than any dog.
10. Is there a singer more good than she is?

PUNCTUATION

Using punctuation correctly will help you to craft clear, convincing sentences.

WRITE GUY *Jeff Anderson, M.Ed.*

CHAPTER 13

WHAT DO YOU NOTICE?

Note the punctuation as you zoom in on these sentences from the story "Chicoria," retold in English by Rudolfo A. Anaya and adapted in Spanish by José Griego y Maestas.

MENTOR TEXT

> When the maids began to dish up the plates of food, Chicoria turned to one of the servers and said, "Ah, my friends, it looks like they are going to feed us well tonight!"

Now, ask yourself the following questions:

- How are the words that Chicoria speaks set off in this sentence?
- Why do you think the author used an exclamation mark at the end of Chicoria's spoken words?

The comma after *said* signals the beginning of Chicoria's spoken words, and the quotation marks indicate the start and finish of his spoken words. The author used an exclamation mark to show that Chicoria was excited about the food.

Grammar for Writers Whether you are writing fiction or nonfiction, including quotations is a fantastic way to add interest. Using proper punctuation for quotations makes them understandable to readers.

Do you think my paper deserves an A?

There's no question about it!

13.1 End Marks

End marks signal the end or conclusion of a sentence, word, or phrase. There are three end marks: the **period (.)**, the **question mark (?)**, and the **exclamation mark (!)**.

Using Periods

A **period** indicates the end of a sentence or an abbreviation.

13.1.1

> **Use a period to end a declarative sentence—a statement of fact or opinion.**

DECLARATIVE SENTENCE This is a beautiful weekend.

13.1.2

> **Use a period to end most imperative sentences—sentences that give directions or commands.**

IMPERATIVE SENTENCE Finish practicing the piano.

13.1.3

> **Use a period to end a sentence that contains an indirect question.**

An **indirect question** restates a question in a declarative sentence. It does not give the speaker's exact words.

INDIRECT QUESTION Janie asked me if I liked the show.

13.1.4

> **Use a period after most abbreviations and initials.**

ABBREVIATIONS Blvd. Jr. Gov. in. Dr.

INITIALS Franklin D. Roosevelt J. K. Rowling

Note: The abbreviation for *inch, in.,* is the only measurement abbreviation that uses a period after it.

When a sentence ends with an abbreviation that uses a period, do not put a second period at the end.

EXAMPLE   Our speaker today is James Young Jr.

> Do not use periods with **acronyms**, words formed with the first or first few letters of a series of words.

EXAMPLES   UN   United Nations

NASA   National Aeronautics and Space
Administration

Using Question Marks

A **question mark** follows a word, phrase, or sentence that asks a question.

> Use a question mark after an **interrogative sentence**—one that asks a direct question.

INTERROGATIVE   Do turtles lay eggs in water?
SENTENCES

What time are you picking me up?

Sometimes a single word or brief phrase is used to ask a direct question. This type of question is punctuated as though it were a complete sentence because the words that are left out are easily understood.

> Use a question mark after a word or phrase that asks a question.

EXAMPLES   I would like to go along with you. When?

See Practice 13.1A

I'll meet you for dinner. How about that?

Using Exclamation Marks

Use an **exclamation mark** to end a word, phrase, or sentence that shows strong emotion.

EXAMPLES

Look at that classic car!

I will not!

Use an exclamation mark after an **imperative** sentence that gives a forceful or urgent command.

IMPERATIVE SENTENCE

Don't burn the eggs!

Hurry up!

While imperative sentences containing forceful commands often end with an exclamation mark, mild imperatives should end with a period.

MILD IMPERATIVES

Please don't get up.

Put the salad in the refrigerator.

Use an exclamation mark after an **interjection** that expresses strong emotion.

INTERJECTIONS

Oh! You ruined the surprise.

Stop! You are going too fast!

Exclamation marks should not be used too often. Overusing them reduces their emotional effect and makes writing less effective.

See Practice 13.1B

 **PRACTICE 13.1A** **Using Question Marks and Periods**

Read the sentences. Rewrite each sentence, adding missing question marks and periods.

EXAMPLE   Mom asked if Dr Chavez was available

ANSWER   *Mom asked if Dr. Chavez was available.*

1. Who invented sails for ships
2. Look for the information in an encyclopedia
3. Mrs Young asked whether I had ever been to Portland
4. How many stars are there in a galaxy
5. Send this form to Mr D H Jackson at the mayor's office
6. Is Gov Lopez the woman in the photo
7. Which planet is farthest from the sun
8. Teresa wondered what was wrong with her skateboard
9. The ocean depths hold many fascinating secrets
10. Has the dog really run away Why

PRACTICE 13.1B **Using Exclamation Marks and Periods**

Read the sentences. Rewrite each sentence, adding missing exclamation marks and periods.

EXAMPLE   Wow What an exciting adventure that was

ANSWER   *Wow! What an exciting adventure that was!*

11. How courageous those mountain climbers are
12. Watch out for that car
13. Please take your seats
14. They'll be here any minute Hurry
15. What a delicious dinner that was
16. Shoot the ball now
17. Ugh That trash smells horrible
18. Whew I'm glad we made it home
19. Tell me the story again
20. What a beautiful morning this is

SPEAKING APPLICATION

Say the following sample sentence three times out loud to your partner, using the different inflections that the three different end marks would give it. Have your partner tell what end mark you are indicating with your voice.
We're not finished yet

WRITING APPLICATION

Write three sentences using at least one period, one question mark, and one exclamation mark correctly.

13.2 Commas

End marks signal a full stop. **Commas** signal a brief pause. A comma may be used to separate elements in a sentence or to set off part of a sentence. Include a comma in your writing when you want your reader to group information in your sentence.

Using Commas in Compound Sentences

A **compound sentence** consists of two or more main or independent clauses that are joined by a coordinating conjunction, such as *and, but, for, nor, or, so,* or *yet.*

RULE 13.2.1

> **Use a comma before the conjunction to separate two main or independent clauses in a compound sentence.**

COMPOUND SENTENCE

My puppy has learned to stay in the yard**,** but I always use his leash when we go for a walk.

Use a comma before a conjunction only when there are complete sentences on both sides of the conjunction. If the conjunction joins single words, phrases, or subordinate clauses, do not use a comma.

SINGLE WORDS   Soccer and lacrosse are growing in popularity.

PHRASES   Tony likes both soccer and football.

SUBORDINATE CLAUSES   Look for someone who can follow directions but also likes to try new things.

In some compound sentences, the main or independent clauses are very brief, and the meaning is clear. When this occurs, the comma before the conjunction may be omitted.

EXAMPLE   Gil was here but he left quickly.

See Practice 13.2A

Avoiding Comma Splices

A **comma splice** occurs when two or more sentences have been joined with only a comma between them.

> Avoid **comma splices** by making sure all of your ideas are properly linked.

INCORRECT   The players arrived in the morning **,** they gathered on the field.

CORRECT   The players arrived in the morning **.** They gathered on the field.

Using Commas in a Series

Sometimes, a sentence lists a number of single words or groups of words. When three or more of these items are listed, the list is called a **series.** Separate the items in a series with commas.

> Use commas to separate three or more words, phrases, or clauses in a **series.**

A comma follows each of the items except the last one in a series. The conjunction *and* or *or* is added after the last comma.

SERIES OF WORDS   A gorilla's diet includes roots **,** stems **,** leaves **,** and fruit.

SERIES OF PHRASES   Cleaning my room included sweeping the floor **,** making the bed **,** and hanging up the clothes.

There are two exceptions to this rule. If each item except the last one in a series is followed by a conjunction, do not use commas. Also, do not use a comma to separate groups of words that are considered to be one item.

EXAMPLES   We didn't see any birds or insects or spiders.

The sandwich choices are peanut butter and jelly **,** ham and cheese **,** or turkey and cheese.

See Practice 13.2B

Using Commas Between Adjectives

Sometimes, two or more adjectives are placed before the noun they describe.

RULE 13.2.4

Use commas to separate adjectives of equal rank.

There are two ways to tell whether adjectives in a sentence are of equal rank:

- If the word *and* can be placed between the adjectives without changing the meaning, the adjectives are of equal rank.

- If the order of the adjectives can be changed, they are of equal rank.

EXAMPLE

She left detailed**,** precise instructions for me.
(*Detailed and precise instructions* does not change the sentence's meaning. *Precise, detailed instructions* also does not change the meaning.)

RULE 13.2.5

Do not use commas to separate adjectives that must appear in a specific order.

Do not use a comma if adding *and* or changing the order of the adjectives would result in a sentence that makes no sense.

INCORRECT   An experienced and desert guide led our tour.

INCORRECT   A desert-experienced guide led our tour.

CORRECT   An experienced desert guide led our tour.

RULE 13.2.6

Do not use a comma to separate the last adjective in a series from the noun it modifies.

INCORRECT   A young**,** efficient**,** kind**,** nurse took care of her.

CORRECT   A young**,** efficient**,** kind nurse took care of her.

See Practice 13.2C
See Practice 13.2D

PRACTICE 13.2A **Using Commas in Compound Sentences**

Read the sentences. Rewrite each sentence, adding commas where they are needed.

EXAMPLE   The fans were getting restless for the kickoff was delayed.

ANSWER   *The fans were getting restless, for the kickoff was delayed.*

1. The courses are organized and the instructors are excellent.

2. It was January yet the days were mild.

3. I know Hector is a good musician but do you think he is ready for the symphony?

4. We stayed an extra day in Phoenix for there were many more sites to see.

5. Will Judy be your partner for the science project or are you paired with someone else?

6. Mr. Garcia loves to entertain so he has a barbecue every weekend in the summer.

7. The runner was exhausted yet he was determined to finish the marathon.

8. The bathroom has been remodeled and it now looks modern and has more storage space.

9. The sign said the store was open until 8:00 P.M. but the doors were locked.

10. Snow fell all night and by morning it had blanketed the hills.

PRACTICE 13.2B **Using Commas in a Series**

Read the sentences. Rewrite each sentence, adding commas as needed.

EXAMPLE   Jason wrote the script played the main role and directed the other actors.

ANSWER   *Jason wrote the script, played the main role, and directed the other actors.*

11. A second language can be useful in business for travel or in almost any profession.

12. We play soccer at school in the park or in the backyard.

13. Then the boat slowed down changed course and went in a different direction.

14. Staying alert being calm and removing distractions will make you a better driver.

15. We need a screwdriver a pair of pliers and a hammer and nails for this project.

16. Maine New Hampshire Vermont and Massachusetts are famous for fall foliage.

17. The trail starts in the foothills winds up the mountain and stretches along the crest.

18. On the nature hike, Chandra saw birds snakes wildflowers and various insects.

19. The television the CD player and the refrigerator are all new.

20. The raccoon lumbered down the sidewalk across the road and into a drainage opening.

SPEAKING APPLICATION

Read the following compound sentence to your partner without the comma. Then, add the comma by pausing, and have your partner tell how the sentence sounds different. *They wanted to visit the museum but it was closed.*

WRITING APPLICATION

Write three sentences using various types of items in series. Use commas correctly.

PRACTICE 13.2C Using Commas Between Adjectives

Read the sentences. Rewrite the sentences, adding commas where necessary. If no comma is needed, write *correct*.

EXAMPLE   On the porch was a large ornate planter with colorful flowers.

ANSWER   *On the porch was a large, ornate planter with colorful flowers.*

1. My friend Serena is a thoughtful kind and reliable person.

2. The car already has several minor problems.

3. Four small boys were playing in the sandbox.

4. We heard a low steady hum coming from the cellar.

5. The noisy slow-moving train made its way up the hill.

6. Suddenly, a loud ghastly shriek pierced the night air.

7. Dad bought a beautiful stained-glass lamp for the living room.

8. She stated her demands in a strong forceful voice.

9. Those solid gold bracelets are not for sale.

10. On a damp and chilly morning, we started our journey.

PRACTICE 13.2D Proofreading Sentences for Commas

Read the sentences. Rewrite each sentence, adding commas where they are needed.

EXAMPLE   The sheep moved on the road in a tight shifting mass.

ANSWER   *The sheep moved on the road in a tight, shifting mass.*

11. I like reading suspenseful well-written mystery novels.

12. What is this coarse sturdy fabric called?

13. I'd like to exchange this dirty torn shirt for one that is new and crisp and clean.

14. The hikers carried simple nutritious snacks and fresh drinking water.

15. To Cassandra, golf is a relaxing challenging pastime.

16. Those birds have made a strong protective nest in which to raise their babies.

17. The rocks at the bottom of the stream were covered with a brown slimy substance.

18. We adopted the dog because he seemed playful smart and affectionate.

19. Terri is a genuine caring and kind girl.

20. A mysterious stranger appeared in the tiny quiet village.

SPEAKING APPLICATION

Say the following two sentences to a partner. Have your partner tell which sentence needs a comma and why.
They noticed faint, eerie music coming from the other room.
The soft jazz music was very soothing.

WRITING APPLICATION

Write two sentences with adjectives that require commas and two with adjectives that do not need commas.

Using Commas After Introductory Words, Phrases, and Clauses

When a sentence begins with an introductory word, phrase, or other structures, that word or phrase is usually separated from the rest of the sentence by a comma.

> **Use a comma after most introductory words, phrases, or dependent clauses.**

13.2.7 RULE

KINDS OF INTRODUCTORY MATERIAL	
Introductory Word	Hey, listen to the great idea I have for our final project.
	Mom, would you please pass me the bread and butter?
	Well, I have never seen anything like that.
	Ariel, where are we going?
Introductory Phrase	To save money, we are packing our lunch instead of eating out.
	After practicing for two hours, the team was glad to take a long break.
	In the center of the city, there are many art galleries.
	To visit China, you will need a passport.
Introductory Adverbial Clause	Although we had missed the introduction, we were able to see the rest of the ceremony.
	When Dominic got on the bus, all of the seats were already taken.
	When Devin arrived, they needed more room at the table.

When a prepositional phrase of only two words begins a sentence, a comma is not absolutely necessary.

EXAMPLES At night we heard the owls hoot.

In August we go to the beach.

For hours she worked at the computer.

See Practice 13.2E

Using Commas With Parenthetical Expressions

A **parenthetical expression** is a word or phrase that is not essential to the meaning of the sentence. These words or phrases generally add extra information to the basic sentence.

> Use commas to set off **parenthetical expressions** from the rest of the sentence.

A parenthetical expression in the middle of a sentence needs two commas. A parenthetical expression at the end of a sentence needs only one.

KINDS OF PARENTHETICAL EXPRESSIONS	
Names of People Being Addressed	Sit down, Brock, while I explain my reasons. Please come straight home, Chung.
Certain Adverbs	The beach, therefore, is easily accessible. His plan will not work, however.
Common Expressions	I understand your actions, of course. They are not old enough to go alone, in my opinion.
Contrasting Expressions	That problem is yours, not mine. These letters, not those, are ready to be mailed.

See Practice 13.2F
See Practice 13.2G

Using Commas With Nonessential Expressions

To determine when a phrase or clause should be set off with commas, decide whether the phrase or clause is **essential** or **nonessential** to the meaning of the sentence. Nonessential expressions can be left out without changing the meaning of the sentence.

> Use commas to set off **nonessential** expressions from the main clause. Do not set off **essential** material with commas.

Appositives and Appositive Phrases

Appositives are often set off with commas, but only when their meaning is not essential to the sentence. In the first example below, the appositive *the Hurricanes* is not set off with commas because it clarifies which team is being discussed.

ESSENTIAL   The winning team the Hurricanes prepared for the parade.

NONESSENTIAL   The Hurricanes **,** the winning team **,** prepared for the parade.

Participial Phrases

Like appositives, participial phrases are set off with commas when their meaning is nonessential. In the first example below, *standing in the room* is essential because it tells which man is the teacher.

ESSENTIAL   The man standing in the room is my teacher.

NONESSENTIAL   My teacher **,** standing in the room **,** asked us to be seated.

Adjectival Clauses

Adjectival clauses, too, are set off with commas only if they are nonessential. In the second example below, *which likes to play ball* is nonessential because it adds information about Rocket. The main clause in the sentence is about Bea and her sister being thrilled, not about what Rocket can do.

ESSENTIAL   Bea and her sister wanted a dog that could play ball with them.

NONESSENTIAL   Bea and her sister are thrilled with Rocket **,** their new dog, which likes to play ball.

See Practice 13.2H

Using Commas After Introductory Words, Phrases, or Clauses

Read the sentences. Rewrite each sentence, adding the comma needed after the introductory word, phrase, or dependent adverbial clause.

EXAMPLE   As visitors entered the museum they saw a huge dinosaur replica.

ANSWER   *As visitors entered the museum, they saw a huge dinosaur replica.*

1. Why that island is the most beautiful place I've ever seen.

2. Reading about ancient Rome I learned some surprising facts.

3. Yes there is an original sculpture in the hall.

4. When the play was over we all met out front.

5. To preserve the environment humans will have to be diligent.

6. Before the walls can be painted they will need to be cleaned and primed.

7. In every room of the house colorful tapestries decorated the walls.

8. Hey you're blocking my view of the screen.

9. At small booths lining the midway vendors were selling their crafts.

10. Refreshed by our cold beverages we resumed the game.

Proofreading a Passage for Commas

Read the paragraphs. Rewrite the paragraphs, adding commas where they are needed.

EXAMPLE   When we visited New Mexico Aunt Lucy took us to a Native American pueblo.

ANSWER   *When we visited New Mexico, Aunt Lucy took us to a Native American pueblo.*

Driving to Acoma Sky City we saw beautiful scenery and even some wildlife. The pueblo sits on the top of a 367-foot sandstone mesa. This site was chosen because it provided a natural defense against enemies. Why can you imagine how difficult it would be to attack a village that was that high up?

During the one-hour walking tour a tribal member told us stories about the history of Acoma. I was amazed to learn the village was built around 1150 A.D. According to the guide it has been continuously inhabited the entire time. To continue the pueblo life tribal members must stay true to their culture. I think I will remember what I learned on the tour because I was able to see that culture.

SPEAKING APPLICATION

Read the following sentences to a partner. Discuss where to add the comma.
At the fork in the road we turned to the right.
No that's not what I meant.

WRITING APPLICATION

Write one sentence with an introductory word, one with an introductory phrase, and one with an introductory clause. Use commas correctly in your sentences.

PRACTICE 13.2G Using Commas With Parenthetical Expressions

Read the sentences. Rewrite each sentence, adding commas as needed to set off parenthetical expressions.

EXAMPLE   He decided therefore to enter the contest.

ANSWER   *He decided, therefore, to enter the contest.*

1. Take the lid off Carmen or the water will boil over.

2. She thought nevertheless that the job would be hers.

3. The fire we believe was a result of bad wiring.

4. The older daughter not the younger one is getting married.

5. Everyone was in good spirits of course.

6. The flight attendant not the pilot greeted the passengers.

7. Gina could you please hand me that paintbrush?

8. The wait at the bus stop however was extremely long.

9. Have you ever gone snowboarding Jared?

10. The debate therefore has been postponed.

PRACTICE 13.2H Using Commas With Nonessential Expressions

Read the sentences. Rewrite the sentences, adding commas where needed. If a sentence is punctuated correctly, write *correct.*

EXAMPLE   The first contestant a juggler did not impress the judges.

ANSWER   *The first contestant, a juggler, did not impress the judges.*

11. Charles Dickens a famous British author wrote *A Tale of Two Cities.*

12. The store was hiring only people who had experience.

13. The famous actor Tom Hanks was in that film.

14. This sweater a birthday gift is warm but somewhat scratchy.

15. The song "Neon Moon" was very popular.

16. This stopwatch which was inexpensive is good for timing sprints.

17. This is a painting of George Washington crossing the Delaware River.

18. The woman standing in the back of the room is the high school principal.

19. We took the subway which is pretty fast to the downtown area.

20. The little girl grinning broadly reached out for the balloon.

SPEAKING APPLICATION

Briefly tell a partner about public transportation in your town. Your partner should listen for and name two parenthetical expressions.

WRITING APPLICATION

Write two sentences, one with a nonessential expression and one with an essential phrase or clause. Use commas correctly with the nonessential expression.

Using Commas With Dates and Geographical Names

Dates usually have several parts, including months, days, and years. Commas prevent dates from being unclear.

> **When a date is made up of three parts, use a comma after each item, except in the case of a month followed by a day.**

Notice in the examples that commas are not used to set off a month followed by a numeral standing for a day. Commas are used when both the month and the date are used as an appositive to rename a day of the week.

EXAMPLES   On June 12, 2009, I celebrated my thirteenth birthday with my family.

Monday, October 3, is the date our class is going on a field trip to the history museum.

When a date contains only a month and a year, commas are unnecessary.

EXAMPLES   She will receive her award in May 2015.

Most of the storms we experienced in April 2007 caused severe flooding.

> **When a geographical name is made up of a city and a state, use a comma after each item except when the state ends a sentence.**

EXAMPLES   They lived in Albany, New York, for several years and then moved to Santa Fe, New Mexico.

My family went to San Francisco, California, to visit our many relatives in the area.

See Practice 13.2I

Using Commas in Numbers

Numbers of one hundred or less and numbers made up of two words (for example, *three thousand*) are generally spelled out in words. Other large numbers (for example, 8,463) are written in numerals. Commas make large numbers easier to read.

> **With large numbers of more than three digits, count from the right and add a comma to the left of every third digit to separate it from every fourth digit.**

13.2.12 RULE

EXAMPLES

3,056 miles

782,956 applicants

a population of 1,256,364

> **Use commas with three or more numbers written in a series.**

13.2.13 RULE

EXAMPLES

My book is missing pages 112, 113, and 114.

I think player number 8, 9, or 12 scored the goal.

> **Do not use a comma with ZIP Codes, telephone numbers, page numbers, years, serial numbers, or house numbers.**

13.2.14 RULE

ZIP CODE   02114

TELEPHONE NUMBER   (617) 723-0987

PAGE NUMBER   on page 4529

YEAR   the year 2006

SERIAL NUMBER   504 33 0923

See Practice 13.2J   HOUSE NUMBER   1579 Brookdale Road

PRACTICE 13.2I Using Commas in Dates and Geographical Names

Read the sentences. Rewrite each sentence, adding commas where they are needed.

EXAMPLE   He will arrive in San Juan Puerto Rico on Tuesday February 17.

ANSWER   *He will arrive in San Juan, Puerto Rico, on Tuesday, February 17.*

1. The new furniture was delivered on Friday March 13 at noon.

2. The family drove to San Francisco California and then to Reno Nevada.

3. The couple was married on Saturday June 25 in Richmond Virginia.

4. The application must be sent to Albuquerque New Mexico by May 21 2010.

5. March 15 is the day we moved to Austin Texas.

6. The Declaration of Independence was approved by Congress on July 4 1776.

7. My mother remembers the May 18 1980 eruption of Mount St. Helens.

8. In May 2007 they moved from Portland Oregon to York Pennsylvania.

9. Andrew's ancestors come from Yorkshire England.

10. The reception is scheduled for Saturday May 5.

PRACTICE 13.2J Using Commas in Numbers

Rewrite each number, adding commas where needed. If no commas are needed, write *correct*.

EXAMPLE   123854 square miles

ANSWER   *123,854*

11. 1500 pages

12. 67000 troops

13. 4876 audience members

14. page 1122

15. a population of 1540967

16. 3000 homes

17. a distance of 13809 miles

18. 1905 Jones Street

19. 31989 students

20. 11277 feet

WRITING APPLICATION

Write four sentences that include the following: a date that requires commas, a date that does *not* require commas, a number that requires commas, and a number that does *not* require commas.

WRITING APPLICATION

Write a brief announcement about an event in your community or at your school. Include at least one date, one geographical name, and one number with at least four digits. Use commas correctly.

Using Commas With Addresses and in Letters

Commas are also used in addresses, salutations of friendly letters, and closings of friendly or business letters.

> **Use a comma after each item in an address made up of two or more parts.**

RULE 13.2.15

In the following example, commas are placed after the name, street, and city. There is no comma between the state and the ZIP Code.

EXAMPLE   Please write to Manuela Rosa, 13 Irving Road, Chicago, Illinois 60613.

Fewer commas are needed when an address is written in a letter or on an envelope.

EXAMPLE   Joan Walsh
119 Hastings Boulevard
Oklahoma City, Oklahoma 73146

> **Use a comma after the salutation in a personal letter and after the closing in all letters.**

RULE 13.2.16

See Practice 13.2K
See Practice 13.2L

SALUTATION   Dear Aunt Adda,   CLOSING   Best wishes,

Using Commas With Direct Quotations

Commas are also used to separate **direct quotations** from other phrases in a sentence.

> **Use commas to set off a direct quotation from the rest of a sentence.**

RULE 13.2.17

EXAMPLES   Ted said, "Let's work on our poster now."

"Maybe later, " replied Seth, "I have to go to my dentist now."

PRACTICE 13.2K ▶ Using Commas in Addresses and Letters

Read the items. Rewrite each item, adding commas where needed. If no commas are needed, write *correct*.

EXAMPLE   Max Jones
            515 Poplar Street
            New Haven CT 06501

ANSWER   *Max Jones*
            515 Poplar Street
            New Haven, CT 06501

1. Dear Aunt Teresa

2. 9410 Bryce Avenue

3. I am writing to my friend Sam Meyer 609 Anderson Avenue Austin Texas 78710.

4. Sincerely yours

5. 84 Mimosa Terrace

6. My dearest Stephanie

7. Fondest regards

8. Shawn Wheton
   102 Bear Avenue
   Hanover PA 17331

9. 902 Fairbanks Lane

10. Kate's address is 2121 Green Spring Road Baltimore Maryland 21201.

PRACTICE 13.2L ▶ Revising a Letter by Adding Commas

Read the letter. Rewrite the letter, adding commas where necessary.

EXAMPLE   The letter was mailed on Tuesday June 2.

ANSWER   *The letter was mailed on Tuesday, June 2.*

Tamesa Glen
1470 Mountain Road
Chapel Hill, NC 27514

June 2 2010

Dear Tamesa

It was good to get your last letter, and I'm glad to hear you are making some new friends in Chapel Hill North Carolina.

All is well with me. I am busy getting ready for our family vacation to New England. We'll be staying in Boston Massachusetts for three nights and in Burlington Vermont for four nights. I'm looking forward to spending time outdoors in Vermont, and I can't wait to see all the old buildings.

I hope you will be able to visit later this summer. How does the week of August 2 through August 8 sound to you?

Your friend

Keiko

WRITING APPLICATION

Use items 3 and 8 as models, and write an address in a sentence and an address for an envelope.

WRITING APPLICATION

Write a brief letter to a friend or relative who lives in a different town. Use commas correctly.

13.3 Semicolons and Colons

The **semicolon (;)** joins related **independent clauses** and signals a longer pause than a comma. The **colon (:)** is used to introduce lists of items and in other special situations.

Using Semicolons to Join Independent Clauses

Sometimes two **independent clauses** are so closely connected in meaning that they make up a single sentence, rather than two separate sentences.

> Use a **semicolon** to join related **independent clauses** that are not joined by the conjunctions *and, or, nor, for, but, so,* or *yet.*

13.3.1 RULE

INDEPENDENT CLAUSES	The winding river has many hazards.
	It is full of snakes and alligators.
CLAUSES JOINED BY SEMICOLONS	The winding river has many hazards ; it is full of snakes and alligators.

A semicolon should be used only when there is a close relationship between the two independent clauses. If the clauses are not very closely related, they should be written as separate sentences with a period or another end mark to separate them or joined with a coordinaring conjunction.

Note that when a sentence contains three or more related independent clauses, they may still be separated with semicolons.

EXAMPLES	We packed our bags ; we packed the car ; we're ready to go on our vacation.
	My dog won first prize in the show ; Larry's dog won second prize ; Noah's dog did not win a prize.

Using Semicolons to Join Clauses Separated by Conjunctive
Adverbs or Transitional Expressions
Semicolons help writers show how their ideas connect.

RULE 13.3.2

> Use a semicolon to join independent clauses separated by
> either a **conjunctive adverb** or a **transitional expression.**

CONJUNCTIVE ADVERBS	*also, besides, consequently, first, furthermore, however, indeed, instead, moreover, nevertheless, otherwise, second, then, therefore, thus*
TRANSITIONAL EXPRESSIONS	*as a result, at this time, for instance, in fact, on the other hand, that is*
EXAMPLE	He arrived late at the train station that morning **; as a result ,** he missed the beginning of the concert.

Remember to place a comma after the conjunctive adverb or
transitional expression. The comma sets off the conjunctive
adverb or transitional expression, which acts as an introductory
expression to the second clause.

Using Semicolons to Avoid Confusion

Sometimes, to avoid confusion, semicolons are used to separate
items in a series.

RULE 13.3.3

> Consider the use of semicolons to avoid confusion when items
> in a series already contain commas.

Place a semicolon after all but the last complete item in a series.

EXAMPLES	The children **,** laughing **;** the clowns **,** juggling **;** and the lions **,** roaring loudly **,** all contributed to the noise at the circus.
	Three important dates in Jamestown history are April 30 **,** 1607 **;** September 10 **,** 1607 **;** and January 7 **,** 1608.

See Practice 13.3A

Using Colons

The **colon (:)** is used to introduce lists of items and in certain special situations.

> **Use a colon after an independent clause to introduce a list of items.**

The independent clause that comes before the colon often includes the words *the following, as follows, these,* or *those.*

EXAMPLE   I am planning to pack the following supplies for the trip : a backpack , a tent , and a sleeping bag.

Remember to use commas to separate three or more items in a series.

> **Do not use a colon after a verb or a preposition.**

INCORRECT   Tyler always brings : a sandwich , fruit , and juice.

CORRECT   Tyler always brings a sandwich , fruit , and juice.

> **Use a colon to introduce a long or formal quotation.**

EXAMPLE   The sign stated the fire code : "No campfires allowed from July 1 to September 30."

SOME ADDITIONAL USES OF THE COLON	
To Separate Hours and Minutes	4:40 P.M. 7:00 A.M.
After the Salutation in a Business Letter	To Whom It May Concern : Dear Dr. Ross :
On Warnings and Labels	Notice : Classes Canceled Warning : Trespassers will be prosecuted. Danger : No Swimming

See Practice 13.3B

PRACTICE 13.3A **Using Semicolons**

Read the sentences. Rewrite each sentence, adding any necessary semicolons.

EXAMPLE   Mara decided not to ride her bike to practice it was too far.

ANSWER   *Mara decided not to ride her bike to practice; it was too far.*

1. Training sessions will take place on Thursday, February 26 Tuesday, March 3 and Thursday, March 5.

2. I thought Brent's poem was excellent in fact, it should have won an award.

3. Shakespeare created many great plays he also wrote some memorable sonnets.

4. Jonathan Ryder, brother of the bride Gregory Pope, cousin of the groom and Eric Chavez, friend of the groom, were the three ushers.

5. The team played with a lot of heart nevertheless, they could not win the championship.

6. Paul enjoys hiking Samuel likes fishing.

7. If Jake is not awake by 6:30 A.M., wake him up otherwise, he will miss the bus.

8. Josie failed to take care of her bicycle as a result, it is falling apart.

9. Sarah's favorite sport is basketball Julia enjoys volleyball.

10. Some of the students were asked to serve food others had the task of cleaning up.

PRACTICE 13.3B **Using Colons**

Read the sentences. Rewrite each sentence, adding any necessary colons. If no colon is needed, write *correct*.

EXAMPLE   The club offers several activities hiking, skiing, boating, and climbing.

ANSWER   *The club offers several activities: hiking, skiing, boating, and climbing.*

11. The Rileys have lived in three different states Missouri, Illinois, and Colorado.

12. The Romance languages include Spanish, Portuguese, French, Italian, and Romanian.

13. Warning Do not allow direct contact with the eyes.

14. The flight is scheduled to leave at 830 A.M.

15. The principal introduced the guest speaker "It is my pleasure to introduce a pillar of the community, Mr. Martin Montoya."

16. He has received acceptance letters from Harvard, Columbia, and Princeton.

17. The following breeds are herding dogs the Collie, the Kelpie, and the Briard.

18. Dad gave me three options finish the paper now, work on it at Grandma's, or stay home.

19. He began the letter "Dear Sir or Madam" and then stated his question.

20. The times of the trains for Denver are as follows 1015 A.M., 1215 P.M., and 430 P.M.

SPEAKING APPLICATION

Take turns telling a partner about a trip you have taken. Your partner should listen for a list that requires a colon.

WRITING APPLICATION

Write two sentences that require semicolons and two that require colons. Then, tell a partner why the semicolons and colons are needed.

13.4 Quotation Marks, Underlining, and Italics

Quotation marks (" ") set off direct quotations, dialogue, and certain types of titles. Other types of titles may be <u>underlined</u> or set in *italics,* a slanted type style.

Using Quotation Marks With Quotations

Quotation marks identify the spoken or written words of others. A **direct quotation** represents a person's exact speech or thoughts. An **indirect quotation** reports the general meaning of what a person said or thought.

Both types of quotations are acceptable when you write. Direct quotations, however, generally result in a livelier writing style.

> **Direct quotations should be enclosed in quotation marks.**

RULE 13.4.1

EXAMPLES Stan said, "I decided to try out for the swim team."

"May I finish my project later?" asked Meg.

> **Indirect quotations do not require quotation marks.**

RULE 13.4.2

EXAMPLES My uncle promised that he would watch my game.

The teacher said that my class was going to be the first class to work in the new computer lab.

Using Direct Quotations With Introductory, Concluding, and Interrupting Expressions
Commas help you set off introductory information so that your reader understands who is speaking. Writers usually identify a speaker by using words such as *he asked* or *she said* with a quotation. These expressions can introduce, conclude, or interrupt a quotation.

Direct Quotations With Introductory Expressions

Commas are also used to indicate where **introductory expressions** end.

> **RULE 13.4.3**
>
> When an **introductory expression** precedes a direct quotation, place a comma after the introductory expression, and write the quotation as a full sentence.

EXAMPLES   My sister begged my mother, "May I go on the hike with my class?"

Nate thought, "I wonder how long the hike will take and how far we will go."

If an introductory expression is very long, set it off with a colon instead of a comma.

EXAMPLE   At the end of the hike, Salim concluded: "The acorn is one of the most important sources of food in the woods."

Direct Quotations With Concluding Expressions

Direct quotations may sometimes end with **concluding expressions.**

> **RULE 13.4.4**
>
> When a **concluding expression** follows a direct quotation, write the quotation as a full sentence ending with a comma, question mark, or exclamation mark inside the quotation mark. Then, write the concluding expression. Be sure to use end punctuation to close the sentence.

Concluding expressions are not complete sentences; therefore, they do not begin with capital letters. Notice also that the closing quotation marks are always placed outside the punctuation at the end of direct quotations.

EXAMPLE   "What activities does your camp offer?" inquired Kamilla.

Direct Quotations With Interrupting Expressions
You may use an interrupting expression in a direct quotation,
which is also called a **divided quotation.** Interrupting
expressions help writers clarify who is speaking and can also
break up a long quotation.

> When the direct quotation of one sentence is interrupted,
> end the first part of the direct quotation with a comma and
> a quotation mark. Place a comma after the **interrupting**
> **expression,** and then use a new set of quotation marks
> to enclose the rest of the quotation.

EXAMPLES   "My grandparents are coming for dinner , "
            explained Jade , "so I want to hurry home after
            school . "

            "Do you think , " questioned Kyle , "that I could
            help prepare dinner ? "

Do not capitalize the first word of the second part of the sentence.

> When two sentences in a direct quotation are separated by an
> **interrupting expression,** end the first quoted sentence with
> a comma, question mark, or exclamation mark and a quotation
> mark. Place a period after the interrupter, and then write the
> second quoted sentence as a full quotation.

EXAMPLES   "This is Carter's Grove Plantation , " the
            guide said. "It is an fine example of a
            mid-eighteenth–century mansion . "

See Practice 13.4A
See Practice 13.4B

            "What would it have been like to live there ? "
            asked Corrina. "Can you imagine it ? "

PRACTICE 13.4A **Using Quotation Marks With Direct Quotations**

Read the sentences. If the sentence contains a direct quotation, write *D*. If it contains an indirect quotation, write *I*. Then, rewrite each sentence that contains a direct quotation, adding the quotation marks where needed.

EXAMPLE   My older brother is studying graphic design, said Rachel.

ANSWER   *D — "My older brother is studying graphic design," said Rachel.*

1. Marcus asked, Did you ever read anything by James Joyce?

2. The coach told us that a goalie must have especially good reflexes.

3. I like spring better than summer, Hakeem said.

4. Is it true that green chili peppers will help you recover from a cold? asked Darryl.

5. Joel told me that learning to swim was a great experience for him.

6. Emily Dickinson was very talented, Mrs. Hudson explained.

7. The vendor shouted, Get your popcorn here!

8. Gwen asked, Where are the balloons?

9. The little girl kept repeating that she wanted her mommy.

10. Kelsey wonders whether marine biology would interest him.

PRACTICE 13.4B **Punctuating With Expressions**

Read the sentences. Rewrite each sentence, adding commas and quotation marks where needed.

EXAMPLE   At dusk the guide explained the Sandia Mountains sometimes look pink.

ANSWER   *"At dusk," the guide explained, "the Sandia Mountains sometimes look pink."*

11. This spring said Masako I will plant pansies along the front sidewalk.

12. Be careful what you say Jamal remarked or you might be sorry.

13. Watch your step said the bus driver.

14. Have you ever Mrs. Polk asked seen such beautiful Native American pottery?

15. The doctor said You are healthy.

16. These caves claimed Jaime were once inhabited by ancient peoples.

17. The concert at the park has been canceled announced Clarice.

18. I hope it doesn't rain whined Ramona.

19. Being on time said the teacher is very important.

20. I've always thought said Mom that wolves are beautiful creatures.

WRITING APPLICATION

Write two sentences with direct quotations and two with indirect quotations.

WRITING APPLICATION

Using Sentence 20 as a model, write two more sentences with direct quotations interrupted by expressions.

Using Quotation Marks With Other Punctuation Marks

You have seen that a comma or period used with a direct quotation goes inside the final quotation mark. In some cases, however, end marks should be placed outside of quotation marks.

> Always place a comma or a period inside the final quotation mark.

RULE 13.4.7

EXAMPLES   "We are helping to clean up the park**,** " said Neal**.**

Mando added**,** "Our class is meeting by the playground on Saturday morning**.** "

> Place a **question mark** or an **exclamation mark** inside the final quotation mark if the end mark is part of the quotation. Do not use an additional end mark outside the quotation marks.

RULE 13.4.8

EXAMPLES   Retha asked**,** "When may I have a pet**?** "

Dad looked at the footprints and protested loudly**,** "I just finished washing the floor**!** "

> Place a **question mark** or **exclamation mark** outside the final quotation mark if the end mark is part of the entire sentence, not part of the quotation.

RULE 13.4.9

EXAMPLES   Did I hear you say**,** "I did my homework but forgot to bring it to school**"** **?**

See Practice 13.4C

Please don't tell me the excuse**,** "I forgot**"** **!**

Using Single Quotation Marks for Quotations Within Quotations

Double quotation marks are used to enclose the main quotation. The rules for using commas and end marks with **single quotation marks (' ')** are the same as they are with double quotation marks.

Single quotation marks are used to separate a quote that appears inside of another quotation.

RULE 13.4.10

> Use **single quotation marks** to set off a quotation within a quotation.

EXAMPLES "Do you know if it was Katy who called, 'Come back!' as I was leaving?" I asked.

Liam moaned, "I heard someone say, 'Watch out!' as I began to fall."

Punctuating Explanatory Material Within Quotes

Sometimes it is necessary to add information to a quotation that explains the quote more fully. In that case, brackets tell your reader which information came from the original speaker and which came from someone else. (See Section 13.7 for more information on brackets.)

RULE 13.4.11

> Use brackets to enclose an explanation located within a quotation to show that the explanation is not part of the original quotation.

EXAMPLES The principal announced, "Two clubs [the Chess Club and the History Club] worked together to plan the tournament."

"We [the faculty of Central High School] dedicate this plaque to all the student athletes."

See Practice 13.4D

 **PRACTICE 13.4C** **Using Quotation Marks With Other Punctuation Marks**

Read the sentences. Decide whether the missing punctuation goes inside or outside the quotation marks. Then, rewrite each sentence, adding the proper punctuation for quotations.

EXAMPLE   "When did you become interested in gardening" Miguel asked Tina.

ANSWER   *"When did you become interested in gardening?" Miguel asked Tina.*

1. "How are we going to get this desk up the stairs" asked Consuela.

2. "The sun sets at 6:45 tonight" he stated.

3. Jim announced, "The movie is starting in ten minutes"

4. Who said, "A penny saved is a penny earned"

5. Donna actually said to me, "You are not welcome here"

6. Did someone say, "This experiment was a disaster"

7. Ami excitedly announced, "I passed the test"

8. Jenny asked, "How many miles is a marathon"

9. Then the host said, "All of our contestants have been fooled"

10. The driver of the boat yelled, "Hold on tight"

PRACTICE 13.4D **Punctuating Quotations Within Quotations and Explanatory Material**

Read the sentences. Rewrite each sentence, adding single quotation marks or brackets where needed.

EXAMPLE   "I heard the boy yell, Watch out! after he threw the ball," said Mason.

ANSWER   *"I heard the boy yell, 'Watch out!' after he threw the ball," said Mason.*

11. "Did he really say, My iguana has escaped?" asked Nolan.

12. Tyrell announced to the class, "Ms. Hartin said, Read the first three pages only."

13. "Who said, Let's start with an outline?" asked Mr. Lorenzo.

14. "I heard Mom tell you, The laundry is now your job," said Melissa.

15. The city councilman said, "This intersection 12th St. and Hill Dr. is too dangerous."

16. "Did he say, There's the pin, or There's the pen?" asked Perry.

17. Rosita said, "I thought I heard you say, The milk is sour."

18. "Our highest priority," said Senator Smiley, "is to pass this legislation House Bill 7172"

19. The camp director told us, "No one in the cabin Cabin 12 heard or saw anything."

20. "Then she yelled, Take cover!" said Julio.

WRITING APPLICATION

Write four sentences in which you correctly use punctuation inside and outside quotation marks.

WRITING APPLICATION

Write two sentences including quotations within quotations, and punctuate them correctly.

Using Quotation Marks for Dialogue

A conversation between two or more people is called a **dialogue.** Adding dialogue makes your writing lively because it brings different points of view into your work. It makes your work sound like speech, so dialogue makes your reader feel involved in the scene you describe.

> **When you are writing a dialogue,** indent to begin a new paragraph with each change of speaker. Also be sure to add quotation marks around a speaker's words. When a new speaker is quoted, be sure to indicate the change to your reader by adding information that identifies the new speaker.

RULE 13.4.12

EXAMPLE

"Will you be going with us on the family trip again this summer ? " Noreen asked her cousin .

Gwen hesitated before answering . "I'm afraid so . My parents think I enjoy the experience of traveling with our whole family . "

"You fooled me , too , " Noreen replied . "Maybe the trip will be better this year . I think we're going to places that have large parks . If we're lucky , we might even be able to go on a few rides . "

"Well , at least it can't be any worse , " sighed Gwen . "On the last trip , we waited in line for one hour at three different historic homes in one day ! "

"I remember those lines , " said Noreen . "Didn't you get sunburned while we were waiting? "

Notice that each sentence is punctuated according to the rules discussed earlier in this section.

See Practice 13.4E
See Practice 13.4F

PRACTICE 13.4E ▶ **Using Quotation Marks in Dialogue**

Read the dialogue. Then, rewrite the dialogue. Use proper spacing for quotations and create additional paragraphs where needed. Be sure to use quotation marks and other punctuation correctly.

EXAMPLE Where have Alisa and Mario gone asked Mom. They went to the nursery answered Dad.

ANSWER *"Where have Alisa and Mario gone?" asked Mom.*

"They went to the nursery," answered Dad.

This nursery is huge Mario said. Where should we start? I want to look at flowers for the front yard first said Alisa. Okay, said Mario, we can get a flat of marigolds and one of pansies. I know you also want to buy some seeds to start pepper plants and tomato plants said Alisa. Yes Mario replied. That would be great. Look at all the gardening tools over there exclaimed Alisa. They seem to have everything we need here. I don't even need any tools, said Mario. Well, I do, said Alisa. I need some hand tools to plant those flowers. Let's get started said Mario. This will be fun.

PRACTICE 13.4F ▶ **Revising Dialogue for Punctuation and Paragraphs**

Read the dialogue. Then, rewrite the dialogue. Add quotation marks and begin new paragraphs where needed.

EXAMPLE How did you enjoy your trip to Chicago? asked Malcolm. It was great, but I didn't get to see everything, Nick answered.

ANSWER *"How did you enjoy your trip to Chicago?" asked Malcolm.*

"It was great, but I didn't get to see everything," Nick answered.

Did you get to spend much time outdoors? Malcolm asked. Oh, yes, said Nick. The weather was great, and we went to the Lincoln Park Zoo and to Navy Pier. How about the Botanic Garden? asked Malcolm. I heard that was worth seeing. No, Nick replied. On the very last day, we had to choose between Navy Pier and the Botanic Garden, and almost everyone in the family chose Navy Pier. What did you do at Navy Pier? asked Malcolm. Oh, there was so much to do there. We spent the whole day. What I remember most is riding the huge Ferris wheel. I hope I get to see Chicago someday, said Malcolm. It sounds pretty exciting.

SPEAKING APPLICATION

With a partner, take turns reciting a brief dialogue. Your partner should listen for and point out each time a paragraph break would be needed.

WRITING APPLICATION

Write a brief dialogue between two friends who are discussing their plans for the weekend. Make sure to punctuate each quotation correctly, and start a new paragraph each time the speaker changes.

Using Quotation Marks in Titles

Quotation marks are generally used to set off the titles of shorter works.

RULE 13.4.13

Use **quotation marks** to enclose the titles of short written works and around the title of a work that is mentioned as part of a collection.

WRITTEN WORKS THAT USE QUOTATION MARKS	
Title of a Short Story	"The Gift of the Magi"
Chapter From a Book	"The Test Is in the Tasting" from *No-Work Garden Book*
Title of a Short Poem	"Lucy"
Title of an Article	"How to Build a Birdhouse"
Title Mentioned as Part of a Collection	"Uncle Vanya" in *Eight Great Comedies*

RULE 13.4.14

Use **quotation marks** around the titles of episodes in a television or radio series, songs, and parts of a long musical composition.

ARTISTIC WORKS THAT USE QUOTATION MARKS	
Title of an Episode	"The Nile" from *Cousteau Odyssey*
Title of a Song	"The Best Things in Life Are Free"
Title of a Part of a Long Musical Work	"The Storm" from the *William Tell Overture*

Using Underlining and Italics in Titles

Underlining and **italics** help make titles and other special words and names stand out in your writing. Underlining is used only in handwritten or typewritten material. In printed material, italic (slanted) print is used instead of underlining.

UNDERLINING <u>Treasure Island</u>   ITALICS *Treasure Island*

Underline or **italicize** the titles of long written works and publications that are published as a single work.

13.4.15

WRITTEN WORKS THAT ARE UNDERLINED OR ITALICIZED	
Title of a Book or Play	*To Kill a Mockingbird, Chicago*
Title of a Long Poem	*Beowulf*
Title of a Magazine or Newspaper	*Newsweek, Chicago Tribune*

Underline or **italicize** the titles of movies, television and radio series, long works of music, and art.

13.4.16

ARTISTIC WORKS THAT ARE UNDERLINED OR ITALICIZED	
Title of a Movie	*Star Wars*
Title of a Television Series	*Happy Days*
Title of a Long Work of Music	*Moonlight Sonata*
Title of a Music Album	*Pet Sounds*
Title of a Painting	*Christina's World*
Title of a Sculpture	*The Discus Thrower*

Underline or **italicize** the names of individual air, sea, and spacecraft.

13.4.17

EXAMPLES   *Voyager 2*   the *Mayflower*

Underline or **italicize** words and letters used as names for themselves and foreign words.

13.4.18

EXAMPLES   Do you know how to spell *Victoria?*

See Practice 13.4G
See Practice 13.4H

An *obi* is a sash worn with traditional Japanese dress.

PRACTICE 13.4G Underlining Titles, Names, and Words

Read the sentences. Rewrite each sentence, underlining titles, names, and words where needed. You can use italics if you are typing your answers.

EXAMPLE   This year the high school drama club will present Romeo and Juliet.

ANSWER   *This year the high school drama club will present <u>Romeo and Juliet</u>.*

1. My sister is reading The Scarlet Letter, a novel by Nathaniel Hawthorne.

2. An au pair is a person who cares for a family's children in exchange for room and board.

3. I always forget how to spell occasion.

4. The cast gave a good performance in Charlie and the Chocolate Factory.

5. Kimberly is learning to play the koto, a traditional stringed instrument from Japan.

6. The pilgrims had a miserable journey aboard the Mayflower.

7. Remember not to use their when you mean there.

8. Have you ever seen a performance of Hamlet?

9. The Starry Night is one of Van Gogh's famous paintings.

10. Sally Ride, the first American woman to fly in space, was a crew member of the space shuttle Challenger.

PRACTICE 13.4H Using Underlining and Quotation Marks

Read the sentences. Rewrite each sentence, enclosing the titles in quotation marks or underlining them. You can use italics if you are typing your answers.

EXAMPLE   The collection We'll Always Have Paris includes the short story The Twilight Greens.

ANSWER   *The collection <u>We'll Always Have Paris</u> includes the short story "The Twilight Greens."*

11. My music teacher has composed a piece called Opus of George.

12. In class we are discussing The Landlady, a short story by Roald Dahl.

13. The poem The Cremation of Sam McGee appears in The Best of Robert Service.

14. The teacher has assigned one chapter, Below the Equator, for homework.

15. That episode was titled Archie Helps Out.

16. Langston Hughes wrote the short poem Refugee in America.

17. Mom is reading Your Child's First Dog, an article in Dog Fancy.

18. The song I'm Yours always puts me in a good mood.

19. The Dying Cowboy is an old American ballad.

20. My brother titled his school newspaper article Baseball Team Needs Help.

WRITING APPLICATION

Write one sentence about a short story you read and one about a movie you saw. Make sure to punctuate the titles correctly.

WRITING APPLICATION

Write a sentence about a ship and one about a spacecraft. You may make up the names if you want, but be sure to use underlining correctly.

13.5 Hyphens

Hyphens (-) are used to combine words and to show a connection between the syllables of words that are broken at the ends of lines.

Using Hyphens in Numbers

Hyphens are used to join compound numbers and fractions.

> **Use a hyphen when you write two-word numbers from twenty-one through ninety-nine.**

EXAMPLES   twenty-one   thirty-eight

> **Use a hyphen when you use a fraction as an adjective but not when you use a fraction as a noun.**

13.5.2 RULE

ADJECTIVE   The bus is two-thirds full.

NOUN   Two thirds of voters agree with the plan.

Using Hyphens for Prefixes and Suffixes

Many words with common prefixes are no longer hyphenated. The following prefixes are often used before proper nouns: *ante-*, *anti-*, *post-*, *pre-*, *pro-*, and *un-*. Check a dictionary when you are unsure about using a hyphen.

> **Use a hyphen after a prefix that is followed by a proper noun or adjective.**

EXAMPLES   pre-Civil War   mid-January

> **Use a hyphen in words with the prefixes *all-*, *ex-*, and *self-* and the suffix *-elect*.**

EXAMPLES   self-employed   governor-elect

Using Hyphens in Compound Words

Compound words are two or more words that must be read together to create a single idea.

> Use a **hyphen** to connect two or more nouns that are used as one compound word, unless a dictionary gives a different spelling.

EXAMPLES   six - year - olds   mother - in - law

Using Hyphens With Compound Modifiers

Hyphens help your reader group information properly.

> Use a hyphen to connect a **compound modifier** that comes before a noun. Do not use a hyphen with a compound modifier that includes a word ending in -*ly* or in a compound proper adjective.

EXAMPLE   In the basket were seven well - fed puppies.

INCORRECT   freshly - baked bread   Native - American art

CORRECT   freshly baked bread   Native American art

A hyphen is not necessary when a compound modifier follows the noun it describes.

MODIFIER
BEFORE NOUN   The never - ending sound of cheering filled the hall.

MODIFIER
AFTER NOUN   The sound of cheering in the hall was never ending.

However, if a dictionary spells a word with a hyphen, the word must always be hyphenated, even when it follows a noun.

EXAMPLE   We plan to visit the park in the off - season.

See Practice 13.5A
See Practice 13.5B

PRACTICE 13.5A Using Hyphens in Numbers and Words

Read the following items. Write each item, adding hyphens where needed. If an item is already correct, write *correct*.

EXAMPLE   in mid September
ANSWER   *in mid-September*

1. carefully chosen words
2. the post Elizabethan era
3. a two thirds majority
4. twenty two people
5. a well built wall
6. his brother in law
7. a self confident girl
8. a wall that is well built
9. a four story building
10. user friendly instruction manual

PRACTICE 13.5B Proofreading for Hyphens

Read the sentences. Rewrite each sentence, adding hyphens where needed.

EXAMPLE   The debate team now has twenty one members.
ANSWER   *The debate team now has twenty-one members.*

11. The senator elect is eager to begin serving his state.
12. Our great aunt usually comes to visit in the summer.
13. A low cost plan was presented to the council.
14. We began our cross country trip in New York City.
15. About three quarters of the voters attend the once a month meeting.
16. The famous author illustrator is giving a book signing tomorrow.
17. I returned to my half finished lunch after the fire drill.
18. A well maintained car will usually be reliable.
19. The ex congressman now works in radio.
20. The thirty eight members who voted "yes" made up a two thirds majority.

WRITING APPLICATION

Write three sentences. Include at least three compound nouns or adjectives that need hyphens, and hyphenate them correctly.

WRITING APPLICATION

Write a sentence that contains one hyphenated fraction and one fraction that is not hyphenated.

Using Hyphens at the Ends of Lines

Hyphens serve a useful purpose when they are used to divide words at the ends of lines. They should not, however, be used more often than is necessary because they can make reading feel choppy.

Avoid dividing words at the end of a line whenever possible. If a word must be divided, always divide it between syllables.

EXAMPLE   You must not feel that your contrib-
ution was insignificant.

Check a dictionary if you are unsure how a word is divided into syllables. Looking up the word *seriously*, for example, you would find that its syllables are *se-ri-ous-ly*.

A hyphen used to divide a word should never be placed at the beginning of the second line. It must be placed at the end of the first line.

INCORRECT   His taste in music is quite sophis
-ticated.

CORRECT   His taste in music is quite sophis-
ticated.

Using Hyphens Correctly to Divide Words

One-syllable words cannot be divided.

Do *not* divide one-syllable words even if they seem long or sound like words with two syllables.

INCORRECT   wh-eel   pl-ease   shr-ink
CORRECT   wheel   please   shrink

RULE

Do *not* divide a word so that a single letter stands alone.

| INCORRECT | a‑long | i‑con | air‑y |
| CORRECT | along | icon | airy |

Also avoid placing *-ed* at the beginning of a new line.

INCORRECT   The list of the new team members was post‑
ed on the wall of the gym.

CORRECT   The list of the new team members was
posted on the wall of the gym.

Avoid dividing proper nouns or proper adjectives.

| INCORRECT | Jenni‑fer | Span‑ish |
| CORRECT | Jennifer | Spanish |

Divide a hyphenated word only immediately following the existing hyphen.

INCORRECT   John gave the class an up‑to‑the‑min‑
ute report each morning.

See Practice 13.5C
See Practice 13.5D

CORRECT   John gave the class an up‑to‑the‑
minute report each morning.

PRACTICE 13.5C Using Hyphens to Divide Words

Read the following words. Rewrite each word. Then, draw vertical lines between syllables that can be divided at the end of a line. Do nothing to words that cannot be divided.

EXAMPLE   baseball

ANSWER   *base | ball*

1. Daniel
2. highway
3. self-respect
4. steady
5. swallow
6. interrupt
7. stopped
8. panted
9. skillfully
10. intended

PRACTICE 13.5D Using Hyphens in Words in Sentences

Read the sentences. If a word has been divided correctly, write *correct*. If not, rewrite the sentence, dividing the word correctly or writing it as one word if it cannot be divided.

EXAMPLE   The wallpaper had dia-mond-shaped patterns.

ANSWER   *The wallpaper had diamond-shaped patterns.*

11. Mr. Ramirez traveled to Cincinnati for a busi-ness meeting.
12. While we were out of town, Terrence water-ed our plants.
13. Several family members have Decem-ber birthdays.
14. Yoko will spend most of her vaca-tion in South Dakota.
15. New York City attracts man-y tourists each year.
16. Tyrell found satisfaction in compl-eting the recycling project.
17. Aisha spends most Saturdays volun-teering at the animal shelter.
18. On the plate sat one lone strawber-ry dipped in yogurt.
19. The outcome of the tourna-ment did not surprise anyone.
20. Miguel wanted to buy a T-shirt, so he bro-ught some extra money with him.

SPEAKING APPLICATION

With a partner, sound out these words and have your partner determine where the syllables break: *shoveling, dismiss, appointment, popular.* Then, check the syllable breaks in a dictionary.

WRITING APPLICATION

Write four sentences. Break each sentence in the middle of a word to show one place it would be correct to divide a word at the end of a line.

13.6 Apostrophes

The **apostrophe (')** is used to show possession or ownership. It is also used in shortened forms of words called contractions. In a contraction, the apostrophe marks the place where letters have been omitted.

Using Apostrophes With Possessive Nouns

Apostrophes are used with nouns to show ownership or possession.

> **Add an apostrophe and -s to show the possessive case of most singular nouns and plural nouns that do not end in -s or -es.**

13.6.1 RULE

EXAMPLES   Wayne's brother was the first one in line.

The children's game is in the afternoon.

Even when a singular noun already ends in -s, you can usually add an apostrophe and -s to show possession.

EXAMPLE   The first grade class's play was very funny.

In classical or ancient names that end in -s, it is common to omit the final -s to make pronunciation easier.

EXAMPLE   Zeus' thunderbolt is a symbol in Greek mythology.

> **Add an apostrophe to show the possessive case of plural nouns ending in -s or -es. Do not add an -s.**

13.6.2 RULE

EXAMPLE   The witnesses' testimonies were very helpful.

RULE 13.6.3

Add an apostrophe and *-s* (or just an apostrophe if the word is a plural ending in *-s*) to the last word of a compound noun to form the possessive.

EXAMPLES　　My brother-in-law**'**s school

the Girl Scouts**'** ceremony

See Practice 13.6A

Using Apostrophes With Pronouns

Both indefinite and personal pronouns can show possession.

RULE 13.6.4

Use an apostrophe and *-s* with indefinite pronouns to show possession.

EXAMPLES　　everyone**'**s opinion　　everybody**'**s food

RULE 13.6.5

Do not use an apostrophe with possessive personal pronouns.

POSSESSIVE PERSONAL PRONOUNS		
	SINGULAR	PLURAL
First Person	I, me, my, mine	we, us, our, ours
Second Person	you, your, yours	you, your, yours
Third Person	he, him, his; she, her, hers; it, its	they, them; their, theirs

Some of these pronouns act as adjectives.

EXAMPLES　　The cat held a ball of yarn in its paws.

Our car is being repaired.

Others act as subjects, objects, and subject complements.

EXAMPLES　　Mine is the red-and-white uniform.

The red-and-gray uniform is his.

See Practice 13.6B

Using Apostrophes With Contractions

Contractions are used in informal speech and writing, especially in dialogue because they create the sound of speech.

> Use an **apostrophe** in a **contraction** to show where one or more letters have been omitted.

RULE 13.6.6

COMMON CONTRACTIONS		
Verb + *not*	is not = isn't	cannot = can't
Noun or Pronoun + *will*	I will = I'll	we will = we'll
Noun or Pronoun + *be*	you are = you're	Andy is = Andy's
Noun or Pronoun + *would*	she would = she'd	who would = who'd

> Avoid using contractions in formal speech and writing.

RULE 13.6.7

Contractions may be used in dialogue and in informal speech and writing, but they should be avoided in formal usage.

INFORMAL WRITING   Where's the fire?

FORMAL WRITING   Where is the fire?

Using Apostrophes to Create Plurals

Do not use an apostrophe to form plurals, except in specific instances.

> Use an **apostrophe** and *-s* to create the plural form of a letter, numeral, or a word used as a name for itself.

RULE 13.6.8

See Practice 13.6C
See Practice 13.6D

EXAMPLES   There are two 5's in his phone number.

People can confuse *a*'s and *an*'s.

Using Apostrophes to Show Ownership

Read each phrase. Write the possessive form of each item.

EXAMPLE   the computer of my mother

ANSWER   *my mother's computer*

1. the tasks of Hercules
2. the thoughts of the men
3. the doors of the nursery school
4. the cellphone of his brother-in-law
5. the clothing of the children
6. the works of the artists
7. the nest of the mice
8. the speech of the governor-elect
9. the coat of her cousin
10. the eyes of the praying mantis

Using Apostrophes With Pronouns

Read the sentences. If all pronouns in a sentence are used correctly, write *correct*. If one or more pronouns are used incorrectly, rewrite the sentence correctly.

EXAMPLE   This pencil is mine, and that one is your's.

ANSWER   *This pencil is mine, and that one is yours.*

11. The books in this backpack are his', not mine.
12. Somebodys' dog was digging in our garden while our's was sleeping inside.
13. The doctor examined the girl and discovered her hand was broken.
14. Ours was the best presentation, even though their's was also excellent.
15. Consider his song idea before you accept hers.
16. It will soon be too late to buy your' mother a gift.
17. Their's is always the first driveway to have it's snow cleared.
18. Is this her scarf, or is it someone else's?
19. Of all the performances, her's was the most impressive.
20. The chair was turned over on it's side.

WRITING APPLICATION

Write three sentences that contain possessive forms of nouns, and punctuate the possessives correctly.

WRITING APPLICATION

Write three sentences that contain the possessive forms of pronouns, and punctuate the possessives correctly. Include at least one personal pronoun and one indefinite pronoun.

PRACTICE 13.6C Using Apostrophes in Contractions

Read the sentences. Each sentence contains a word group that can be written as a contraction. Write the contractions.

EXAMPLE   Who is going to go to the game?

ANSWER   *Who's*

1. Mom and Dad have not given their permission yet.

2. If you do not want the granola bar, give it to me.

3. Of all the pets we have had, our new parrot is the noisiest.

4. Helen could not remember who was in the movie.

5. We are all in agreement about the chore list.

6. Perry is running across the field.

7. What is the easiest way to get to the mall?

8. If you set the table, I will fix the sandwiches.

9. Where is the key to this lock?

10. Serena wanted to know who would be driving her home.

PRACTICE 13.6D Proofreading for Apostrophes

Read the sentences. Rewrite each sentence, adding apostrophes where needed.

EXAMPLE   Ive been waiting here for an hour.

ANSWER   *I've been waiting here for an hour.*

11. I wont be at practice on Tuesday.

12. My niece thinks counting by 2s is fun.

13. Aileen has been ill, but shell be back in school next week.

14. Mrs. Richards suggested that I use fewer *howevers* in my writing.

15. Whats wrong with Cynthia today?

16. The detectives cant seem to solve this case.

17. If you want to get As, youll have to work harder.

18. That little boy shouldnt be crossing the street by himself.

19. His speaking has so many *ums* that it is hard to listen to him sometimes.

20. The play wont be over until at least 10:00.

SPEAKING APPLICATION

With a partner say the following pairs of sentences. Your partner should note how much more casual the second pair sounds.
I will not be late. / I won't be late.
We cannot make a mistake. / We can't make a mistake.

WRITING APPLICATION

Write two sentences with contractions, and make sure each contraction is spelled correctly. Then, write two sentences with plural forms that require apostrophes.

13.7 Parentheses and Brackets

Parentheses and **brackets** enclose explanations or other information that may be omitted from the rest of the sentence without changing its basic meaning or construction.

Parentheses

Parentheses are used to separate information from the rest of a sentence or paragraph.

RULE 13.7.1

Use a **parenthesis** to set off explanations or other information that is loosely related to the rest of the sentence.

EXAMPLE   Abraham Lincoln **(**1809–1865**)** led the United States during the Civil War.

RULE 13.7.2

A **parenthetical sentence** within another sentence should not begin with a capital letter unless the parenthetical sentence begins with a word that should be capitalized.

EXAMPLE   We jumped into the pool **(**the water was freezing**)** and climbed out immediately.

RULE 13.7.3

A **parenthetical sentence** within another sentence may end with a question mark or exclamation mark if applicable, but it should not end with a period.

INCORRECT   The class trip **(**we all want to go**.** **)** is planned for the same day as our game**.**

CORRECT   The class trip **(**are you going**?** **)** is planned for the same day as our game**.**

Parenthetical Sentences That Stand on Their Own
Parenthetical sentences add information to another sentence or
a paragraph.

> **A parenthetical sentence** that stands on its own should
> begin with a capital letter and end with an end mark before the
> closing parenthesis.

RULE 13.7.4

EXAMPLE The class trip is planned for the same day as our

game **.** **(** Do you think they will change the date **?** **)**

Brackets

Brackets have one major use: to enclose a word or words into a
quotation that were not spoken by the person or source that is
quoted.

> Use **brackets** to enclose an explanation located within a quote
> to show that the explanation is not part of the original quote.

RULE 13.7.5

EXAMPLE Mr. Johnson exclaimed, "This is the first time the

baseball team has lost the playoffs since I became

coach **[** in 2003 **]** ."

> Use **brackets** to enclose an explanation that is located within
> parenthetical text.

RULE 13.7.6

EXAMPLE John Adams **(** the second president of the United

States **[** 1797–1801 **]** **)** was defeated for reelection

See Practice 13.7A
See Practice 13.7B

by Thomas Jefferson.

PRACTICE 13.7A Using Parentheses and Brackets

Read the sentences. Rewrite the sentences, adding parentheses or brackets where appropriate.

EXAMPLE   The longer route it follows the river is more scenic.

ANSWER   *The longer route (it follows the river) is more scenic.*

1. Zora Neale Hurston 1891–1960 was influential during the Harlem Renaissance.

2. The entire team all 32 members piled onto the old bus.

3. Principal Yang said, "This fine woman the youth volunteer coordinator can answer your questions."

4. The Earth Day Festival wasn't the weather perfect? was a big success.

5. Queen Elizabeth (she ruled England for 65 years 1558–1603) was the last monarch of the Tudor dynasty.

6. Dr. Gardner stated, "Courses in paleontology the study of dinosaurs are offered at the state college."

PRACTICE 13.7B Proofreading for Parentheses and Brackets

Read the paragraph. Rewrite the paragraph, adding parentheses or brackets where appropriate.

EXAMPLE   The trapping of wild parrots they are sold as pets and loss of habitat have reduced parrot populations.

ANSWER   *The trapping of wild parrots (they are sold as pets) and loss of habitat have reduced parrot populations.*

There are about 372 species a species is the most specific unit of biological classification of parrots. Most parrots have a strong curved bill, very strong legs, and zygodactyl having two toes in the front and two in the back feet. Parrots are usually brightly colored, but some the cockatoo species, to be specific, are white, gray, or black. According to zookeeper Kara Paulson, "Parrots are one of the most diverse bird species in terms of size. Their length can vary from 8 cm 3.2 inches to 1 meter 3.3 feet." Parrots are found mostly in places with tropical climates (areas with warm, moist conditions Brazil and Hawaii, for example).

SPEAKING APPLICATION

With a partner, read the following sentence aloud twice, first without and then with appropriate pauses. *These burritos (they have spinach in them) are delicious.* Discuss which version was easier to understand and why.

WRITING APPLICATION

Write one sentence with information requiring parentheses and one with information requiring brackets.

13.8 Ellipses and Dashes

An **ellipsis** (. . .) shows where words have been omitted from a quoted passage. It can also mark a pause in dialogue. A **dash** (—) shows a strong, sudden break in thought or speech.

Using the Ellipsis

An **ellipsis** consists of three evenly spaced periods, or ellipsis points, in a row. There is a space before the first ellipsis point, between ellipsis points, and after the last ellipsis point. The plural form of the word *ellipsis* is *ellipses*.

> Use an **ellipsis** to show where words have been omitted from a quoted passage. Including an ellipsis shows the reader that the writer has chosen to omit some information.

13.8.1 RULE

QUOTED PASSAGE	"Four score and seven years ago our fathers brought forth on this continent a new nation conceived in liberty and dedicated to the proposition that all men are created equal." –Abraham Lincoln, *The Gettysburg Address,* November 19, 1863
QUOTED PASSAGE WITH WORDS OMITTED	"Fourscore and seven years ago our fathers brought forth . . . a new nation . . . dedicated to the proposition that all men are created equal."

Ellipses in Advertising

Ellipses are commonly used in ads for movies and other media. When you see an ellipsis in an ad, think about what might have been omitted. You might want to find the original review because the ad might be giving a different impression from what the reviewer intended.

ORIGINAL REVIEW	"The news article is neither accurate nor well written and is not recommended reading."
AD WORDING	" . . . accurate . . . well written . . . recommended"

RULE
13.8.2

> Use an **ellipsis** to mark a pause in a dialogue or speech.

EXAMPLE

"But, in a larger sense, we can not dedicate ... we can not consecrate ... we can not hallow ... this ground."

RULE

> It is not necessary to use an **ellipsis** to show an omission at the beginning of material you are quoting. However, if you choose to omit any words *within* material you quote, you must use an ellipsis to show where information has been omitted.

UNNECESSARY

" ... Now we are engaged in a great civil war, testing whether that nation, or any nation, so conceived and so dedicated, can long endure."

CORRECT

"Now we are engaged in a great civil war, testing whether that nation, or any nation so conceived and so dedicated, can long endure."

RULE
13.8.4

> Use an **ellipsis** to show an omission, pause, or interruption in the middle of a sentence.

EXAMPLE

"But, in a larger sense, we cannot dedicate ... this ground."

RULE

> Use an **ellipsis** and an end mark to show an omission or a pause at the end of a sentence.

EXAMPLE

"I want to make sure that everyone understood what I just said. We need to ... ."

If you omit words from a source you are quoting, omit the punctuation that accompanies the words unless it is correct in your sentence.

See Practice 13.8A

Dashes

Like commas and parentheses, **dashes** separate certain words, phrases, or clauses from the rest of the sentence or paragraph. Dashes, however, signal a stronger, more sudden interruption in thought or speech than commas or parentheses. A dash may also take the place of certain words before an explanation.

> Use a dash to show a strong, sudden break in thought or speech.

13.8.6 RULE

EXAMPLE   I can't believe how many goals she scored — she must be the star of the team!

If the interrupting expression is in the middle of the sentence, use a dash on either side of it to set it off from the rest of the sentence.

EXAMPLE   I read an article — you might have seen it — about the new arena they are building downtown.

> Use a dash in place of *in other words, namely,* or *that is* before an explanation.

13.8.7 RULE

EXAMPLES   Dana skateboarded for one reason — pure enjoyment.

To finish her project before the deadline — that is why she is working so hard.

Dashes can also be used to set off nonessential appositives or modifiers.

EXAMPLE   The recycling program — run by the students — has made a real difference is the amount of garbage collected.

See Practice 13.8B

PRACTICE 13.8A > Using Ellipses

Read the sentences. For each sentence, tell whether ellipses (or ellipsis points) are used to indicate a *pause* or an *omission*.

EXAMPLE   The text continued, "For thousands of years . . . dogs and men have depended on each other."

ANSWER   *omission*

1. Does this bleak landscape . . . I don't know . . . make you feel melancholy?

2. The speech began, "In our hands is a grand opportunity . . . which we must grasp tightly."

3. According to the review, the book is "a peek into . . . the private lives of nobility."

4. The councilman was famous for this statement: "Progress . . . must never come at the expense of people's dignity."

5. I think . . . to tell you the truth, I'm not sure.

6. It was a day-dreamy kind of day, and . . . my mind was wandering.

7. "Where in this land . . . have we seen no war?" is the first line of the book.

8. Is this . . . the way to the fairgrounds?

9. The letter ended, "And so, my dear friend . . . I will say farewell for now."

10. That painting is so realistic it is as though I can . . . I can . . . actually smell the summer rain.

PRACTICE 13.8B > Using Dashes

Read the sentences. Rewrite each sentence, adding dashes where they are needed.

EXAMPLE   There is just one thing I ask of you that you be honest with me.

ANSWER   *There is just one thing I ask of you—that you be honest with me.*

11. The periwinkle I never knew this has many medicinal uses.

12. Hans needed just one more thing to complete his costume a large feather for the hat.

13. Fran told me a story I forget the beginning about a homeless terrier.

14. The software had a bug, and oh, I don't have time to explain.

15. Daffodils at least I think that's what they were adorned every table.

16. June has a reason for waking up so early to have time for a jog in the morning.

17. I'll probably see the hey, Jared, wait up!

18. An entomologist that's someone who studies insects spoke to our science class today.

19. Hydrangeas are interesting plants leafy green shrubs with clumps of tiny white flowers.

20. It's time to wait, don't step there.

SPEAKING APPLICATION

With a partner, read the following two sentences. See if your partner can tell which sentence has an ellipsis and which has a dash. *It was time to go . . . but we lingered by the fire.*
Close that—oh, no, the dog has already run off!

WRITING APPLICATION

Write one sentence using ellipses correctly and one sentence using dashes correctly.

CHAPTER 14

CAPITALIZATION

Capitalizing the correct words in your sentences will add a final polish to your writing.

WRITE GUY *Jeff Anderson, M.Ed.*

WHAT DO YOU NOTICE?

Spot the capital letters as you zoom in on this sentence from "Choice: A Tribute to Martin Luther King, Jr." by Alice Walker.

MENTOR TEXT

> In 1960, my mother bought a television set, and each day after school I watched Hamilton Holmes and Charlayne Hunter as they struggled to integrate—fair-skinned as they were—the University of Georgia.

Now, ask yourself the following questions:

- Why is one of the pronouns capitalized?
- Why are certain nouns capitalized while others are not?

The pronoun *I* is always capitalized. The author capitalizes *Hamilton Holmes* and *Charlayne Hunter* because they name specific people. Similarly, because *University of Georgia* is the name of a specific place, the individual nouns in its title are capitalized. Common nouns in the sentence, such as *mother*, *television set*, and *school*, are not capitalized.

Grammar for Writers Capitalization helps a writer highlight specific people, places, and things for readers. When you use capital letters correctly, you guide readers through your writing.

Should I be capitalized?

Yes, but you should not be.

14.1 Using Capitalization

Capital letters are used for the first words in all sentences and in many quotations. They are also used for the word *I*, whatever its position in a sentence.

The Word *I*

RULE 14.1.1

The pronoun *I* is always capitalized.

EXAMPLE   **I** worked for two years as an apprentice before **I** received a promotion.

Sentences

One of the most common uses of a capital letter is to signal the beginning of a sentence. The first word in a sentence must begin with a capital letter.

RULE 14.1.2

Capitalize the first word in **declarative, interrogative, imperative,** and **exclamatory** sentences.

DECLARATIVE   **S**trong gusts of wind made it dangerous to walk outside.

INTERROGATIVE   **W**ho found the book I left on the bus this morning?

IMPERATIVE   **T**hink carefully before you respond.

EXCLAMATORY   **W**hat an amazing result this is!

Sometimes only part of a sentence is written. The rest of the sentence is understood. In these cases, a capital is still needed for the first word.

EXAMPLES   **W**ho?   **H**ow so?   **I**ndeed!

Quotations

A capital letter also signals the first word in a **direct quotation,** a person's exact words.

> **Capitalize the first word in a quotation if the quotation is a complete sentence.**

14.1.3 RULE

EXAMPLES   Several people shouted, "**S**top the train!"

"**S**he really wants to go to the concert," Linda confided.

Abby asked, "**D**oes anyone want to play tennis after school?"

> **When a quotation consists of one complete sentence in two parts, only capitalize the first part of the quotation.**

14.1.4 RULE

EXAMPLES   "**H**ow much longer," asked Bill, "**i**s this meal going to last?"

"**T**he elephant," he said, "**i**s a symbol of wisdom in Asian cultures and is famed for its memory and intelligence."

> **If a quotation contains more than one sentence, the first word of each sentence begins with a capital.**

14.1.5 RULE

EXAMPLES   "**P**lease distribute these outlines to everyone," said the manager. "**T**hey show the topics we will discuss this afternoon."

See Practice 14.1A
See Practice 14.1B

"**I**'m finished with the science homework," said Sophie. "**I** will need it for class tomorrow."

PRACTICE 14.1A Supplying Capitalization

Read the sentences. Rewrite each sentence, adding the missing capitals.

EXAMPLE "please clean the table," Yolanda said. "we have visitors on the way."

ANSWER *"Please clean the table," Yolanda said. "We have visitors on the way."*

1. that arrowhead is thousands of years old.

2. "the decision," Jamal insisted, "is yours."

3. where did you put the new photographs?

4. she and i have been friends for five years.

5. "this assignment is pretty challenging," thought Clarissa.

6. a bus stopped near the corner and let off a little girl.

7. yikes! the cat is tearing up the carpet!

8. consider all the features before you buy a computer.

9. Greta asked, "may Jason and i please have some grapes?"

10. "all the supplies are ready," he said. "we can start painting."

PRACTICE 14.1B Proofreading for Capitalization

Read the sentences. Rewrite each sentence, adding the missing capitals.

EXAMPLE i lost the ring somewhere. but where?

ANSWER *I lost the ring somewhere. But where?*

11. what time does the animal shelter open?

12. refer to a dictionary for word origins and spellings.

13. next month? i thought the pool had already been finished.

14. Tamara whispered, "are you awake? i can't sleep."

15. how brave he was!

16. his in-line skates broke the first day he had them.

17. "the yard is clean," she said, "but we still need to mow the grass."

18. "return the book to the library," Julio said. "it is overdue."

19. what? you have to leave already?

20. "we can wait at the subway terminal," said Mr. Romero.

WRITING APPLICATION

Write one declarative sentence, one imperative sentence, and one interrogative sentence. Use capital letters correctly.

WRITING APPLICATION

Use sentences 17, 18, and 20 as models, and write three more sentences with direct quotations, and capitalize them correctly.

Using Capitalization for Proper Nouns

An important use of capital letters is to show that a word is a **proper noun.** Proper nouns name specific people, places, or things.

> Capitalize all **proper nouns.**

EXAMPLES
Jim **T**horpe

Cedar **B**reaks **N**ational **M**onument

Golden **G**ate **B**ridge

Sky **T**ower

Names of People

> Capitalize each part of a person's full name, including initials.

EXAMPLES
Barbara **A**nn **M**eninger

William **J**. **T**. **J**ackson

B. **J**. **M**ingle

When a last name has two parts and the first part is *Mac, Mc, O',* or *St.,* the second part of the last name must also be capitalized.

EXAMPLES
Mac**Gr**egor

Mc**G**rath

O'**L**eary

St. **J**ames

See Practice 14.1C

For two-part last names that do not begin with *Mac, Mc, O',* or *St.,* the capitalization varies. Check a reliable source, such as a biographical dictionary, for the correct spelling.

Geographical Places

Any specific geographical location listed on a map should be capitalized.

RULE 14.1.8

> **Capitalize geographical names.**

GEOGRAPHICAL NAMES	
Streets	Warren Street, Carlton Avenue, Interstate 10
Cities	Baltimore, London, Memphis, Tokyo
States	Arizona, Florida, Hawaii, Idaho
Nations	Italy, Canada, Kenya, France, Peru, South Korea
Continents	North America, Asia, Africa, Antarctica
Deserts	Sahara, Negev, Mojave
Mountains	Mount Everest, Rocky Mountains
Regions	Great Plains, Appalachian Highlands, Northwest
Islands	Canary Islands, Fiji Islands
Rivers	Mississippi River, Amazon River
Lakes	Lake Michigan, Great Salt Lake, Lake Erie
Bays	Hudson Bay, Baffin Bay, Biscayne Bay
Seas	Black Sea, Mediterranean Sea, North Sea
Oceans	Atlantic Ocean, Arctic Ocean

Regions and Map Directions

Names of regions, such as the South and the Northeast, are capitalized because they refer to a specific geographical location. Map directions that do not refer to a specific geographical location are not capitalized.

RULE 14.1.9

> **Do not capitalize compass points, such as north, southwest, or east, when they simply refer to direction.**

REGION   Someday I would like to visit the Southeast.

DIRECTION   The train traveled east for about an hour.

Specific Events and Time Periods

> **Capitalize the names of specific events, periods of time, and documents.**

The following chart contains examples of events, periods of time, and documents that require capitalization.

SPECIFIC EVENTS AND TIMES	
Historical Periods	**A**ge of **E**nlightenment, **M**iddle **A**ges, **t**he **R**enaissance
Historical Events	**W**orld **W**ar II, **B**oston **T**ea **P**arty, **B**attle of **L**exington
Documents	**B**ill of **R**ights, **T**reaty of **P**aris, **D**eclaration of **I**ndependence
Days	**W**ednesday, **S**aturday
Months	**D**ecember, **O**ctober
Holidays	**T**hanksgiving, **L**abor **D**ay
Religious Days	**C**hristmas, **P**assover, **R**amadan
Special Events	**F**iddlers' **C**onvention, **B**oston **M**arathon, **S**uper **B**owl

Names of Seasons

The names of the seasons are an exception to this rule. Even though they name a specific period of time, the seasons of the year are not capitalized unless they are part of a title or an event name.

SEASONS   In the **f**all, we like to go hiking.

           I take most of my vacation in the **s**ummer.

TITLE   Last **w**inter, I read *Driftwood* **S**ummer.

EVENT   It was so hot at the **F**all Festival it felt like **s**ummer.

See Practice 14.1D

 **PRACTICE 14.1C** Using Capitalization for Names of People

Read the sentences. Write each name, adding the missing capitals.

EXAMPLE   The teacher assigned jeremy mcnabb as allison's lab partner.

ANSWER   *Jeremy McNabb, Allison*

1. The class is studying poetry by walt whitman.

2. Frowning, trina st. paul approached the counter.

3. Mom sent flowers to irene mckinney, who is in the hospital.

4. The letter was addressed to rosa m. garcia.

5. The author walter dean myers was raised by foster parents.

6. She can play music by mozart on the piano.

7. According to sheryl, that story by w. w. jacobs is very suspenseful.

8. Deliver the package to larry o'boyle on the third floor.

9. Have you read anything by julia alvarez?

10. The coach encouraged terri, carlos, and me.

PRACTICE 14.1D Using Capitalization for Geographical Places, Specific Events, and Time Periods

Read the sentences. Write each geographical place name specific event, or time period, adding the missing capitals.

EXAMPLE   Who is moving into the house on ridgecrest avenue?

ANSWER   *Ridgecrest Avenue*

11. The last two states to be admitted to the united states were alaska and hawaii.

12. Gregory dreams of one day moving to the pacific northwest.

13. The family drove to philadelphia to see a hockey game.

14. My family visited williamsburg, virginia, to learn about the american revolution.

15. The guadalupe river runs through austin, texas.

16. We were amazed by the size of yellowstone national park.

17. The countries of bolivia and peru both border argentina.

18. Are you going to the fall festival next weekend?

19. I just learned that baffin island is part of canada.

20. The scenery on the drive through the san fernando valley was breathtaking.

WRITING APPLICATION

Write three sentences that include people's names, and capitalize them correctly.

WRITING APPLICATION

Write three sentences using at least three different types of geographical names. Make sure to capitalize the names correctly.

Specific Groups

Proper nouns that name specific groups also require capitalization.

> **Capitalize the names of various organizations, government bodies, political parties, and nationalities, as well as the languages spoken by different groups.**

RULE 14.1.11

EXAMPLES   The **P**eace **C**orps helps promote a better understanding of other cultures.

Switzerland's four official languages are **G**erman, **F**rench, **I**talian, and **R**umantsch.

John F. Kennedy was the first **B**oy **S**cout to ever become president of the United States.

The proper nouns shown in the chart are groups with which many people are familiar. All specific groups, however, must be capitalized, even if they are not well known.

SPECIFIC GROUPS	
Clubs	**K**iwanis **C**lub **R**otary **C**lub
Organizations	**N**ational **G**overnors **A**ssociation **N**ational **O**rganization for **W**omen
Institutions	**M**assachusetts **I**nstitute of **T**echnology **S**mithsonian **I**nstitution
Businesses	**S**imon **C**hemical **C**orporation **F**ido's **F**avorite **P**et **F**oods
Government Bodies	**U**nited **S**tates **C**ongress **S**upreme **C**ourt
Political Parties	**D**emocrats **R**epublican **P**arty
Nationalities	**C**hinese, **G**erman **N**igerian, **I**ranian
Languages	**E**nglish, **S**panish **K**orean, **S**wahili

See Practice 14.1E

Religious References

Use capitals for the names of the religions of the world and certain other words related to religion.

> **RULE 14.1.12** Capitalize references to religions, deities, and religious scriptures.

The following chart presents words related to five of the world's major religions. Next to each religion are examples of some of the related religious words that must be capitalized. Note that the name of each religion is also capitalized.

RELIGIOUS REFERENCES	
Christianity	God, Lord, Father, Holy Spirit, Bible, books of the Bible (Genesis, Deuteronomy, Psalms, and so on)
Judaism	Lord, Father, Prophets, Torah, Talmud, Midrash
Islam	Allah, Prophet, Mohammed, Qur'an
Hinduism	Brahma, Bhagavad Gita, Vedas
Buddhism	Buddha, Mahayana, Hinayana

Note in the following examples, however, that the words *god* and *goddess* in references to mythology are not capitalized. A god's or goddess's name, however, is capitalized.

EXAMPLES   In Roman mythology, the god of the sea was Neptune.

The goddess Diana was the daughter of Jupiter and was the goddess of the moon.

Specific Places and Items

Monuments, memorials, buildings, celestial bodies, awards, the names of specific vehicles, and trademarked products should be capitalized.

> **Capitalize the names of specific places and items.**

14.1.13 RULE

OTHER SPECIAL PLACES AND ITEMS	
Monuments	**S**tatue of **L**iberty **W**ashington **M**onument
Memorials	**W**inston **C**hurchill **M**emorial **V**ietnam **V**eterans **M**emorial
Buildings	**H**ouston **M**useum of **F**ine **A**rts **E**mpire **S**tate **B**uilding **t**he **C**apitol **B**uilding (in Washington, D.C.)
Celestial Bodies (except the moon and sun)	**E**arth, **M**ilky **W**ay **J**upiter, **A**ries
Awards	**N**ewbery **M**edal **N**obel **P**eace **P**rize
Air, Sea, and Space Craft	*S*pirit of *S*t. *L*ouis *M*onitor *V*oyager 2 *M*etroliner
Trademarked Brands	**K**razy **K**orn **E**co-**F**riendly **C**leanser
Names	**Z**enox **K**ermit **t**he **F**rog **t**he **G**reat **H**oudini

> **Capitalize the names of awards.**

14.1.14 RULE

Notice that *the* is not capitalized in these examples.

EXAMPLES   **t**he **G**rammy **A**wards

                the **G**ates **S**cholarship

                the **R**ookie of the **Y**ear **A**ward

                the **G**ood **C**onduct **M**edal

See Practice 14.1F

 **PRACTICE 14.1E** **Using Capitalization for Groups and Organizations**

Read the sentences. Write each group or organization, adding the missing capitals.

EXAMPLE   Each state has two representatives in the u.s senate.

ANSWER   *U.S. Senate*

1. Dad recently joined the cedar crest garden club.

2. Mario is a member of the police athletic league.

3. My older sister is attending the university of tennessee.

4. She has always enjoyed the comedy of the british.

5. For more information, contact the national association of broadcasters.

6. Being able to speak portuguese is an advantage in her job.

7. The closest dry cleaner is heights cleaners.

8. Dr. Sanchez is a member of the american medical association.

9. Leila's dad has just started working for the corel corporation.

10. The american kennel club Web site is a good place to start researching dog breeds.

PRACTICE 14.1F **Using Capitalization for Religious References and Specific Items and Places**

Read the sentences. Write each term that should be capitalized, adding the missing capitals.

EXAMPLE   Crowds of people stood on the steps of the lincoln memorial.

ANSWER   *Lincoln Memorial*

11. The actress won an oscar for her performance.

12. Try clean coat shampoo on your dog.

13. The scriptures of hinduism include the tantras and the agama, among others.

14. The planet venus was named for the Roman goddess of love.

15. In 1985 the space shuttle *atlantis* had its first flight.

16. The tower of london is actually a group of buildings along the Thames River.

17. How many books are there in the new testament?

18. Mom cried when she visited the vietnam veterans memorial.

19. Jan's muslim friend studies the qur'an.

20. One main branch of buddhism is mahayana.

SPEAKING APPLICATION

Read the following sentence aloud to your partner, and have him or her identify each word that should be capitalized.
Scientists used Voyager 2 *to study Triton, a moon of Neptune.*

WRITING APPLICATION

Write three sentences including the following: the name of a specific group or organization, the name of a monument or memorial, and the name of an award.

Using Capitalization for Proper Adjectives

When a proper noun or a form of a proper noun is used to describe another noun, it is called a **proper adjective.** Proper adjectives usually need a capital letter.

> **Capitalize most proper adjectives.**

14.1.15 RULE

In the following examples, notice that both proper nouns and proper adjectives are capitalized. Common nouns that are modified by proper adjectives, however, are not capitalized.

PROPER NOUNS

Korean **W**ar

Cuba

PROPER ADJECTIVES

a **K**orean **W**ar **v**eteran

a **C**uban **s**andwich

The names of some countries and states must be modified to be used as proper adjectives. For example, something from Kenya is Kenyan, someone from Texas is Texan, a chair from Spain is a Spanish chair, and a building in France is a French building.

Brand Names as Adjectives

Trademarked brand names are considered to be proper nouns. If you use a brand name to describe a common noun, the brand name becomes a proper adjective. In this case, capitalize only the proper adjective and not the common noun.

> **Capitalize brand names used as adjectives.**

14.1.16 RULE

PROPER NOUN

Fruit and **R**ice

PROPER ADJECTIVE

Fruit and **R**ice **c**ereal

Notice that only the proper adjective *Fruit* and *Rice* is capitalized. The word *cereal* is not capitalized because it is a common noun; it is not part of the trademarked name.

See Practice 14.1G

Using Capitalization for Titles of People

A person's title shows his or her or relationship to other people. Whether a title is capitalized often depends on how it is used in a sentence.

Social and Professional Titles

Social and professional titles may be written before a person's name or used alone in place of a person's name.

> **Capitalize the title of a person when the title is followed by the person's name or when it is used in place of a person's name in direct address.**

BEFORE A NAME   **P**rofessor Walsh and **D**ean Smith have approved.

IN DIRECT ADDRESS   Look, **C**orporal, here is the missing weapon!

TITLES OF PEOPLE	
Social	**M**ister, **M**adam or **M**adame, **M**iss, **M**s., **S**ir
Business	**D**octor, **P**rofessor, **S**uperintendent
Religious	**R**everend, **F**ather, **R**abbi, **B**ishop, **S**ister
Military	**P**rivate, **E**nsign, **C**aptain, **G**eneral, **A**dmiral
Government	**P**resident, **S**enator, **R**epresentative, **G**overnor, **M**ayor, **P**rince, **Q**ueen, **K**ing

In most cases, do not capitalize titles that are used alone or that follow a person's name—especially if the title is preceded by the articles *a, an,* or *the.*

EXAMPLES   James Goodman, your **a**ttorney, will meet you at the closing.

Tell your **d**octor if you do not feel better soon.

My sister Mary, who is a **p**rivate in the army, will be home on leave soon.

Government Officials

> **Capitalize the titles of government officials when they immediately precede the name of specific officials. If no person is named, these titles should be written in lower case.**

14.1.18 RULE

EXAMPLES   **C**ongressman **C**lark will throw the honorary first pitch at the new stadium.

Our **c**ongresswoman will throw the honorary first pitch at the new stadium.

Governor **P**aterson is the highest executive authority in the state government.

The **g**overnor is the highest executive authority in a state government.

Note: Certain honorary titles are always capitalized, even if the title is not used with a proper name or direct address. These titles include the First Lady of the United States, Speaker of the House of Representatives, Queen Mother of England, and the Prince of Wales.

Titles for Family Relationships

> **Capitalize titles showing family relationships when the title is used with the person's name or as the person's name—except when the title comes after a possessive noun or pronoun.**

14.1.19 RULE

BEFORE A NAME   We agree with **U**ncle Bob's position.

IN PLACE OF A NAME   Is **G**randma going to join us?

AFTER POSSESSIVES   Kaitlyn's **b**rother is the team mascot.

See Practice 14.1H

Notice that the family title *brother* used in the last example is not capitalized because it is used after the possessive word *Kaitlyn's*.

PRACTICE 14.1G Using Capitalization
for Proper Adjectives

Read the sentences. Write the proper adjectives, adding the correct capitalization.

EXAMPLE   Judith is training her dog, an irish setter, in agility.

ANSWER   *Irish*

1. In the living room stood an antique victorian armchair.

2. Who is your favorite character from the arthurian legends?

3. The family usually buys american cars.

4. Does that japanese restaurant serve sushi?

5. Heather was looking for a translated version of that french novel.

6. Doesn't swiss cheese taste good on a turkey sandwich?

7. The professor speaks with a strong german accent.

8. Sometimes these montana winters are harsh.

9. The manhattan skyline looked magical at twilight.

10. Kayla loves studying roman mythology.

PRACTICE 14.1H Using Capitalization
for Titles of People

Read the sentences. If the title in each sentence is correctly capitalized, write *correct*. If it is not, rewrite the title correctly.

EXAMPLE   Have you seen superintendent Ferguson this morning?

ANSWER   *Superintendent*

11. Please, colonel, tell us the plan.

12. Has mayor Gomez held elective office before?

13. The queen, Elizabeth, looked over a crowd of her subjects.

14. Excuse me, mr. Jackson, but I need to get through.

15. We took aunt Crystal out for her birthday.

16. The ceremony was conducted by reverend Hill.

17. I really miss my cousin Darius since he moved out of town.

18. Keith told mom you would be late.

19. Paul Rubenstein, the sergeant on duty, will return your call.

20. The president and his family live in the White House.

WRITING APPLICATION

Write three sentences with proper adjectives, and capitalize them correctly.

WRITING APPLICATION

Write two sentences with titles of people, one that requires a capital and one that does not.

Using Capitalization for Titles of Works

Capital letters are used for the titles of things such as written works, pieces of art, and school courses.

> **Capitalize the first word and all other key words in the titles of books, newspapers, magazines, short stories, poems, plays, movies, songs, and artworks.**

RULE 14.1.20

Do not capitalize articles (*a, an, the*), prepositions (*of, to*), and conjunctions (*and, but*) that are fewer than four letters long unless they begin a title. Verbs and personal pronouns, no matter how short, are always capitalized in titles.

EXAMPLE   "**N**ot **W**anted" by Anton Chekhov

> **Capitalize the title of a school course when it is followed by a course number or when it refers to a language. Otherwise, do not capitalize school subjects.**

RULE 14.1.21

EXAMPLES   **S**panish   **B**iology 250   **H**istory II

I have **h**istory in the afternoon.

Using Capitalization in Letters

Several parts of friendly and business letters are capitalized.

> **In the heading, capitalize the street, city, state, and the month.**

RULE 14.1.22

EXAMPLES   **S**econd **S**treet   **B**illings   **M**ontana   **A**pril

> **In the salutation, capitalize the first word, any title, and the name of the person or group mentioned. In the closing, capitalize the first word.**

RULE 14.1.23

See Practice 14.1I
See Practice 14.1J

SALUTATIONS   **M**y **d**ear **F**rancis,   **D**ear **U**ncle **R**udy,

CLOSINGS   **Y**our **p**artner,   **Y**ours **f**orever,   **L**ove,

PRACTICE 14.1I > Using Capitalization for Titles of Things

Read the sentences. Write the titles, adding the correct capitalization.

EXAMPLE   The show *are you afraid of the dark?* ran for five seasons in the 1990s.

ANSWER   *Are You Afraid of the Dark?*

1. Jared has seen *spider-man* several times.

2. The *daily tribune* has an article about the election.

3. Mom reads each issue of *modern housekeeping* from cover to cover.

4. Pablo drew illustrations to go with his poem "ode to the snail on the wall."

5. Hannah is taking sociology 101 and computer science 141 at the community college.

6. For my science report I consulted *the handy weather answer book.*

7. Tamesa read the chapter "rise of the empire" for social studies class.

8. One of Jack London's most famous works is the novel *the call of the wild.*

9. *The boating party,* by Mary Cassatt, will be one of the paintings featured in the exhibit.

10. My five-year-old nephew loves to sing "if you're happy and you know if."

PRACTICE 14.1J > Using Capitalization for Titles of Things

Read the sentences. Rewrite each sentence, adding the missing capitals.

EXAMPLE   Consider taking chemistry 101 and also psychology.

ANSWER   *Consider taking Chemistry 101 and also psychology.*

11. "when you wish upon a star" is still one of my mother's favorite songs.

12. Isn't *my fair lady* a musical based on George Bernard Shaw's play *pygmalion?*

13. I really like the characters in *sword of the rightful king.*

14. In biology we are reading the chapter "cells and how they work."

15. Hector's sculpture, *cats napping on rugs,* won first prize at the art show.

16. Mom has renewed her subscription to *the dillsburg journal.*

17. Mr. Tanger teaches algebra II and also calculus.

18. "all summer in a day" is a short story by science-fiction writer Ray Bradbury.

19. Megan enjoyed reading Donald Hall's poem "names of horses."

20. Who starred in the movie *angels in the outfield?*

WRITING APPLICATION

Write the titles of your favorite movie, your favorite television show, your favorite book, and your favorite song. Capitalize each title correctly.

WRITING APPLICATION

Write three sentences with titles of things, and use capitalization correctly.

Using Capitalization in Abbreviations, Acronyms, and Initials

An **abbreviation** is a shortened form of a word or phrase. An **acronym** is an abbreviation of a phrase that takes one or more letters from each word in the phrase being abbreviated.

> In general, capitalize **abbreviations, acronyms,** and **initials** if the words or names they stand for are capitalized.

 RULE 14.1.24

INITIALS	**R** . **U** . Goodman
TITLES	**R** ev. Adam Clayton Powell **J** r.
ACADEMIC DEGREES	Mark Greene, **M.D.** , Ben Casey, **Ph.D.**
ACRONYMS	**NAFTA** , **MIA**

Abbreviations for most units of measurement are not capitalized.

EXAMPLES	**c** m (centimeters) **g** al (gallons)

> Capitalize **abbreviations** that appear in addresses.

RULE 14.1.25

Use a two-letter state abbreviation without periods only when the abbreviation is followed by a ZIP Code. Capitalize both letters of the state abbreviation.

EXAMPLE	Albany, **NY** 12207

> Capitalize **acronyms** that stand for proper nouns, such as businesses, government bodies, and organizations.

RULE 14.1.26

Spell out the name of an organization and include its acronym in parentheses the first time you use it. Use only the acronym in later references.

EXAMPLE	Have you heard of the Federal Bureau of Investigation (**FBI**)? The **FBI** protects and defends the United States against foreign threats.

See Practice 14.1K
See Practice 14.1L

PRACTICE 14.1K Using Capitalization for Abbreviations

Read the items. Rewrite each item, adding capitals as needed. If the item is already correct, write *correct*.

EXAMPLE   mrs. Lillian Munson

ANSWER   *Mrs. Lillian Munson*

1. mt. Hood
2. Dan Jones, m.d.
3. Polk's Sporting Goods, ltd.
4. Santa Fe, nm 87501
5. 3366 Fairbanks rd.
6. mr. Kenneth Young jr.
7. 3 ft 5 in.
8. dr. Rosita Jimenez
9. Mary Ellen Morrison, ph.d.
10. a speed limit of 35 mph

PRACTICE 14.1L Using Capitalization for Initials and Acronyms

Read the sentences. Write the initials and acronyms, adding capitals as needed. If a sentence is correct, write *correct*.

EXAMPLE   The Federal Housing Administration, usually referred to as the fha, insures home loans.

ANSWER   *FHA*

11. Mrs. Johnson belongs to the nea (that stands for National Education Association).
12. That medication has not yet been approved by the fda.
13. Arthur w. t. McFearson is my grandfather.
14. The Super Bowl is the biggest event in the nfl each year.
15. Astronauts for nasa have completed years of studying and training.
16. What is the difference between the fbi and the cia?
17. Jaime's mom belongs to the Society of Professional Accountants (spa).
18. I never knew the word *radar* was originally an acronym for *radio detection and ranging*.
19. The Tennessee Volunteers will play in the ncaa tournament this year.
20. That poem about cats is by T. S. Eliot.

WRITING APPLICATION

Write two sentences with abbreviations that require capitals and two with abbreviations that do not need capitals.

WRITING APPLICATION

Write a short paragraph containing two acronyms and two other kinds of abbreviations. (You may make up the acronyms if you wish, but make sure to tell what they stand for.) Use correct capitalization in your paragraph.

PRACTICE 1 ▶ Using Periods, Question Marks, and Exclamation Marks

Read the sentences. Then, rewrite the sentences, adding periods, question marks, and exclamation marks where needed.

1. Lou Jr lives on S Congress St in Tucson
2. Where is the central headquarters of the CIA
3. Please be seated
4. What a delicious meal this is
5. She asked if we were comfortable
6. Don't go near that alligator
7. Is he helping with the invitations
8. Oops Did I forget the picnic basket
9. How wonderful our vacation was
10. The coach is taking notes Why

PRACTICE 2 ▶ Using Commas Correctly

Read the sentences. Then, rewrite the sentences, adding commas where needed. If a sentence is correct as is, write *correct*.

1. The albatross a large bird is central to the poem.
2. He called "Hey Bella when are you coming?"
3. Before you drop by please give me a call.
4. I asked my friends but no one knew the answer.
5. Her rough chapped hands need lotion of course.
6. The address is 49 Washington Street Newark New Jersey 07102.
7. I left it in my pocket on the table or in my bag.
8. The store had 1224 customers on May 4 2009.
9. I knitted those two blue hats in January 2008.
10. "To get here" Bud explained "take Route 90."

PRACTICE 3 ▶ Using Colons, Semicolons, and Quotation Marks

Read the sentences. Then, rewrite the sentences, using colons, semicolons, and quotation marks where needed. If a sentence is correct as is, write *correct*.

1. What poet said, Whatever is, is right?
2. Buy the following items pens, pads, and a ruler.
3. Well, said Shari, the concert starts at 730.
4. The curry was delicious, I love Indian food.
5. Terry asked me for help with the computer.
6. Warning Stay seated until the train stops.
7. Beth asked, Where are you going?
8. How very much I like that poem The Raven!
9. Joe was late, however, we still found good seats.
10. The kosher restaurant served borscht, a soup, knishes, an appetizer, and blintzes, a dessert.

PRACTICE 4 ▶ Using Apostrophes Correctly

Read the sentences. Then, rewrite the sentences, adding or removing apostrophes as needed. If a sentence is correct as is, write *correct*.

1. The cat closes it's eyes when its happy.
2. Gregs late and wont help with Kims party.
3. Only three students grades were lower than Cs.
4. Greek mythology tells of Hades' dark regions.
5. This is Alexis's seat, not someone elses.
6. Show me whats ours and whats hers.
7. Theirs is the best stall in the vegetable market.
8. Lana could'nt ever come on Monday's.
9. I wont say hes wrong, but I cant say hes right.
10. The team has its picture in the 2009 yearbook.

Continued on next page ▶

PRACTICE 5 Using Underlining (or Italics), Hyphens, Dashes, Parentheses, Brackets, and Ellipses

Read the sentences. Then, rewrite the sentences, adding underlining (or italics if you type your answers on a computer), hyphens, dashes, brackets, parentheses, and ellipses. If a sentence is correct as is, write *correct*.

1. I asked Nino he just moved here from Italy if he would tell us about his childhood.

2. Her brother in law is thirty four years old.

3. Who wrote the novel Friendly Persuasion?

4. The film is set during the Civil War 1861–1865.

5. Her nicely written columns won a Pulitzer Prize.

6. The Titanic, a famous luxury cruise ship, sank after hitting an iceberg.

7. The Preamble says that "We, the people . . . establish this Constitution of the United States."

8. Congress voted on the bill. Click here for a list of members' votes H.R. 301.

9. Becky's dream a modeling career got off to a rocky start.

10. In his speech the librarian said, "She meaning Mrs. Finch is our most generous patron."

PRACTICE 6 Using Correct Capitalization

Read the sentences. Then, rewrite each sentence, using capital letters where they are needed.

1. on sunday mom heated a can of joy luck soup.

2. in the midwest, we stayed near lake superior.

3. the treaty of ghent ended the war of 1812.

4. w. b. yeats, an irish poet, wrote the poem "the lake isle of innisfree."

5. "the first time i visited doctor rivera," said harry, "was in april of 2004."

6. the planet neptune is named for the roman god neptune, whom the greeks called poseidon.

7. the clark art institute is just west of route 7 at 225 south street in williamstown, massachusetts.

8. was grandmother once a spy for the cia?

9. Katie lives in an apartment building called city towers.

10. novelist pearl s. buck won the nobel prize.

11. former president teddy roosevelt left the republican party to form the bull moose party.

12. my sister takes geology 101 at emory university.

13. the statue of liberty was a gift from the french.

14. what bible text did reverend lee cite on sunday?

15. "i met tom," said nina, "last winter in ohio."

PRACTICE 7 Writing Letters With Correct Capitalization and Punctuation

Write an imaginary business letter with the following information. Use correct capitalization and punctuation.

1. your return address, followed by today's date

2. the addressee (any real city's or town's visitors' information bureau—you can invent the bureau's exact name and address)

3. any appropriate greeting, beginning with *dear*

4. a body of four or five sentences asking about specific tourist sites in the city or town

5. a closing, beginning with *very* or *most*

6. your signature

Modes
of Writing

Writing is a process that begins with the exploration of ideas and ends with the presentation of a final piece of writing. Often, the types of writing we do are grouped into modes according to their form and purpose.

Narration

Whenever writers tell any type of story, they are using narration. Most narratives share certain elements, such as characters, a setting, a sequence of events, and, often, a theme. The following are some types of narration:

● **Autobiographical Writing**
Autobiographical writing tells a true story about an important period, experience, or relationship in the writer's life.

Effective autobiographical writing includes:
- *A series of events that involve the writer as the main character*
- *Details, thoughts, feelings, and insights from the writer's perspective*
- *A conflict or an event that affects the writer*
- *A logical organization that tells the story clearly*

Types of autobiographical writing include personal narratives, autobiographical sketches, reflective essays, eyewitness accounts, and memoirs.

● **Short Story** A short story is a brief, creative narrative.

Most short stories contain:
- *Details that establish the setting in time and place*
- *A main character who undergoes a change or learns something during the course of the story*
- *A conflict or a problem to be introduced, developed, and resolved*
- *A plot—the series of events that make up the action of the story*
- *A theme or message about life*

Types of short stories include realistic stories, fantasies, historical narratives, mysteries, thrillers, science fiction, and adventure stories.

Description

Descriptive writing is writing that creates a vivid picture of a person, place, thing, or event.

Most descriptive writing includes:

- *Sensory details—sights, sounds, smells, tastes, and physical sensations*
- *Vivid, precise language*
- *Figurative language or comparisons*
- *Adjectives and adverbs that help to paint a word picture*
- *An organization suited to the subject*

Types of descriptive writing include description of ideas, observations, travel brochures, physical descriptions, functional descriptions, remembrances, and character sketches.

Persuasion

Persuasion is writing or speaking that attempts to convince people to accept a position or take a desired action. The following are some types of persuasion:

● **Persuasive Essay**

A persuasive essay presents a position on an issue, urges readers to accept that position, and may encourage a specific action.

An effective persuasive essay:

- *Explores an issue of importance to the writer*
- *Addresses an arguable issue*
- *Is supported by facts, examples, statistics, or personal experiences*
- *Tries to influence the audience through appeals to the readers' knowledge, experiences, or emotions*
- *Uses clear organization to present a logical argument*

Forms of persuasion include editorials, position papers, persuasive speeches, grant proposals, advertisements, and debates.

● **Advertisements**

An advertisement is a planned communication that is meant to be seen, heard, or read. It attempts to persuade an audience to buy or use a product or service. Advertisements may appear in print or broadcast form.

An effective advertisement includes:

- *A concept, or central theme*
- *A devise, such as a memorable slogan, that catches people's attention*
- *Language that conveys a certain view of a product or issue*

Common types of advertisements include public service announcements, billboards, merchandise ads, service ads, and public campaign literature.

Exposition

Exposition is writing that relies on facts to inform or explain. Effective expository writing reflects an organization that is well planned—one that includes a clear introduction, body, and conclusion. The following are some types of exposition:

● **Comparison-and-Contrast Essay**
A comparison-and-contrast essay analyzes similarities and differences between or among two or more things.

An effective comparison-and-contrast essay:
- *Identifies a purpose for comparing and contrasting*
- *Identifies similarities and differences between or among two or more things, people, places, or ideas*
- *Gives factual details about the subjects*
- *Uses an organizational plan suited to the topic and purpose*

● **Cause-and-Effect Essay** A cause-and-effect essay examines the relationship between events, explaining how one event or situation causes another.

A successful cause-and-effect essay includes:
- *A discussion of a cause, event, or condition that produces a specific result*
- *An explanation of an effect or result*
- *Evidence and examples to support the relationship between cause and effect*
- *A logical organization that makes the relationship between events clear*

● **Problem-and-Solution Essay** A problem-and-solution essay describes a problem and offers one or more solutions. It describes a clear set of steps to achieve a result.

An effective problem-and-solution essay includes:
- *A clear statement of the problem, with its causes and effects summarized*
- *A proposal of at least one realistic solution*
- *Facts, statistics, data, or expert testimony to support the solution*
- *A clear organization that makes the relationship between problem and solution obvious*

Research Writing

Research writing is based on information gathered from outside sources.

An effective research paper:
- *Focuses on a specific, narrow topic*
- *Presents relevant information from a variety of sources*
- *Is clearly organized and includes an introduction, body, and conclusion*
- *Includes a bibliography or works-cited list*

In addition to traditional research reports, types of research writing include statistical reports and experiment journals.

Response to Literature

When you write a response to literature, you can discover how a piece of writing affected you.

An effective response:
- *Reacts to a work of literature*
- *Analyzes the content of a literary work*
- *Focuses on a single aspect or gives a general overview*
- *Supports opinion with evidence from the text*

You might respond to a literary work in reader's response journals, literary letters, and literary analyses.

Writing for Assessment

Essays are commonly part of school tests.

An effective essay includes:
- *A clearly stated and well-supported thesis*
- *Specific information about the topic derived from your reading or from class discussion*
- *A clear organization with an introduction, body, and conclusion*

In addition to writing essays for tests, you might write essays to apply to schools or special programs, or to enter a contest.

Workplace Writing

Workplace writing communicates information in a structured format.

Effective workplace writing:
- *Communicates information concisely*
- *Includes details that provide necessary information and anticipate potential questions*

Common types of workplace writing include business letters, memorandums, résumés, forms, and applications.

Writing Effective
Paragraphs

A paragraph is a group of sentences that share a common topic or purpose. Most paragraphs have a main idea or thought.

Stating the Main Idea in a Topic Sentence

The main idea of a paragraph is directly stated in a single sentence called the topic sentence. The rest of the sentences in the paragraph support or explain the topic sentence, providing support through facts and details.

Sometimes the main idea of a paragraph is implied rather than stated. The sentences work together to present the details and facts that allow the reader to infer the main idea.

WRITING MODELS

from **The Secret Language of Snow**
Terry Tempest Williams and Ted Major

Many types of animal behavior are designed to reduce heat loss. Birds fluff their feathers, enlarging the "dead air" space around their bodies. Quails roost in compact circles, in the same manner as musk oxen, to keep warmth in and cold out. Grouse and ptarmigan dive into the snow, using it as an insulating blanket.

> In this passage, the stated topic sentence is highlighted.

from **"The Old Demon"**
Pearl S. Buck

The baker's shop, like everything else, was in ruins. No one was there. At first she saw nothing but the mass of crumpled earthen walls. But then she remembered that the oven was just inside the door, and the door frame still stood erect, supporting one end of the roof. She stood in this frame, and, running her hands in underneath the fallen roof inside, she felt the wooden cover of the iron cauldron. Under this there might be steamed bread. She worked her arm delicately and carefully in. It took quite a long time, but even so, clouds of lime and dust almost choked her. Nevertheless she was right. She squeezed her hand under the cover and felt the first smooth skin of the big steamed bread rolls, and one by one she drew out four.

> In this passage, all the sentences work together to illustrate the implied main idea of the paragraph: The woman searches persistently until she finds food.

Writing a Topic Sentence

When you outline a topic or plan an essay, you identify the main points you want to address. Each of these points can be written as a topic sentence—a statement of the main idea of a topical paragraph. You can organize your paragraph around the topic sentence.

A good topic sentence tells readers what the paragraph is about and the point the writer wants to make about the subject matter. Here are some tips for writing a strong topic sentence.

☑ Review details.

☑ Group related details.

☑ Write a statement that pulls the details together.

Writing Supporting Sentences

Whether your topic sentence is stated or implied, it guides the rest of the paragraph. The rest of the sentences in the paragraph will either develop, explain, or support that topic sentence.

You can support or develop the idea by using one or more of the following strategies:

Use Facts

Facts are statements that can be proved. They support your key idea by providing proof.

- **Topic Sentence:** Our football team is tough to beat.
- **Supporting Fact:** It wins almost all of its games.

Use Statistics

A statistic is a fact, usually stated using numbers.

- **Topic Sentence:** Our football team is tough to beat.
- **Supporting Statistic:** The football team's record is 10–1.

Use Examples, Illustrations, or Instances

An example, illustration, or instance is a specific thing, person, or event that demonstrates a point.

- **Topic Sentence:** Our football team is tough to beat.
- **Illustration:** Last week, the team beat the previously undefeated Tigers in an exciting upset game.

Use Details

Details are the specifics— the parts of the whole. They make your point or main idea clear by showing how all the pieces fit together.

- **Topic Sentence:** Our football team is tough to beat.
- **Detail:** There were only seconds left in last week's game, when the quarterback threw the winning pass.

Placing Your Topic Sentence

Frequently, the topic sentence appears at the beginning of a paragraph. Topic sentences can, however, be placed at the beginning, middle, or end of the paragraph. Place your topic sentence at the beginning of a paragraph to focus readers' attention. Place your topic sentence in the middle of a paragraph when you must lead into your main idea. Place your topic sentence at the end of a paragraph to emphasize your main idea.

Paragraph Patterns

Sentences in a paragraph can be arranged in several different patterns, depending on where you place your topic sentence. One common pattern is the TRI pattern (Topic, Restatement, Illustration).

- **T**opic sentence (State your main idea.)
- **R**estatement (Interpret your main idea; use different wording.)
- **I**llustration (Support your main idea with facts and examples.)

T	Participating in after-school clubs is one of the ways you can meet new people. Getting involved in extracurricular activities brings you in contact with a wide range of individuals. The drama club, for example, brings together students from several different grades.
R	
I	

Variations on the TRI pattern include sentence arrangements such as TIR, TII, IIT, or ITR.

I	This month alone the service club at our high school delivered meals to thirty shut-ins. In addition, members beautified the neighborhood with new plantings. If any school-sponsored club deserves increased support, the service club does.
I	
T	

Paragraphs
in Essays
and other Compositions

To compose means "to put the parts together, to create." Most often, composing refers to the creation of a musical or literary work—a composition. You may not think of the reports, essays, and test answers you write as literary works, but they are compositions. To write an effective composition, you must understand the parts.

The Introduction

The introduction does what its name suggests. It introduces the topic of the composition. An effective introduction begins with a strong lead, a first sentence that captures readers' interest. The lead is followed by the thesis statement, the key point of the composition. Usually, the thesis statement is followed by a few sentences that outline how the writer will make the key point.

The Body

The body of a composition consists of several paragraphs that develop, explain, and support the key idea expressed in the thesis statement. The body of a composition should be unified and coherent. The paragraphs in a composition should work together to support the thesis statement. The topic of each paragraph should relate directly to the thesis statement and be arranged in a logical organization.

The Conclusion

The conclusion is the final paragraph of the composition. The conclusion restates the thesis and sums up the support. Often, the conclusion includes the writer's reflection or observation on the topic. An effective conclusion ends on a memorable note, for example, with a quotation or call to action.

Recognizing Types of Paragraphs

There are several types of paragraphs you can use in your writing.

Topical Paragraphs

A topical paragraph is a group of sentences that contain one key sentence or idea and several sentences that support or develop that key idea or topic sentence.

Functional Paragraphs

Functional paragraphs serve a specific purpose. They may not have a topic sentence, but they are unified and coherent because the sentences (if there is more than one) are clearly connected and follow a logical order. Functional paragraphs can be used for the following purposes:

- **To create emphasis** A very short paragraph of one or two sentences focuses the reader on what is being said because it breaks the reader's rhythm.
- **To indicate dialogue** One of the conventions of written dialogue is that a new paragraph begins each time the speaker changes.
- **To make a transition** A short paragraph can help readers move between the main ideas in two topical paragraphs.

WRITING MODEL

from **"The Hatchling Turtles"**

by Jean Craighead George

One morning each small turtle fought for freedom within its shell.

They hatched two feet down in the sand, all of them on the same day. As they broke out, their shells collapsed, leaving a small room of air for them to breathe. It wasn't much of a room, just big enough for them to wiggle in and move toward the sky. As they wiggled they pulled the sand down from the ceiling and crawled up on it. In this manner the buried room began to rise, slowly, inch by inch.

The highlighted functional paragraph emphasizes the struggle of the turtles to emerge from their shells.

Paragraph Blocks

Sometimes, you may have so much information to support or develop a main idea that it "outgrows" a single paragraph. When a topic sentence or main idea requires an extensive explanation or support, you can develop the idea in a paragraph block—several paragraphs that work together and function as a unit. Each paragraph in the block supports the key idea or topic sentence. By breaking the development of the idea into separate paragraphs, you make your ideas clearer.

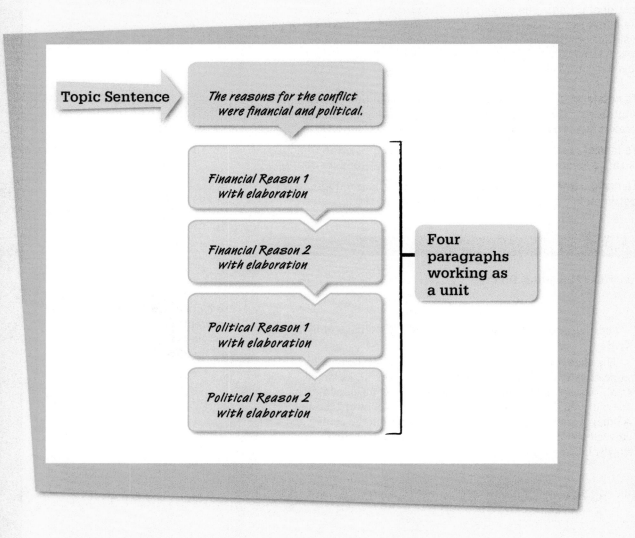

Qualities
of Good Writing

The quality of your writing depends on how well you develop six important traits: ideas, organization, voice, word choice, sentence fluency, and conventions.

Organization

Organization refers to the way in which the ideas and details are arranged in a piece of writing. To enable readers to follow your ideas, choose an organization that makes sense for your topic, and stick with that organization throughout the piece of writing.

Ideas

Good writing begins with interesting ideas. Explore topics that you find interesting and that you think will interest others. Focus on presenting information that will be new and fresh to readers.

Voice

Just as you have a distinctive way of expressing yourself when you speak, you can develop a distinctive voice as a writer. Your voice consists of the topics you choose, the attitude you express toward those topics, the words you use, and the rhythm of your sentences. By developing your own voice, you let your personality come through in your writing.

Conventions

Conventions refer to the grammatical correctness of a piece of writing. Don't let errors in grammar, usage, mechanics, and spelling interfere with your message.

Word Choice

Words are the building blocks of a piece of writing. By choosing precise and vivid words, you will add strength to your writing and enable readers to follow your ideas and picture the things that you describe.

Sentence Fluency

In a piece of writing, it is important that sentences flow well from one to another. By using a variety of sentences—different lengths and different structures—and using transitions to connect them, you will create smooth rhythm in your writing.

Stages of the Writing Process

Writing is called a process because it goes through a series of changes or stages. These five stages are:

PREWRITING DRAFTING REVISING EDITING PUBLISHING

- In **prewriting**, you explore an idea by using various prewriting techniques, such as brainstorming and questioning.

- In **drafting**, you get your ideas down on paper or on the computer in roughly the format you intend.

- Once you finish your first draft, you decide on the changes, or **revisions**, you want to make.

- Finally, when you are happy with your work, you **edit** it, checking the accuracy of facts and for errors in spelling, grammar, usage, and mechanics.

- You then make a final copy and **publish** it, or share it with an audience.

You will not always progress through these stages in a straight line. You can backtrack to a previous stage, repeat a stage many times, or put the stages in a different sequence to fit your needs. To get an idea of what the writing process is like, study the following diagram. Notice that the arrows in the drafting and revising sections can lead you back to prewriting.

Prewriting
- Using prewriting techniques to gather ideas
- Choosing a purpose and an audience
- Ordering ideas

Drafting
- Putting ideas down on paper
- Exploring new ideas as you write

Publishing
- Producing a final polished copy of your writing
- Sharing your writing

Revising
- Consulting with peer readers
- Evaluating suggested changes
- Making revisions

Editing
- Checking the accuracy of facts
- Correcting errors in spelling, grammar, usage, and mechanics

Prewriting
• Using prewriting techniques to gather ideas
• Choosing a purpose and an audience
• Ordering ideas

Prewriting

No matter what kind of writing assignment you are given, you can use prewriting techniques to find and develop a topic. Some prewriting techniques will work better than others for certain kinds of assignments.

Choosing a Topic

Try some of the following ways to find topics that fit your assignment.

● **Look Through Newspapers and Magazines** In the library or at home, flip through recent magazines or newspapers. Jot down each interesting person, place, event, or topic you come across. Review your notes and choose a topic that you find especially interesting and would like to learn more about.

● **Keep an Events Log** Every day you probably encounter many situations about which you have opinions. One way to remember these irksome issues is to keep an events log. For a set period of time—a day or a week—take a small notebook with you wherever you go. Whenever you come across something you feel strongly about, write it down. After the specified time period, review your journal and select a topic.

● **Create a Personal Experience Timeline** Choose a memorable period in your life and map out the events that occurred during that period. Create a timeline in which you enter events in the order they occurred. Then, review your timeline and choose the event or events that would make the most interesting topic.

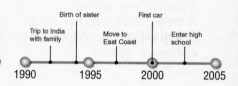

Narrowing Your Topic

Note that narrowing a topic is not an exact science. It is part of the creative process of writing, which involves experimentation and leads to discovery. Here are some specific techniques you can use.

● **Questioning** Asking questions often helps narrow your topic to fit the time and space you have available. Try asking some of the six questions that journalists use when writing news stories: *Who? What? When? Why? Where?* and *How?* Then, based on your answers, refocus on a narrow aspect of your topic.

● **Using Reference Materials** The reference materials you use to find information can also help you narrow a broad topic. Look up your subject in an encyclopedia, or find a book on it at the library. Scan the resource, looking for specific, narrow topics. Sometimes a resource will be divided into sections or chapters that each deal with a specific topic.

● **Using Graphic Devices** Another way to narrow a topic is to combine questioning with a graphic device, such as a cluster or inverted pyramid. Draw one in your notebook or journal, and write your broad topics across the top of the upside-down pyramid. Then, as the pyramid narrows to a point, break down your broad topic into narrower and narrower subcategories. The following graphic shows how questions can be used to do this.

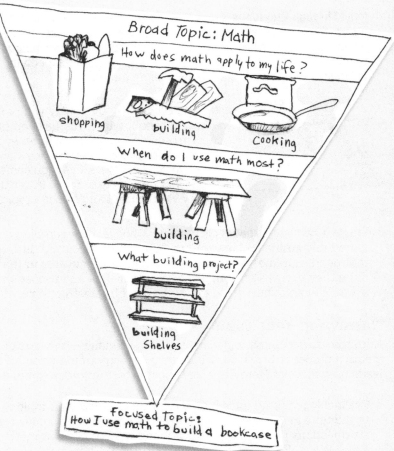

Broad Topic: Math

How does math apply to my life?

shopping   building   cooking

When do I use math most?

building

What building project?

building Shelves

Focused Topic:
How I use math to build a bookcase

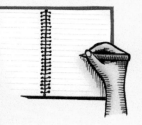

Purpose and Audience

Every piece of writing is written for an audience. Even when you write a secret in your journal, you are writing for an audience of one—yourself. To succeed in any writing task, you have to understand what your audience wants and needs to know.

Pinpointing your purpose is also essential when you write. Sometimes you write to fulfill an assignment; at other times you decide to whom you will write and why. For example, you might decide to write a letter to your sister about your bunkmates at camp. Your purpose might be to describe your bunkmates' looks and personalities. Another time you might write a letter to your principal about cell phones. Your purpose might be to convince her to ban cell phones inside your school.

- **Defining Your Purpose and Audience** Answering certain questions can help you define your purpose for writing and identify your audience.

> - *What is my topic?*
> - *What is my purpose for writing?*
> - *Who is my audience?*
> - *What does my audience already know about this topic?*
> - *What does my audience need or want to know?*
> - *What type of language will suit my audience and purpose?*

Gathering Details

After finding a topic to write about, you will want to explore and develop your ideas. You can do this on your own or with classmates. The following techniques may help you.

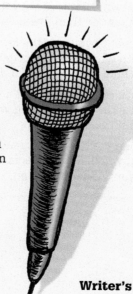

- **Interview a Classmate** Questioning a classmate can help both of you develop your topics. You can interview a friend who has a special skill. Find out how she or he developed that skill. You could also find an interview partner and question each other on an acceptable topic.

● **Fill In an Observation Chart** To come up with details to develop a piece of descriptive writing or to help you create the setting and characters for a narrative, you can fill in an observation chart. A writer created the chart that follows while wondering how to describe the school cafeteria at lunch time.

Once you have completed your own observation chart, circle the details you want to include in your piece of writing.

SUBJECT: CAFETERIA AT LUNCHTIME

See	Hear	Touch	Smell	Taste
swirl of motion	kids' voices	hot melted cheese	stuff they wash the floors with	tart juice
fluorescent lights	thuds and clunks of chairs and trays	wet plastic trays	delicious aroma of pizza	pepperoni
colors of plastic trays	scraping of chairs	cold, wet milk cartons	apple crisp baking	mild cheese

● **Do a Focused Freewriting** Freewriting can be used to either find or develop a topic. When it is used to develop a topic, it is called focused freewriting. Follow these four steps as you use focused freewriting to develop a topic:

1 Set a time limit. (Until you get used to freewriting, write for no more than five minutes at a time.)

2 Repeat to yourself the key words of your topic, and then write whatever comes to mind about them. Do not stop; do not read or correct what you write.

3 If you get stuck, repeat a word (even the word *stuck*), or write the last word you wrote until new ideas come. You can be sure they will.

4 When the time is up, read what you wrote. Underline parts that you like best. Decide which of these parts you will use in your piece of writing.

Drafting

Drafting
- Putting ideas down on paper
- Exploring new ideas as you write

In writing, an **organizational plan** is an outline or map that shows the key ideas and details that you want to include in the order that you want to include them. Following such a plan can help you structure your writing so that it makes a clearer and stronger impression on your audience.

Organizing Your Ideas

Often, a piece of writing lends itself to a particular order. For instance, if you are describing a scene so that readers can visualize it, spatial order may be your best option. However, if you are describing a person, you might compare and contrast the person with someone else you and your readers know, or you might reveal the person's character by describing a series of past incidents in chronological order.

ORGANIZATIONAL PLANS

Chronological Order	Events or details are arranged in the order in which they occur. Words showing **chronological order** include *first, next,* and *finally.*
Spatial Order	Details are given by location so that readers can visualize the scene, object, or person. Expressions showing **spatial order** include *to the right (or left), in the middle, nearby, in front of, on, beside, behind,* and *next to.*
Order of Importance	Events and details are arranged from the least to the most significant, or vice versa. Expressions showing **order of importance** include *most important, above all,* and *also.*
Logical Order	Each point that is made builds on previous information, and ideas are clearly linked. Expressions showing **logical order** include *it follows that, for example,* and *therefore.*

Introductions

The introduction to your paper should include a **thesis statement**, a sentence about your central purpose or what you plan to "show" in your paper. Here is a thesis statement for a paper on the ancient Kingdom of Ghana:

> Ghana was one of the strongest, richest kingdoms of its time.

An effective written introduction draws your readers into your paper and interests them in the subject. The way you introduce your paper depends on the goal you want to achieve and the type of writing you are doing. The following are some possibilities.

GOAL	TYPE OF INTRODUCTION	COULD BE USED FOR
Be clear and direct	a statement of the main point	• an informative paper • a research report • an editorial
Appeal to readers' senses	a vivid description	• a description of a scene • an observation report • a character sketch
Get readers' attention	a startling fact or statistic	• an informative paper • a persuasive essay • a research report
Lure readers into the story quickly	dialogue	• a story • a personal narrative
Make readers wonder	a question	• an informative paper • a persuasive essay • a research report
Give your writing authority	a quotation	• a persuasive essay • an informative paper • a research report • a book review or report

Elaboration

Sometimes what you write seems to be only the bare bones of a composition. In order to flesh out your work, you must add the right details. This process is called **elaboration**.

Certain types of elaboration are more effective for certain forms of writing, but there are no hard-and-fast rules about which type of elaboration to use. You can use facts and statistics in a poem if you want to! Some types of elaboration include the following:

Facts and Statistics	Facts are statements that can be proved true. Statistics are facts that you express as numbers.
Sensory Details	Sensory details are details that appeal to the five senses— sight, hearing, touch, smell, and taste.
Anecdotes	An anecdote is a short account of an interesting or funny incident.
Examples	An example is an instance of something.
Quotations	A quotation is someone's words—often those of an expert or public figure.
Personal Feelings	Personal feelings are thoughts and emotions that are yours alone.
Memories	Memories are recollections from the past.
Observations	Observations are things you have seen or noticed firsthand.
Reasons	Reasons are explanations of why something is true.

● **Uses of Elaboration** Here is a chart showing the types of elaboration you can use and what each is used for.

TYPE OF ELABORATION		USED FOR
facts and statistics	➡	essays news stories feature articles business letters	advertisements reviews research reports
sensory details	➡	observations poems personal essays advertisements	stories plays descriptions
anecdotes	➡	journal entries personal letters news stories	personal essays feature articles
examples	➡	essays news stories business letters editorials advertisements poems	responses to literature book reports research reports feature articles reviews
quotations	➡	news stories feature articles essays	responses to literature book reports
personal feelings	➡	journal entries personal letters personal essays poems	editorials observations responses to literature persuasive essays
memories	➡	journal entries personal letters personal essays poems	descriptions observations stories
observations	➡	journal entries personal letters personal essays poems	reviews feature articles stories plays
reasons	➡	essays business letters reviews book reports news stories feature articles	editorials advertisements research reports responses to literature personal essays

- **Uses of Elaboration** Here is a chart showing the types of elaboration you can use and what each is used for.

TYPE OF ELABORATION	USED FOR	
facts and statistics	essays news stories feature articles business letters	advertisements reviews research reports
sensory details	observations poems personal essays advertisements	stories plays descriptions
anecdotes	journal entries personal letters news stories	personal essays feature articles
examples	essays news stories business letters editorials advertisements poems	responses to literature book reports research reports feature articles reviews
quotations	news stories feature articles essays	responses to literature book reports
personal feelings	journal entries personal letters personal essays poems	editorials observations responses to literature persuasive essays
memories	journal entries personal letters personal essays poems	descriptions observations stories
observations	journal entries personal letters personal essays poems	reviews feature articles stories plays
reasons	essays business letters reviews book reports news stories feature articles	editorials advertisements research reports responses to literature personal essays

Revising

Revising
- Consulting with peer readers
- Evaluating suggested changes
- Making revisions

When you have included all your ideas and finished your first draft, you are ready to revise it. Few writers produce perfect drafts the first time around. You can almost always improve your paper by reworking it. Here are some hints to help you revise your work.

● **Take a Break** Do not begin to revise right after you finish a draft. In a few hours or days you will be better able to see the strengths and weaknesses of your work.

● **Look It Over** When you reread your draft, look for ways to improve it. Use a pencil to mark places where an idea is unclear or the writing is jumpy or disjointed. Also, remember to let yourself know when you have written an effective image or provided a wonderful example. Write Good! next to the parts that work well.

● **Read Aloud** Your ear is a wonderful editor. Read your work aloud and listen for dull, unnecessary, or awkward parts that you did not notice when you read your work silently. Are there any passages that you stumble over as you read aloud? Try different wordings and then read them aloud with expression, emphasizing certain words. Listen and identify which wording sounds best.

● **Share Your Work** Your friends or family members can help you by telling you how your work affects them. Ask them whether your ideas are clear. What is interesting? What is boring?

When it is time to revise a draft, many writers are tempted to just correct a few spelling mistakes and combine a sentence or two. Eliminating surface errors, however, is only a small part of revising. After all, what good is a neat and perfectly spelled paper if it does not make sense or prove a point? The word *revise* means "to see again" or "to see from a new perspective." In order to revise your work, you need to rethink your basic ideas.

Revising by Rethinking

Taking a close look at the ideas in your draft is the most important part of revising. Usually, you will spot some "idea" problems. When you do, it is time to get to work. Here are some strategies to help you rethink your draft.

PROBLEM	STRATEGY	REVISION
My topic is boring.	Look for topics that are too general or vague, such as "My Typical Day."	Select a specific focus. If you are writing "What I Did on My Summer Vacation," focus on one event.
My opening puts me to sleep.	Look for openings that state the obvious, such as "I am going to tell you about sailing."	Begin with an interesting anecdote, fact, or question.
The focus of my draft is unclear.	Read your introduction and your conclusion. If they seem unrelated, your main idea may be unclear.	Add an introductory sentence to present the main idea. Reorder your paragraphs to develop the main idea or story in a logical way. Make sure your conclusion sums up your main idea.
I have left out key points, ideas, or events that my readers need to know.	Pretend that you know nothing about your topic, and then reread your draft.	Wherever your readers might ask who? what? when? where? why? or how? add a sentence or paragraph to your draft that provides the answer. Put the new information in logical order.
Relationships among ideas or events in my narrative are unclear.	Look for sections of the text you have to reread in order to get the meaning.	Use a graphic device such as a chart or story map to rethink the flow of ideas. Use transition words such as because, therefore, next, and finally to show the connections between ideas.

Revising by Elaborating

When you are sure your ideas are clear and in order, it is time to judge whether you have provided enough appropriate details. Remember, elaborating means developing and expanding on ideas by adding the right details. These details will help develop your ideas in clear and interesting ways.

You might choose any of the following types of details explained on page **TK**:

- *facts and statistics*
- *sensory details*
- *anecdotes*
- *examples*
- *quotations*
- *personal feelings*
- *memories*
- *observations*
- *reasons*

Revising by Reducing

Just as you need to add specific details when you revise your draft, you sometimes need to get rid of material that is unnecessary. Following are some ways you can solve revision problems by removing unneeded words.

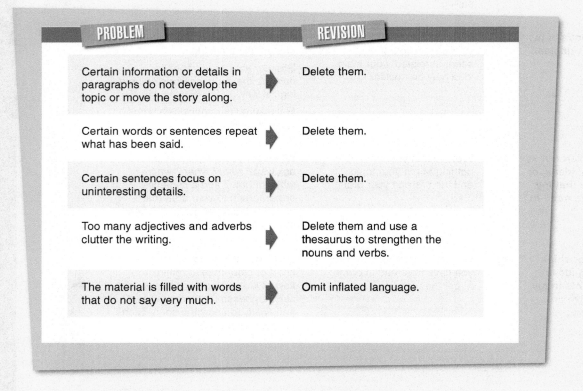

PROBLEM	REVISION
Certain information or details in paragraphs do not develop the topic or move the story along.	Delete them.
Certain words or sentences repeat what has been said.	Delete them.
Certain sentences focus on uninteresting details.	Delete them.
Too many adjectives and adverbs clutter the writing.	Delete them and use a thesaurus to strengthen the nouns and verbs.
The material is filled with words that do not say very much.	Omit inflated language.

Revising by Rewording

Choosing the right words is essential to good writing. As a final step in revising, improve your choice of words. At times, a better word will spring to mind. At other times, use a thesaurus to find words. As you rework your draft, you will reveal your own style.

The following chart can help you find the right word.

PROBLEM

Have I used the most effective word possible?

REVISION ACTIVITIES:

Choose specific nouns.
General: I wish I had some food.
Specific: I wish I had some pizza.

Choose active, colorful verbs.
General: The sick man walked to his bed.
Specific: The sick man hobbled to his bed.

Avoid the word _be_.
General: My horse is a good jumper.
Specific: My horse easily jumps four feet.

Choose the active voice.
General: Chocolate should never be fed to dogs.
Specific: Never feed dogs chocolate.

Editing
• Checking the accuracy of facts
• Correcting errors in spelling, grammar, usage, and mechanics

Editing

Editing is the process of finding and correcting errors in grammar, usage, and mechanics. When you have finished drafting and revising your paper, here is how to edit your work.

Here are some specific editing strategies that may help you.

General Tips
- Look first for mistakes that you typically make.
- Proofread your paper for one type of error at a time.
- Read your work aloud word for word.
- When in doubt, use reference sources to help you.

SPECIFIC TASKS	STRATEGY
Check Your Grammar	
Have you written any run-on sentences or fragments?	Check that each sentence has a subject and verb. Use a comma and conjunction to connect main clauses.
Do your subjects and verbs agree?	Make sure that singular subjects have singular verbs and plural subjects have plural verbs.
Check Your Usage	
Have you used the past forms of irregular verbs correctly?	Watch out for irregular verb forms such as *seen, done, gone,* and *taken.*
Have you used subject and object pronouns correctly?	Check that the pronouns *me, him, her, us,* and *them* are used only after verbs or prepositions.
Check Your Punctuation	
Does each sentence have the correct end mark?	Look for inverted word order that may signal a question.
Have you used apostrophes in nouns, but not in pronouns, to show possession?	Use a phrase with *of* to check for possession.
Have you used quotation marks around words from another source?	Avoid plagiarism by checking your notecards to be sure.
Check Your Capitalization	
Did you begin each sentence or direct quotation with a capital letter?	Look for an end mark and then check the next letter.
Have you capitalized proper nouns?	Look for the name of specific people and places.
Check Your Spelling	
Did you correctly spell all words?	Use a dictionary. Look for your common errors.

Publishing

Once you have made a final, clean copy of a piece of writing that pleases you, you may want to share it with others. What you have to say might be important or meaningful to someone else. Here are some ways you can publish your writing—that is, bring it to the public eye.

- Submit your work to a school newspaper or magazine.

- Have a public reading of your work. Perform it in one of the following ways:
  - Over the school P.A. or radio system
  - In a school assembly or talent show
  - In a group in which members take turns reading their work
  - At your local library or community center

- If your work is a play or skit, have a group of classmates or the drama club present it.

- Work with classmates to put together a class collection of written work. You can have it copied and bound at a copy shop.

- Submit your piece to a local or national writing contest.

- Send your writing to a local newspaper or area magazine.

- Publish your own work and the writings of classmates by using a computer with a desktop publishing program.

Reflecting

Your writing can help you learn about your subject or the writing process—or even yourself. Once you have completed a writing assignment, sit back and think about the experience for a few minutes.

Ask yourself questions such as the following:

- What did I learn about my subject through my writing?

- Did I experiment with writing techniques and forms? If so, were my experiments successful? If not, what held me back?

- Am I pleased with what I wrote? Why or why not?

- Did I have difficulty with any part of the writing process? If so, which part gave me trouble? What strategies did I use to overcome my difficulties?

This resource section contains tips on writing in English and information on grammar topics that are sometimes challenging for English learners.

The numbered arrows in the side margins also appear on other pages of the Grammar Handbook that provide information on writing or instruction in these same grammar topics.

EL1

Understand the Demands of Writing in a Second Language

Talk with other writers.

When you write in an unfamiliar situation, it may be helpful to find a few examples of the type of writing you are trying to produce. For example, if you are writing a letter to the editor of a magazine, look at letters from readers that the magazine has published. Notice the various ways that readers presented their views in writing.

Use your native language as a resource.

You can also use your native language to develop your texts. Many people, when they cannot find an appropriate word in English, write down a word, a phrase, or even a sentence in their native language and consult a dictionary later. Incorporating key terms from your native language is also a possible strategy.

A Japanese term adds perspective to this sentence.

"Some political leaders need to have *wakimae*—a realistic idea of one's own place in the world."

Use dictionaries.

Bilingual dictionaries are especially useful when you want to check your understanding of an English word or find equivalent words for culture-specific concepts and technical terms. Some bilingual dictionaries also provide sample sentences.

Learner's dictionaries, such as the *Longman Dictionary of American English,* include information about count/non-count nouns and transitive/intransitive verbs. Many of them also provide sample sentences.

Understand English idioms.

Some English idioms function like proverbs. In the United States, for example, if someone has to "eat crow," that person has been forced to admit he or she was wrong about something. *Simpler* examples of idiomatic usage—word order, word choice, and combinations that don't follow any obvious set of rules—are common in even the plainest English. If you are unsure about idioms, use Google or another search engine to find out how to use them.

INCORRECT IDIOM	Here is the answer **of** your question.
ACCEPTED IDIOM	Here is the answer **to** your question.
INCORRECT IDIOM	I had jet **legs** after flying across the Pacific.
ACCEPTED IDIOM	I had jet **lag** after flying across the Pacific.

Understand Nouns in English

Perhaps the most troublesome conventions for nonnative speakers are those that guide usage of the common articles *the, a,* and *an.* To understand how articles work in English, you must first understand how the language uses **nouns.**

Proper nouns and common nouns

EL2

There are two basic kinds of nouns. A **proper noun** begins with a capital letter and names a unique person, place, or thing: *Elvis Presley, Russia, Eiffel Tower.*

The other basic kind of noun is called a **common noun.** Common nouns such as *man, country* and *tower,* do not name a unique person, place, or thing. Common nouns are not names and are not capitalized unless they are the first word in a sentence.

PROPER NOUNS
Beethoven   Michael Jordan   Honda
South Korea   Africa
Empire State Building

COMMON NOUNS
composer   athlete   vehicle   country
continent   building

Count and non-count nouns

EL3

Common nouns can be classified as either **count** or **non-count**. Count nouns can be made plural, usually by adding the letter *s* (*finger, fingers*) or by using their plural forms (*person, people; datum, data*).

Non-count nouns cannot be counted directly and cannot take the plural form (*information,* but not *informations; garbage,* but not *garbages*). Some nouns can be either count or non-count, depending on how they are used. *Hair* can refer to either a strand of hair, when it serves as a count noun, or a mass of hair, when it becomes a non-count noun.

Count nouns usually take both singular and plural forms, while non-count nouns usually do not take plural forms and are not counted directly. A count noun can have a number before it (as in *two books, three oranges*) and can be qualified with adjectives such as *many* (as in *many books*), *some* (as in *some schools*), and *few* (as in *few people volunteered*).

Non-count nouns can be counted or quantified in only two ways: either by general adjectives that treat the noun as a mass (*much* information, *some* news) or by placing another noun between the quantifying word and the non-count noun (two *kinds* of information, a *piece* of news).

CORRECT USE OF HAIR *AS A COUNT NOUN*
Three blonde hairs were in the sink.

CORRECT USE OF HAIR *AS A NON-COUNT NOUN*
My roommate spent an hour combing his hair.

INCORRECT	five horse many accident
CORRECT	five horses many accidents
INCORRECT	three breads I would like a mustard on my hot dog.
CORRECT	three loaves of bread I would like some mustard on my hot dog.

Understand Articles in English

Articles indicate that a noun is about to appear, and they clarify what the noun refers to. There are only two kinds of articles in English, definite and indefinite.

1. **the:** *The* is a **definite article,** meaning that it refers to (1) a specific object already known to the reader, (2) one about to be made known to the reader, or (3) a unique object.

2. **a, an:** The **indefinite articles** *a* and *an* refer to an object whose specific identity is not known to the reader. The only difference between *a* and *an* is that *a* is used before a consonant sound (*a man, a friend, a yellow toy*), while *an* is used before a vowel sound (*an orange, an old shoe*).

Look at these sentences, which are identical except for their articles, and imagine that each is taken from a different newspaper story.

Rescue workers lifted **the** man to safety.

Rescue workers lifted **a** man to safety.

By using the definite article *the*, the first sentence indicates that the reader already knows something about the identity of this man. The news story has already referred to him.

The indefinite article *a* in the second sentence indicates that the reader does not know anything about this man. Either this is the first time the news story has referred to him, or there are other men in need of rescue.

RULES FOR USING ARTICLES

1. *A* or *an* is not used with non-count nouns.

   INCORRECT The crowd hummed with **an** excitement.
   CORRECT The crowd hummed with excitement.

2. *A* or *an* is used with singular count nouns whose identity is unknown to the reader or writer.

   INCORRECT Detective Johnson was reading book.
   CORRECT Detective Johnson was reading **a** book.

3. *The* is used with most count and non-count nouns whose particular identity is known to readers.

   CORRECT I bought a book yesterday. **The** book is about kayaking.

4. *The* is used when the noun is accompanied by a superlative form of a modifier: for example, *best, worst, highest, lowest, most expensive, least interesting.*

   CORRECT **The** most interesting book about climbing Mount Everest is Jon Krakauer's *Into Thin Air.*

Understand Verbs and Modifiers in English

Verbs, verb phrases, and helping verbs

Verbs in English can be divided between one-word verbs like *run*, *speak*, and *look*, and verb phrases like *may have run*, *have spoken*, and *will be looking*. The words that appear before the main verbs—*may*, *have*, *will*, *do*, and *be*—are called **helping verbs**. Helping verbs help express something about the action of main verbs: for example, when the action occurs, whether the subject acted or was acted upon, or whether or not an action *has* occurred.

Indicating tense with *be* verbs

Like the helping verbs *have* and *do*, *be* changes form to signal tense. In addition to *be* itself, the **be verbs** are *is*, *am*, *are*, *was*, *were*, and *been*.

To show ongoing action, *be* verbs are followed by the present participle, which is a verb ending in *-ing*.	*INCORRECT* I **am think** of all the things I'd rather **be do**.
	CORRECT I **am thinking** of all the things I'd rather **be doing**.
To show that an action is being done to the subject rather than by the subject, follow *be* verbs with the past participle (a verb usually ending in *-ed*, *-en*, or *-t*).	*INCORRECT* The movie **was direct** by John Woo.
	CORRECT The movie **was directed** by John Woo.

Placement of Modifiers

Modifiers will be unclear if your reader can't connect them to the words to which they refer. How close a modifier is to the noun or verb it modifies provides an important clue to their relationship.

Clarity should be your first goal when using a modifier.	*UNCLEAR* Many pedestrians are killed each year by motorists **not using sidewalks**.
	CLEAR Many pedestrians **not using sidewalks** are killed each year by motorists.
An **adverb**—a word or group of words that modifies a verb, adjective, or another adverb—should not come between a verb and its direct object.	*AWKWARD* The hurricane destroyed **completely** the city's tallest building.
	BETTER The hurricane **completely** destroyed the city's tallest building.
Try to avoid placing an adverb between *to* and its verb. This construction is called a **split infinitive**.	*AWKWARD* The water level was predicted **to not rise**.
	BETTER The water level was predicted **not to rise**.

Understand English Sentence Structure

Words derive much of their meaning from how they function in a sentence.

With the exception of **imperatives** (commands such as *Watch out!*), sentences in English usually contain a *subject* and a *predicate*. A subject names who or what the sentence is about; the predicate tells what the subject is or does.

The **lion** **is asleep.**
subject   predicate

A predicate consists of at least one main verb. If the verb is **intransitive,** like *exist,* it does not take a direct object. Some verbs are **transitive,** which means they require a **direct object** to complete their meaning.

INCORRECT   The bird saw.
CORRECT   The bird saw a cat.

Some verbs (*write, learn, read,* and others) can be both transitive and intransitive, depending on how they are used.

INTRANSITIVE   Pilots fly.
TRANSITIVE   Pilots fly airplanes.

Formal written English requires that each sentence includes a subject and a verb, even when the meaning of the sentence would be clear without it. In some cases you must supply an expletive, such as *it* and *there*.

INCORRECT   Is snowing in Alaska.
CORRECT   It is snowing in Alaska.